THE JEWISH HERITAGE IN BRITISH HISTORY:
ENGLISHNESS AND JEWISHNESS

THE
JEWISH HERITAGE
IN
BRITISH HISTORY
Englishness and Jewishness

Edited by
TONY KUSHNER

FRANK CASS

First published 1992 in Great Britain by
FRANK CASS & CO. LTD.
Gainsborough House, Gainsborough Road,
London E11 1RS, England

and in the United States of America by
FRANK CASS
c/o International Specialized Book Services Ltd,
5602 N.E. Hassalo Street
Portland, OR 97213-3640

British Library Cataloguing in Publication Data

A catalogue record for this book is available from the British Library.

ISBN 0-7146-3464-6 (hardback)
ISBN 0-7146-4086 7 (paperback)

Library of Congress Cataloging in Publication Data

The Jewish heritage in British history : Englishness and Jewishness /
edited by Tony Kushner.
    p.   cm.
    Published also as v. 10, no. 1 of Immigrants and minorities.
    Includes index.
    ISBN 0-7146-3464-6. — ISBN 0-7146-4086-7 (pbk.)
    1. Jews—Great Britain—Historiography.   2. Great Britain—Ethnic
relations—Historiography.   3. Synagogues—Great Britain–
–Conservation and restoration.   I. Kushner, Tony (Antony Robin
Jeremy)
DS135.E5A2328   1992   92-12873
941'.004924—dc20   CIP

This group of studies first appeared in a Special Issue on 'The Jewish
Heritage in British History: Englishness and Jewishness' of *Immigrants
and Minorities*, Vol. 10, Nos. 1 & 2, published by Frank Cass & Co. Ltd.

Typeset by Regent Typesetting, London
Printed by Antony Rowe Ltd, Chippenham

To
Bill Williams
for dragging Anglo-Jewish historiography
and heritage preservation into the late
twentieth century

Contents

Notes on Contributors

Susie Barson is an architectural historian working in the London Region of English Heritage. She has prepared general guidelines for the listing of synagogues.

David Cesarani is Director of Studies at the Institute of Contemporary History and Wiener Library. His publications include *The Making of Modern Anglo-Jewry* (1990).

Judy Glasman is senior lecturer in historical and contextual studies in the Department of Art and Design, Nene College, Northampton. She has recently been the visual art critic for *New Moon* magazine.

Sharman Kadish is a Researcher in the Department of History, Royal Holloway and Bedford New College, University of London. She organized the conference 'The Future of Jewish Monuments in the British Isles' in October 1991 and her *Bolsheviks and British Jews* has just been published by Frank Cass (1992). She is chairman of the Working Party on Jewish Monuments in the UK and Ireland.

David S. Katz is Professor of History, Tel Aviv University. Among his many publications is *Philo-Semitism and the Readmission of the Jews to England, 1603–1655* (1982).

Tony Kushner is Parkes Lecturer in Jewish Studies at the University of Southampton. His writing includes *The Persistence of Prejudice* (1989) and he is convenor of the Working Party on Jewish Archives in the United Kingdom.

Lara Marks is a Research Fellow in Queen Mary and Westfield College, University of London. She has written extensively on Anglo-Jewish women's history and has completed a doctorate thesis which is being revised for publication on 'Irish and Jewish women's experience of childbirth and infant care in East London 1870–1939'.

Colin Richmond is Professor of Medieval History at Keele University where he also teaches a special subject on the Holocaust. His latest book is *The Paston Family in the Fifteenth Century: The First Phase* (1990).

Bill Williams was the first chairman of the Manchester Jewish Museum Trust and is now its honorary president and historical adviser. Currently he is working on a sequel to *The Making of Manchester Jewry* and is supervising the interviewing of Holocaust survivors for the National Life Story Collection.

Editor's Note

In July 1990 the Parkes Library with the Working Party on Jewish Archives organized a national conference: 'Preserving the Jewish Heritage'. Over 50 papers were delivered at the conference which was a successful venture in creating awareness of the dangers facing Jewish records, libraries, buildings and even popular memory in the United Kingdom. *The Jewish Heritage in British History: Englishness and Jewishness* does not reproduce these papers, although one or two do come from the conference in a much revised form. It is hoped that all the papers from that conference and some written after it will be published in another volume. Instead, this volume is an attempt to provide a more theoretical framework for the pursuit of Jewish historiography and heritage preservation in this country. It asks what sort of Anglo-Jewish history and heritage has been produced and what are the possibilities for developments in the future. In terms of monuments, it also poses the question of how Jewish buildings developed and the context in which they were created. Moreover, it asks what we are to do with those that survive today. Conservation of records, artefacts, buildings or whatever is thus only the first stage. I hope this volume provides the right balance between theoretical concerns and practical issues.

I should like to take this opportunity to thank all who came to the Southampton conference and particularly the speakers. We were also indebted to the Board of Deputies of British Jews, the Kessler Foundation, the Duke of Devonshire and Frank Cass himself for generous sponsorship. Yet again I take much pleasure in acknowledging the tremendous hard work, patience, efficiency and, most of all, the cheerfulness of Jill Whale who acted as administrator for this project. The inspiration from Bill Williams and all at the Manchester Jewish Museum is made clear elsewhere. The promotion of Stockport County (May 1991) after several decades in the fourth division provided a welcome boost while this volume was being put together. The same cannot be said for the summer '91 performance of the Southampton Cavaliers Cricket team. Thanks are also due to Lydia Linford at Cass, Sybil Lunn for the index and Mag Kushner for helping to check the proofs.

Heritage and Ethnicity: An Introduction

TONY KUSHNER

The 'Heritage Industry' in the United Kingdom has failed to acknowledge the ethnic diversity which as well as being a feature of modern British society is also an important part of the British past. This study explores the reasons behind the neglect of issues concerning immigrants and minorities in history and heritage. It also, with specific regard to Anglo-Jewish history, analyses how minorities have regarded their own history in contrast and as a response to Gentile society. It illustrates the benefits as well as potential dangers that may emerge from a new, inclusive approach to the study and representation of British history.

In the contemporary British context 'heritage' is a highly politicized and contentious term – to the extent that the authors of the National History Curriculum 'have been careful to minimise [its] use . . . because it has various meanings and is in danger of becoming unhelpfully vague'. The pressures operating on its authors were immense and it is not surprising they wanted to avoid controversy and thus confronting the 'heritage' debate. The heated debate on the curriculum, both before and after the publication of the *Final Report* reflect that 'history is a profoundly ideological subject'.[1] Those associated with the 'New Right' wished the History Curriculum to be part of a general training for citizenship – one that emphasized the achievements of Britain at home and abroad in the past (or as Margaret Thatcher put it: 'The British character has done so much for democracy, for law, and done so much throughout the world'). Indeed, the critic Neal Ascherson has suggested that 'The heritage industry, like the proposed "core curriculum" of history for English schools, imposes one ruling group's version of history on everyone and declares that it cannot be changed'. Ascherson concludes that the heritage industry, by its very nature, 'is enforcing a one-sided . . . deeply conservative view of the past upon British society'. Robert Hewison, in a pioneer study of the heritage industry published in 1987, acknowledged the tendency for it to lean towards conservatism. Nevertheless he also quoted the curator of Glasgow's People's Palace museum who claimed her collection celebrated and acted as 'the centre for the city's radical heritage'.[2] The debate about 'heritage', then, extended far beyond that of the economics of the subject (although profit making was to play a major role in the development of the 'industry' – one which ran parallel to the extolling of 'enterprise' in British society) – it was also deeply concerned with ideology and how the past could be used to buttress the politics of the present and specifically Britain's national identity.

Hewison, following Patrick Wright, was at pains to stress that whilst 'heritage' was influenced by economic and political pressure, 'economics and politics are themselves culturally conditioned'. Neither of these authors, however, fully confronted the issue of minorities and 'heritage'. It is not an aspect of the 'heritage' debate that is insignificant. Both Hewison and Wright were aware that racial minorities in Britain, whether it had been Jews in the first half of the twentieth century or 'blacks' from the New Commonwealth in the second, had been connected by contemporaries with Britain's decline. Hewison himself equated the existence of one with the presence of the other: 'Decline has been most bitterly experienced in the inner cities where much of the black population is clustered ... Since the riots in Bristol in 1980 the crisis of social control has periodically led to pitched battles with the police, with race as a catalytic factor.'[3] Wright gave more attention to this specific subject than Hewison and provided a more sophisticated analysis. Analysing the inter-war fiction of Mary Butts he discovered 'a particularistic 'England' in which belonging is mystical and intuitive ... It is an England in which to be English is to be *against* necessary outsiders.' Wright then suggests that 'the culture of pre-war anti-Semitism has gone on to serve as a resource for the racisms which in the post-war years have accompanied immigration from the fragments of disintegrating empire'.[4]

Wright, followed by Geoff Dench and Paul Gilroy, had made the important discovery that English national identity in the twentieth century (and how the national past was presented in the present) depended on the exclusion of outsiders – outsiders who were defined by 'race' or, more commonly, by culture. Thus Margaret Thatcher's comments on the *contribution* of the British to world civilization were made in the context of her justification of the control of *coloured* immigration to Britain: 'people are really rather afraid that this country might be swamped by people of a different culture'.[5] Yet, as

David Cesarani argues in this volume, the second half of the equation –
how minorities in Britain have defined their own identities and how
they themselves have played an essential role in the creation and
definition of English 'heritage' – has been ignored by the new
generation of cultural historians. The essays in this collection are
designed to show the importance of this neglected but vital area in the
understanding of the nature of 'heritage' in Britain. They deal not only
with exclusion and the intolerance of difference in the British past and
present, but also with the attempt of one specific minority – the Jews –
to shape their own heritage and history in relation to the rest of society.

I

David Cannadine has recently been described as 'The brightest and
liveliest of our young historians' with a 'range [which] is ... striking –
touching on urban, economic, social, cultural and political history'.
Here, however, is Cannadine on the study of Anglo-Jewry: 'In the
context of international Jewry, the history of British Jewry is neither
very interesting nor very exciting. In the context of British history, it is
just not that important.'[6] Given such an attitude from a progressive
and innovative historian, it is not surprising that Jewish themes (and,
indeed, themes involving other minorities) in British history have, in
general, been ignored by the historical profession in this country. John
Roberts, author of *A History of the World*, was elected on to the
working party for the History National Curriculum. He was clear that
there would be little place for black British history in the curriculum:
'If you ask what has had the most impact on our national history, the
fact of the matter is that until 1950 it was the impact of the English,
Welsh, Scots and Irish on each other. You would be very hard-pressed
to write the history of this country in terms of the ethnic minority
groups.'[7]

In a straightforward numbers game, minorities will always lose out –
as they do in terms of the curriculum *Final Report* (although it is a more
complex beast on this subject than Roberts's thinking would lead us to
expect). Elsewhere in British 'heritage' and history, exclusion is not
hard to detect. The *Final Report* has an option 'Houses and Places of
Worship Throughout History' which contains no mention of synagogues – a neat commentary on the alleged desire of its authors to
prepare pupils for 'so culturally diverse a society as exists in Britain'.[8]
A slip perhaps? Yet the new government heritage scheme to save

Britain's cathedrals follows a similar line: Anglicans, Catholics and Nonconformists can apply. A representative from English Heritage made it clear that there were no plans to extend the scheme to non-Christian religions: 'The Government has indicated that it is for cathedrals and similar buildings.'[9] The logic of such an argument is that in a Christian country, whatever their architectural or historical significance, synagogues, mosques and temples are not 'priority projects'. 'Heritage' tells us who we are and who we are not. Thus in 1988 Margaret Thatcher told the Church of Scotland Assembly in relation to religious teaching at school that 'the Christian religion' is 'a fundamental part of our national heritage. I believe it is the wish of the overwhelming majority of people that this heritage should be preserved and fostered.' Paying the obligatory lip-service to British tolerance, but at the same time reinforcing her emphasis on the Christian basis of British society, she added that 'Peoples with other faiths and cultures have always been welcomed in our land'.[10] In 1987 *The Guardian*'s art critic, Waldemar Januszczak, made the following observation:

> Looking inside the heritage culture home lovingly constructed out of favourite bits and pieces sent in by local grannies you inevitably see the nuclear family in all its unshakeable cohesion. Sleeping babies are in. Troublesome teenagers are out. Heritage homes are the direct descendants of the Christmas crib.
>
>   With one major difference – you never find foreigners in them, no three kings, no blacks, Asians, Jews, no Flemish weavers or Jacobin metal-workers. In the ... regrettable display of jingoism devoted to 'Londoners' at the Museum of London the only foreigners on show were exotic Red Indians brought over as circus exhibits.[11]

The point was echoed by another visitor to the Museum of London: 'The continued omission of the Black experience is unforgivable – when a short walk in the streets of London challenges the idea that all Londoners are white.'[12] If this is true of representations of the metropolis then it is even more the case for the countryside (described by Mike Phillips, a black British writer as 'a last refuge of English nationality, a protection against people who really ought to be foreigners but who somehow seem to have captured part of the island'). The countryside itself is cosmopolitan – flora, fauna and wildlife come from all over the globe.[13] Yet, as Peter Fryer and others have pointed out, the human history of the countryside is also multi-cultural with a black presence since Roman times, including the slaves and servants of the classic 'English' country houses.[14] Even without a black presence, many of the stately homes of England, as Phillips points out, owed their wealth to the Caribbean slave trade. The absence of black faces in the English countryside today is mirrored by their absence in the historical accounts. The actual existence of such hidden diversity is even denied by some, a representative of the Conservative Monday Club commenting that activists were 'saying that England's Celtic, Anglo-Saxon and Norman heritage can no longer be tolerated in its undiluted form and must therefore be restructured multi-ethnically'.[15]

More common than the denial of the black experience in Britain has been an avoidance of it. An African observer of Liverpool, a city built up on the profits of the triangular slave trade, pointed out in the late 1980s with regard to the City Museum that 'Its size and location hint at a desire to sanitise Liverpool's history, to purge the records. Another Liverpool Museum [the Maritime] does not even bother to acknow-ledge the trade's existence.' The same could be argued about the treatment of the Holocaust in British society – denied by only a few (mainly extremists) yet ignored and marginalized by all but a minority. Until the minority – largely, though not exclusively Jewish – protested, the Holocaust, although perhaps the central event of the twentieth century, was kept out of the national curriculum. John Roberts's solution to the problem of dealing with the Holocaust at school 'isolated from its context [which context?!]' was not to teach it at all.[16]

Exclusion of minorities in British history and 'heritage' is thus blatant, an extension of general societal discrimination or colour blindness in a culture based on the principle that 'There Ain't No Black In The Union Jack'.[17] Exclusion is not the whole story, however. Strides have been taken in the pursuit of 'multi-cultural' policies and there is a growing awareness that a white, Christian, middle-class view of the world is only a partial one. Efforts have been made, particularly from the left-liberal world and from ethnic minorities themselves, to make all cultural forms represent the diversity of society as a whole. Local history projects have been at the forefront of such endeavours. For example, here is the introduction to *Connections: Haringey Local-National-World Links* by Sylvia Collicot:

[This book] highlights the constant movement of peoples both

into and out from the parishes of Tottenham and Hornsey. That
movement had as many diverse purposes as the diversity of the
people making the journey ... [It] includes the neglected evidence of the colonised and raises the issue of bias and omission in
the writing of much British history.

A similar project in another London borough, Waltham Forest,
points out 'that valuable evidence about the experience of the black
and ethnic minorities communities can be identified and important
themes recovered and highlighted'. In recent years such efforts have
led to a series of local history publications based on the belief 'that the
experiences of ethnic people ... were not being expressed in historical
publications, exhibitions and educational resources'.[18] It is important
that such work, some of it of a high quality, has been carried out. Yet a
larger question remains: what is to be done with the minority experience once it is found? Rescuing the past presence of groups such as
Afro-Caribbeans, Gypsies or Jews is necessary if 'balanced' history is
to be produced, but is it sufficient? Geoffrey Elton has suggested that
the 'non-existent history of ethnic entities and women' leads to 'in-
coherent syllabuses'. Instead he wanted 'more English history, more
kings and bishops'. It is ironic that Elton, once a child refugee, should
deny the existence of ethnic entities. Nevertheless, Elton was right to
raise the issue of where ethnic history 'fits'.[19]
    To the disappointment of some on the right, the History curriculum
Final Report is neither all English kings and queens nor, for that
matter, overly Anglocentric. Indeed, within the British syllabus distinctive Scottish, Welsh and Irish themes are emphasised. Moreover
the *Final Report* stresses that: 'Processes of migration have added
further languages and cultures to the longer-established ones of
Britain. People have come to Britain from near and far: for example
Celts, Romans, Anglo-Saxons, Vikings, Germans, Jews, Huguenots,
Poles, Ukrainians, people from Africa, from Asia, and from the
Caribbean.'[20]
    If the curriculum options are examined in more detail, it is possible
to see how well the 'richness and variety of British culture and its
historical origins' is dealt with in practice. The options 'Victorian
Britain' includes 'Irish and Jewish immigration'; 'Ships and seafarers
through history' mentions 'Minority ethnic communities in British
ports'; 'Expansion, trade and industry: Britain c. 1750 to c. 1900'
likewise has 'Irish and Jewish immigration. Black people in Britain';

'Britain in the twentieth century' refers to 'Immigration Acts. Race Relations Act, 1965' and, away from modern British history, the option 'Medieval Realms' includes 'Jews in medieval society'. All are placed in the same category – exemplary information in the social and religious sub-section. 'Exemplary information', it should be added, 'is only for the guidance of teachers and is not part of the assessment process; they may or may not use it in their schemes of work'.[21]

In short, minorities are no longer notable by their absence but there is still a degree of marginality taking place – such groups rarely feature in 'Essential information [which] *must* be taught'. Rigid exclusion is replaced by an optional pluralism. In this area, as in so many others, the curriculum offers an uneasy compromise. It rejects an exclusive mono-cultural analysis of British history yet offers little assistance and only lukewarm support over the question of how the study of minorities can be incorporated. On one level the justification of recognizing the presence of immigrants and minorities is straightforward. The historical knowledge of minorities gained and the skills obtained 'should', in the words of the *Final Report*, 'assist in identifying, and thus combatting, racial and other forms of prejudice and stereotypical thinking'. That 'anti-racist' educational initiatives are still required in contemporary Britain, where textbooks are still in use which refer to the 'frizzy haired cannibals' of New Guinea, is unquestionnable. In addition, the use of black or other ethnic figures in historical representations can help raise the prestige and self-image of minority groups. There is, however, a danger with such an approach.[22]

II

In the search to 'reclaim the past', *critical* historical analysis can be forgotten. The search for roots and the 'celebration' of continuous presence take precedence over the need to locate contexts and to provide relevance. Ferdinand Dennis quite rightly chastises British civic museums for their lack of attention to Afro-Caribbean culture and the 'resentment and anger' such exclusion causes amongst black British youth today. He adds that 'The Afro-Caribbeans' right to their history should be given official sanction. The great museums and art galleries of Britain need to be seen to be celebrating it, too.' In short, Dennis wishes to replace the omission of the black experience in art galleries, museums and the like with positive representations of Afro-Caribbean and Asian culture throughout history.[23] There is a risk, it must be suggested, with any attempt to over-compensate for past neglect and distortion. It is at the point where analysis gives way to 'celebration' that history can become 'heritage'. There is a need to move from the first stage of reconstruction – that is re-introducing the minority presence on to the historical stage in a non-patronising, racist form – on to the second – examining where minorities 'fit' into general society and examining their own internal dynamics. There has to be a realisation that minorities are often complex groups, containing their own internal divisions and conflicts, and that responses to them are equally complicated. In fact, the locating of the minority provides only the initial foundation from which the real historical analysis can develop.

David Cannadine, whilst acknowledging that the history lampooned in *1066 and All That* of kings and queens and great events ('the story of of Britain's rise to being top nation'), is no longer acceptable, has made a plea for 'a national framework to make sense of our individual historical experience'. He has suggested that:

> the proliferation of history since the Second World War into a variety of sub-specialisms has further accentuated this profes-sional trend away from the study of the national past. Economic history, social history, urban history, women's history and black history – subjects which have seemed of the greatest contem-porary relevance and concern – are rarely conceptualised or written about by professional scholars in national terms ... The result is a version of the past in which blacks or women or city dwellers have more in common with the same people in other countries than they have with different people in the same country.

On the surface minority studies may lead, as Cannadine fears, to 'a fragmented and piecemeal past'.[24] As we have seen with the History Curriculum *Final Report*, it is easiest to locate minorities on a local level without giving any indication of what larger patterns they illustrate other than a parochial cultural diversity. Yet this approach is the least satisfactory and, as Raphael Samuel has argued, 'multi-cultural' and 'national' history:

> are not necessarily mutually exclusive, and it might be rewarding to study the second in the light of the first ... Likewise the recognition of ethnic diversity in the present might serve to put in

question the notion, so dear to Tory atavism, of some all-English past ... Anti-alien sentiment, though only surfacing occasionally in organised political form, might nevertheless appear (if it were historically examined) a systematic feature of national life.[25]

Samuel is, in fact, suggesting that the study of minorities will itself lead to considerations of Britain's *national* identity in relation to these groups. Similarly, Britain's first proposed degree course in homosexual studies has been criticised as being potentially narrow. In response, Jonathan Dollimore, who designed the MA syllabus on this subject has commented:

> Mention lesbian and gay studies and most people declare it to be irrelevant, but there is no question of it being an isolated subject. The history of sexuality is really the history of society – not that everything is sexual in a Freudian way, but that everything intersects with sexuality ... If lesbian and gay studies is really a minority interest, why is society so obsessed with homosexuality – at all levels, in all forms?[26]

If one takes a subject close to Cannadine's own interests, the British aristocracy in the nineteenth and twentieth centuries, the potential of minority studies is revealed. From the mid-Victorian era through to the 1920s, the elite of Anglo-Jewry, the so-called 'Cousinhood', embarked on an impressive building programme of country houses. They were aware that prestige came from the land and not just from wealth itself. Families such as the Rothschilds and Sassoons wished to establish their place on a level with the 'British' aristocracy.[27] The responses of the aristocracy to these Jewish estates revealed far more than the trivia of the social snobbery of the British upper classes – it indicated their own sense of identity in a rapidly changing world. David Lindsay, twenty-seventh Earl of Crawford and tenth Earl of Balcarres, was a prominent Conservative politician before the First World War and was one of the pioneers of 'heritage' conservation after 1918. His diaries reveal a fascination and attraction for the 'big Jewish houses' yet a simultaneous disgust at their 'overpowering ostentation and vulgarity'. The British aristocracy spent many of their weekends enjoying lavish Jewish hospitality yet agreeing amongst themselves that their surrounds were tasteless, vulgar and, ultimately, 'un-English'. Stephen Doree, examining the aristocracy's response to Sir Philip Sassoon's Trent Park argues that 'His country house may have been authentically classical, even "whig", but it only seemed to throw into sharper relief Sassoon's recent oriental ancestry'. At a stage where their status and wealth in mass, urban society was under threat, British aristocrats could comfort themselves that at least they were not Jewish. At the same time, they gorged themselves on Jewish entertainment to fill the vacuum of their wasted lives.[28]

Such was the function of antisemitism in elite British society – not in creating pogroms which sickened Lindsay and others of his class such as Harold Nicolson, but in providing a sense of national identity in a world in flux. John Vincent, as the editor of Crawford's diaries, does not even mention the constantly recurring references to Jews. Elsewhere, however, he has referred to British anti-Semitism as a vague prejudice, minor in importance and 'even ... benign in attention' leaving 'only a faint and delicate odour in the records'. Yet Jews *mattered* to Crawford and his class and scholars as varied as Vincent, Cannadine and Martin Wiener have done British history a disservice by ignoring the importance of this issue.[29] By studying responses to minorities the identity and nature of majority society comes into focus. In this sense the onus is not just on minority specialists to broaden their work and place it in context. The major danger in fact for historical studies is that its major practitioners will continue with their own narrow vision. As Philip Curtin put it: 'The discipline of history has broadened enormously in the post-war decades, but historians have not ... We have specialists in black history, women's history, and historical demography, but people outside these specialities pay little attention to their work.'[30]

III

It is not difficult, therefore, to justify minority studies as a *broadening* exercise revealing the very nature of national identity. It is important, however, in such studies, as Bill Williams has pointed out, not to ignore the 'rich "inner life" ' in the history of ethnic minorities, which 'certainly relate to British society, but [which have their] own validity and a range of dynamics'. Williams highlights the potential dangers of 'an external perspective on immigrant minorities'. As a result of the 'external' approach 'Rarely do we hear the voices of immigrants speaking to us, never to each other'. It is ironic that it is the *conservative*, but, significantly, the unorthodox historian, Jonathan Clark who has also seen the need to follow the approach advocated by Williams:

the one issue academic historians have still, so far, fought shy [of is] the diverse ethnic composition of the population of these islands. It addresses a society in racial turmoil, one which has still not come to terms with the massive immigration for the un- spoken reason that it still lacks an historical understanding of how and why it happened ... How far have immigrant groups sought to integrate themselves into British history, to appro- priate it, to become its heirs?[31]

There is indeed a rich seam for historians to exploit in the area of British minority experience. Too often, for example, is the post-war Afro-Caribbean presence in Britain seen in problematic terms in history textbooks. A pathological chronology is adopted starting with the arrival of the *Empire Windrush* in 1948 followed by the race riots in Notting Hill ten years later and finally the inner city disturbances of the 1980s. It is an approach which can be seen as a historical parallel to Powellism which allows no room for the exploration of black develop- ment in British society and culture. Instead we are offered just racism and revolt – a sanitised historian's 'rivers of blood'.[32]

To emphasize the potential of ethnic studies it is worth returning briefly to the case of the British aristocracy and the stately home. The use and abuse of Jewish hospitality in the new country seats by the 'English' upper classes has already been commented on. But what of those who provided such amusements? David Cannadine in *The Decline and Fall of the British Aristocracy* is aware of the importance of 'outsiders' and particularly Jews and Americans in buying up estates and building new country houses in the late nineteenth and early twentieth centuries. Nowhere, however, do we get a consideration of the mentality and sense of identity of these newcomers.[33] The work of Chaim Bermant on the Anglo-Jewish gentry and that of Stephen Doree on Philip Sassoon is unfortunately ignored by Cannadine. Doree, in particular, provides a fascinating picture of the dilemmas facing Sassoon:

> He might neglect attendance at synagogue, he might throw weekend parties which, in their timing at least were incompatible with Jewish religious observance, he might accumulate pictures, furniture and *objets d'art* which made no concession to Jewish taste, he might refuse to entertain Jews, profess disinterest in Zionism and show little apparent concern for the fate of Euro- pean Jewry in the 1930s, he might even take steps to dress in such

a way that his Jewish physical features were less obvious – yet he could not, and did not, entirely discard his Jewishness.[34]

British minorities define their own identities. They do so certainly neither in isolation from 'majority' society nor in a simplistic or homogeneous manner, yet their own input cannot be ignored. Philip Sassoon may not ultimately have been accepted in Gentile society, 'he was no part of England' as even his friend Lord Boothby put it, but he had nothing in common and literally lived in a different world to the working class and even middle class Jews of Britain. Sassoon in his own agonized way, which verged on self-hatred, created in Trent Park a monument which we now clearly see as part of the British national heritage.[35] As with the question of identities and closely linked to it, minorities have formed their own definitions of the nature of 'heritage'.

IV

Surprise is often expressed at the neglect by the Jewish minority itself of Anglo-Jewish history in terms of its records, buildings, artefacts and memories. For a people with one of the oldest traditions, Jews have been *on the surface* relatively indifferent to the preservation of their historical past. This has been partly due to historical circumstances where the turbulent nature of Jewish history and, in particular, the constant movement of the diaspora has not been conducive to the preservation of records etc which were inevitably a lower priority than the rescue of the essentials of life. There has also been an ideological factor involved, at least until the modern era, with a concentration on the Hebrew scriptures in Jewish thinking. Lionel Kochan has argued that because God for the Jews in pre-modern times had a fundamentally historical nature

> The record of His doings and promises as narrated in the Hebrew scriptures and appropriately understood, utterly exhausted all putative historical interest. The affirmation of history, embodied in those scriptures, removed all need to study history, for in themselves the scriptures answered all historical questions – where Israel originated, where it stands and where it is going.

When in the eighteenth and nineteenth centuries as messianic Judaism declined and the ideas of the enlightenment came into force, Jewish history not only became possible – for some its study became essential.[36]

The idea of the 'Jewish Heritage' being defined in purely religious terms is still very strong. Dan Cohn-Sherbok's book of that title is, indeed, a history of Jewish religious thought and tradition throughout the ages. One of those speaking at the Southampton conference 'Preserving the Jewish Heritage' (from which this volume emerged) explicitly made the point that at first he expected it to be concerned with the religious education of Jewish youth and future generations of Anglo-Jewry.[37] Yet, as David Cesarani indicates, a strong historical consciousness had developed amongst sections of Anglo-Jewry by the last quarter of the nineteenth century.

On one level it does appear that the Jews of Britain have been proud of their history. In 1993 the Jewish Historical Society of England will be celebrating its centenary; the Anglo-Jewish Historical Exhibition which preceded it by six years was one of the first of its type in Europe. In 1932 the Mocatta Library in University College London was re-launched as a major Jewish studies centre and with it came the Jewish Museum. Since the war another major Anglo-Jewish historical exhibition took place in 1956 to mark the tercentenary of resettlement; Anglo-Jewish Archives was established in the 1960s and more recently two Jewish social history museums as well as a Scottish Jewish project have been added to the historical infrastructure of the community. There is, however, another side to this story – one of neglect, indifference and even embarrassment about the Jewish past in Britain. In 1960 the American historian Lloyd Gartner pointed towards a paradox: 'I venture ... to express the hope that the distinguished and historically conscious Jewry of England will not permit the records of the immigrant period from 1870 to 1914 to be lost or destroyed by neglect. However, this is in a fair way of happening.' At that stage Anglo-Jewry did not lack the cohesiveness or minimal financial requirements to take the action Gartner suggested. Its failure to do so reflected a lack of will, yet Gartner was not mistaken when he pointed to Anglo-Jewry's pride in its history.[38]

What was at stake (and continues to be so since the galvanising of Jewish historiography with the Anglo-Jewish Historical Exhibition) was what kind of Jewish heritage should be presented and preserved. As E.H. Carr stressed 'Before you study the history, study the historian'. The neglect of the East European immigrant experience which Gartner highlighted was no accident. The history and heritage that the Jewish establishment wanted to emphasise reflected their own concerns and interests. Thus at the same point that the Anti-Demolition Movement was set up to preserve the elite Bevis Marks (the oldest surviving synagogue in Britain with close links to the resettlement of the Jews), establishment Anglo-Jewry was trying, as Judy Glasman illustrates, to destroy the tiny informal synagogues, or *shtiebls*, which housed the *chevroth* (societies) of the East End.[39] To the elite it was essential to Anglicize the immigrant masses as soon as possible. It was therefore undesirable to preserve for posterity *in any way*, including for the historical record, the immigrants' radical politics or unEnglish religious habits.

The idea of constructing a Jewish historical heritage existing without ideological underpinnings is naive. Any representation of an ethnic past that does not recognize the possibility of internal conflict or the existence of trends or individuals that were not heroic (or indeed could be construed as embarrassing) is bound to be distorted. The essays in this volume reveal how Jewish themes in *British* heritage and history have been abused or neglected. They also show how exclusion is not the only problem and that there is the potential within the minority's own representation of its heritage for 'the reduction of history to ethnic cheer-leading'.[40]

V

The defensive nature of late nineteenth century Anglo-Jewish historiography is highlighted by David Cesarani in his contribution to *Englishness and Jewishness*. The early practitioners were under the burden of writing in a political atmosphere where Jews were not only attacked for their present activities in Britain but also for those of their historic ancestors in the Middle Ages. For the Jewish Historical Society of England, suggests Cesarani, 'The construction of the Anglo-Jewish past, its heritage, was to stress the rootedness of Jews in English society and their positive contribution to politics, culture and the economy'.[41] That the pioneers of Anglo-Jewish history and later writers such as Cecil Roth were not suffering from paranoia about British society and its historians becomes clear in Colin Richmond's contribution to this volume.

Richmond exposes how Jewish themes permeate the history of medieval England yet how, even today, distinguished historians of that period have been unable or unwilling to deal with the subject. The importance of an anti-Jewish ideology to important figures such as Simon de Montfort or even Edward I has been either ignored or more

often excused by leading twentieth-century writers. The embarrassment of British historians at the existence of ritual murder accusations,
massacres and the eventual expulsion of the Jews has led to that most
English of traits in terms of 'race relations' – blaming the victim. The
removal of the Jews in 1290 by Edward thus becomes in the words of
one scholar an act of 'statesmanship' which it is 'difficult to doubt' or,
in the words of another, carried out 'in a gentlemanly fashion'.
Richmond provides a different interpretation, suggesting that the Jews
were vital in the formation of a national identity: 'it is ... the
[medieval] governing elite who first equate Englishness with non-
Jewishness'. He also adds that whilst 'Jews disappeared from England
in 1290; "the Jew" did not'.[42] The roots of the heritage industry, David
Cesarani reminds us, stretch much further back than its recent critics
have realized. Cesarani concentrates on the crucial period in the last
decades of the nineteenth centuries when the modern idea of 'Englishness' was constructed. Richmond goes back 600 years earlier and to the
construction of the shrine to Little St Hugh in Lincoln Cathedral in the
1290s – a project undertaken by Edward I after he had expelled the
Jews. Here was a demonstration of Edward as the protector of English
Christians against the diabolic Jews, the ritual murderers of children.[43]

   The ritual murder and later blood libel accusation myth led to the
death of hundreds of Jews and the destruction of many Jewish communities in the Middle Ages. The accusation, however, lingered well
beyond its medieval confines even in a country such as England which
for three centuries lacked any real Jewish presence. Just as with the
heritage industry today, economics and ideology with their common
cultural roots provide the explanation of how this could happen. The
first ritual murder accusation occurred in Norwich in 1144. It has been
commented that Norwich had 'the need for a saint' and that 'There
were marked economic advantages to both Norwich Priory and the city
itself in the successful establishment of St. William (the alleged victim)
as a wonder-working saint and martyr.' Gavin Langmuir points also to
the importance of ideology in this first attempt to create the ritual
murder myth through a Benedictine monk, Thomas of Monmouth.[44] In
Lincoln the shrine acted as a constant reminder of the 'true' nature of
the Jews. Equally enduring and with a greater circulation was
Chaucer's 'Prioress' Tale' and the subsequent ballads that developed
from it.[45]

   If we turn to the use of Little St Hugh as twentieth century 'heritage'
the reasons behind the defensive nature of early Jewish historiography

are made clear. In the ballads associated with Little St Hugh the idea that the Jews hid his murdered body in a well became part of legend. To provide it with some substance, a false well was constructed in 'Jews' Court', Lincoln at the turn of the century. The money making potential of the ritual myth was thus alive and well in liberal Britain as late as the 1920s.[46] In the cathedral itself 'the description of the shrine of Little St Hugh of Lincoln openly perpetuated this myth until as recently as 1934'. In that year a vicious and pornographic version of the blood libel reappeared in Nazi Germany. The Jewish Historical Society of England attempted to repair some of the damage by arranging a meeting with the cathedral bodies and Mayor of Lincoln. The Mayor and Chancellor of the Cathedral duly obliged and provided a 'forthright repudiation of the murder myth'. A new plaque condemning the accusation, along with a new guidebook to the city also attacking the libel, were produced by the religious and civic authorities. Cecil Roth was brought in to give a lecture to mark the occasion and his gratitide was made clear from his concluding remarks: 'The city which harbours these magnificent relics of mediaeval Jewry will have nothing to do with the revival of mediaeval anti-Jewish prejudice. The implications of this action are not lost upon us. In the name of the Jewish Historical Society of England, gentleman, I thank you.'

The *Jewish Chronicle* added that the Lincoln gesture 'registers the birth of a saner and happier age. It is a warning to Continental dabblers in medieval mire that, whatever they do, Englishman, at any rate, have broken with the Middle Ages, and do not intend to undo 700 years of moral and intellectual progress.'[47] These constant references to English toleration are a reminder of the insecurity felt by those who practised Anglo-Jewish history. They wrote with the constant fear of anti-Semitism and the need in their writings to combat the negative image of the Jew and, at the very least, not to give any ammunition to anti-Semites.

Whether Britain in the mid-twentieth century had totally 'broken with the Middle Ages' is open to question. In 1948 a school history textbook, *The Plantagenets*, suggested that the evidence did point towards the Jews having committed ritual murder in medieval England. This best-selling textbook was not withdrawn by its various publishers until the late 1980s. On a popular level, Jews in Britain still found the accusation used against them in town and country. In 1962 a vicar in Willoughby wrote to Victor Gollancz protesting about the Jewish method of animal slaughter. He concluded: 'Can you wonder the Little St Hugh Legend arose in this diocese?' More recently (1989) allegations were made that local clergy were repeating the blood libel story to tourists in Lincoln cathedral.[48]

In 1987 a major exhibition, 'The Age of Chivalry' devoted to the medieval period, took place at the Royal Academy. It contained no material directly related to the Jews of England apart from a painting 'Synagogue' of 1290 from York Minster. No caption accompanied the image – a classic representation of Judaism as both blindfolded and dejected.[49] Have then all the efforts of the Jewish Historical Society with regard to the medieval period been in vain? Is there still distortion and neglect? The anniversaries commemorated in 1990 suggest that there is a new, more positive tendency to report in terms of the representation of the medieval Anglo-Jewish heritage. In spring 1990, the 800th anniversary of the massacre of the Jews in York was marked by a series of events in the town. Leading Christians acknowledged the importance of anti-Semitism in their religious tradition and asked for forgiveness. Two exhibitions, 'Jews in Medieval York' and 'The Jewish Way of Life' accompanied the events which included an ecumenical service led by by the Archbishop of York: 'Expressions of Heritage and Hope'. In November 1990 the 700th anniversary of the expulsion of the Jews was also marked – in this case by a major television documentary. In Lincoln, 'Jewish Heritage tours' offers an alternative view of Little St Hugh. In addition to exposing the blood libel accusation, its organizer covers the Jewish settlement of Lincoln: 'a fascinating part of our heritage'.

It is thus possible that the exclusion as in 'The Age of Chivalry' exhibition will no longer be repeated. There is still a long way to go, especially in recognising the importance of the study of medieval Anglo-Jewry, as Richmond indicates. But the genuine interest of historians of the callibre of Barrie Dobson, Robert Stacey and Richmond himself suggests that we may now be moving away from the initial defensive approach to the Jews of medieval England practised by the early Jewish Historical Society.[50]

VI

After the expulsion, the rest of Anglo-Jewish history represented what we have seen the *Jewish Chronicle* describe as '700 years of moral and intellectual progress' on behalf of the English. As David Cesarani suggests, to the Jewish Historical Society 'the readmission, the community of the resettlement and the emancipation period offered the perfect synthesis of Jewish and English heritage'.[51] In similar vein, David Katz here points to the Whiggish nature of Anglo-Jewish historiography and its impact on the study of Jewish themes of the early modern period. The readmission of the Jews of England has been marked by what have been literally celebrations on behalf of Anglo-Jewry. 'Resettlement days' of the 1890s and 1900s were followed by the massive tercentenary events of 1956. Only recently have the *Transactions* of the Jewish Historical Society moved beyond the medieval and early modern periods. Despite or perhaps because of all this attention in exhibitions and writings, huge problems remain in the area of early modern Anglo-Jewish historiography and heritage.

Writing in 1930, Cecil Roth was amazed to find the neglect of the prized historical record of the Jews of early modern England. Major synagogues such as the Great, the Hambro and the New had lost much material and records were 'disappointingly late in date'. Those that had survived were in poor condition and neglected. Only recently have these limited materials been deposited in the hands of a professional public archive.[52] Other Jewish records for the early modern period remain in private hands, lacking proper conservation and cataloguing. Inevitably the neglect of its own heritage and the lack of easy access has made an impact on the standard of historiography. It has not acted as an incentive for 'general' scholars to use specifically Jewish material. Yet this factor does not on its own explain the neglect of Jewish themes in early modern English history writing. Nor does the limited range and general insularity of Jewish historians of this period act as a justification for the marginalization of the subject – one that neatly mirrors that of the medieval period. David Katz, through three interesting case studies, exposes the limitations of past scholarship. He also shows what historians are missing – insights not only into the Jewish minority and all those who had contact with them, but also subtleties and nuances about society and government as a whole. Again the need to take Jewish themes seriously is not a case of special pleading, it is so that we can understand the interests and motivations of contemporary figures – at all stages of British history.

VII

David Katz suggests that Anglo-Jewish historiography has been 'written with one eye on the final destination of the history train, the End of

Anglo-Jewish History – "Emancipation" '. This was certainly the case until the early 1950s whether in representations of the Anglo-Jewish past in writing, exhibitions or museums. Indeed, when Cecil Roth carried out his survey of the records of the United Synagogue in 1930, he suggested 1870 as a cut off point for 'records of historical importance'.[53] 1870 fits Katz's idea of emancipation marking the end of Jewish history and the full entry into the Messianic world of British society. It has also another significance – marking the escalation of immigration of poor Jews from Eastern Europe. Having gained emancipation, the established Jews of England found their own security threatened by hundreds of thousands of alien Jews. It was in this background, as Cesarani points out, that the Jewish Historical Society was formed. It was to take over half a century before the Society could even contemplate writing about the new arrivals. By then, ironically, the process of anglicization had been so successful that much of the East European Jewish immigrant heritage had been wiped out.

As I suggest, although the 1956 Tercentenary Celebration inevitably concentrated on the early modern period and little of its content rose above the self-congratulatory, it did act (if only in a limited way) as a turning point in Jewish historiography and heritage representation. Although peripheral to the main thrusts of the celebration, there were exhibits on aspects of Yiddish culture and immigrant life in Britain. This contrasted with the almost total silence on these subjects in the Anglo-Jewish Exhibition in the Festival of Britain just five years earlier. The major publication that emerged from the celebration, *Three Centuries of Anglo-Jewish History*, reveal the subtle changes that were taking place. Although the illustrations of the book concentrated on the period between readmission and emancipation (with the frontispiece devoted to Menasseh Ben Israel), two map reproductions gave a hint of changes to come. At the front of the book was a plan of 1756 illustrating the Algate Ward of London showing the Bevis Marks, Great, Hambro and New Synagogues. On the very back, however, Russell and Lewis's map of the East End of London in 1900 (representing the proportion of Jewish residents in each street) was reproduced. Between these two maps, of the eight chapters, one was devoted to the 'New Community, 1880–1918'. This chapter by Israel Finestein was one of the first attempts to historicise the East European immigrants to Britain.[54]

In the late 1950s Finestein and Vivian Lipman opened up this new area of Jewish history laying the foundations for the classic scholarship

of Lloyd Gartner – *The Jewish Immigrant in England*. It was no
accident, however, that Gartner was an American, a product of the
historical study of ethnicity in the United States. The restraints operating on Anglo-Jewish scholars did not apply and Gartner was to cover
taboo subjects such as immigrant radicalism and religious life. Lipman, as the most productive Anglo-Jewish scholar at this time, as
Geoffrey Alderman suggests, reflected the dilemmas facing Anglo-
Jewish historiography: 'He was sufficiently aware of the need for
comprehensiveness to be able to escape from the alleged dictates of
communal image that had motivated Roth and others of Roth's
generation. But the escape was never complete.'[55]

Gartner's key work was published in 1960 but little else developed in
that decade to develop or challenge his analysis. Although the East
European immigrant experience was now seen as 'history', huge gaps
and biases were developing. Gartner had studied the lives of the
immigrants themselves as well as the response of establishment Jewry
towards them. He called for the preservation of the records of the
immigrants including their Yiddish papers, personal letters, diaries
and even steamship tickets. Although three years later Anglo-Jewish
Archives was set up by the Jewish Historical Society, it tended to
concentrate on the records of organizations set up to deal with the
immigrants rather than the newcomers' own material. Scholarship also
concentrated on the communal organizations such as the Jewish Board
of Guardians and was uncritical in tone.[56]

Change had taken place by the 1960s, but compared to countries
such as the United States, it was painfully slow in happening. Despite
all the exhibitions and publications, women's history, Jewish
radicalism and other 'deviant' tendencies (let alone class conflict
within Anglo-Jewry) remained untouchable subjects. Moreover, although the immigrant movement before 1914 was, within certain
bounds, an acceptable area of study, the more recent movement from
Nazi Europe remained unexplored beyond a few celebratory accounts.
No academic positions for the study of the Jews of Britain were created
in Jewish studies departments – one suggestion to this end met the
response that 'Anglo-Jewish studies were too parochial' – and there
were few outlets for those who wanted to provide a fresh approach.[57]
The achievements therefore of the Celebration of the Jewish East End
in 1987 were thus all the more remarkable. Through sheer hard work,
most of it voluntary, a new generation of scholars and activists had
managed to pull Anglo-Jewish historiography and heritage out of

obscurity and into the late twentieth century. The study of the Jews of Britain was not only brought up to date in its technique and execution, it was, in many areas, ahead of both general British historiography and Jewish studies scholarship abroad.

Gender themes and Jewish women's history had suffered specific neglect in representations of Anglo-Jewry. From the 1880s to the 1970s, Anglo-Jewish historiography, whatever the subject or period, had managed to ignore women. Such absences, although perhaps extreme in this specific case, reflected the general lack of interest in women's history in Britain and beyond. It is significant, however, as Lara Marks suggests, that those in Britain who have studied gender since the growth of women's studies, have ignored ethnicity and concentrated on class. The reverse is true in the United States, where the study of Jewish women's history is now well established. There, class has been ignored, or as Marks suggests, often confused with ethnicity. Lara Marks' work reveals the strength of the new Anglo-Jewish historiography and its potential for both generalists and students of Jewish studies. Class, gender and ethnicity are combined to provide a complex but ultimately more satisfactory analysis. Rather than representing parochialism, Marks shows how new areas of study can be introduced to historians and how these shed light on broader matters. As she suggests: 'The challenge for historians is to unite the vast literature on the history of Jews in Britain and on gender, and to show how the issues of class, gender and ethnicity affected not only the settlement and migration patterns of Jews but also the social fabric of British society.'[58]

VIII

In the absence of established academic positions, the new generation of Jewish historians in Britain were forced to create their instititions, formal and informal. The most important of these were the new Jewish Museums of England which enabled the flowering of talent which culminated in the East End Celebration. The Anglo-Jewish Historical Exhibition of 1887 was a stimulation for the creation of Jewish museums across Europe yet, ironically, it failed to have the same impact in Britain itself. The low priority given to historical matters explains why the Jewish Museum in London was not created until 1932 and that only now, 60 years later is it on the verge of moving to its own buildings. The Museum, presently located in the communal headquarters of Anglo-Jewry, has a strict collecting policy. Items 'are not normally collected unless they are 100 years old' and the Museum concentrates on expensive ritual items. The focus of the Museum is on religious life. Social history, certainly of the Jewish poor, is not a major concern either in the Museum's permanent display or its exhibitions. In contrast the Manchester Jewish Museum has the aim of being 'by the people, for the people and about the people'.[59]

The Museum was set up after an initiative in the Manchester Studies Department of Manchester Polytechnic in the 1970s. A prime mover in both was Bill Williams who commented at the end of that decade that 'Perhaps the most remarkable aspect of the study of local Anglo-Jewish history over the past two decades has been its singular lack of progress'.[60] Indeed one could add that provincial history had been another of the Jewish Historical Society's blind spots since its creation. The Manchester Jewish Museum did more than put Britain's second largest Jewish community on the historical map. Through Bill Williams himself and Ros Livshin and Rickie Burman new subjects in Jewish historiography such as childhood, women and labour history were approached. In addition the Polytechnic project and then the Museum itself became one of the pioneer practitioners of oral history in Britain, allowing different perspectives on Jewish history, or as Williams suggests 'an "alternative" version of the communal heritage'. Taboo subjects such as British anti-Semitism and Jewish radicalism were not shied away from by the new museum. In terms of historiography the Whiggish apologetic approach was replaced with a more critical interpretation: 'It was not defensive or didactic in the face of anti-semitism.' Here was 'heritage' which incorporated the critical use of history.[61]

The impact of the Manchester Jewish Museum went well beyond its local confines. On a level of individuals, Rickie Burman, the first serious student of Anglo-Jewish women's history, went on to found the Museum of the Jewish East End, now the London Museum of Jewish Life. The new generation of Jewish scholars was influenced by the approach of the Museum and the individuals connected to it. Thus the Celebration of the Jewish East End owed as much to initatives made in the north of England as the capital itself. Yet as Bill Williams illustrates, the battle to create the Museum was a hard one, fought against communal apathy and sometimes even antipathy. The Manchester Jewish Museum has also acted as a pioneer in terms of archive, building and artefact preservation – an area in which the rest of Anglo-Jewry has still a long way to go.

In all areas of conservation the Manchester Jewish Museum had notable successes although there were also some tragic losses. The Museum itself won high recommendation form the Museum of the Year competition for its restoration of the Spanish and Portuguese Synagogue. A few yards down Cheetham Hill Road, the indifference of the Jewish community led to the decline and eventual destruction of the equally impressive Great Synagogue. In London, as Sharman Kadish illustrates in her case study of the East London Synagogue and the capital in general, the Jewish community has been slow to see the danger facing its building heritage. As with so many aspects of the Jewish heritage, the common lack of interest of the general community has reinforced the marginal nature of Jewish buildings. Architectural historians and conservationists have not, until recently, considered Jewish issues – the government cathedral heritage trust referred to earlier is just the latest in a long history of neglect. One good example of this was the damage inflicted on Britain's architectural heritage during the Second World War.

The war remains the most crucial point of reference in modern British identity; the bombing of British cities one of the nation's most poignant memories. The loss the Jewish community suffered in terms of its buildings, and particularly that of the Great Synagogue has, however, rarely been considered. Thus a photograph album of blitzed buildings published in the war itself, whose purpose was 'to put on record those of our national architectural possessions that have become casualties', included hundreds of churches but not the Great Synagogue which was destroyed the same night that damage was inflicted on Westminster Abbey in May 1941. On a less grand scale, many Jewish landmarks in the East End were destroyed in the war, yet it is the destruction without record or controversy of so many buildings after 1945 that is most striking.[62] The solution, as Susie Barson and Sharman Kadish suggest, is for the Jewish community to take the issue of conservation seriously and then to pressurize heritage bodies to take action. It is hard for the general architectural community to take Jewish buildings as a priority if the Jewish community itself appears not to care if they fall into neglect or disappear altogether.

Some interesting ironies have developed in Jewish historical building preservation. The elite Spanish and Portuguese Synagogue building of 1874 (which catered for roughly thirty Sephardi trading families of Manchester) is now devoted to portraying the lives or ordinary Jews who would have been excluded from its doors. The East London Synagogue was designed, as Judy Glasman explains, as an attempt by the Jewish establishment in the late nineteenth century to take the poor Jews away from their subversive *chevroth* of Whitechapel. In its abandoned state it is now one of the few legacies of the rich and vibrant culture of the immigrant Jews and their children of the East End. There is a danger with building conservation that it preserves an ideal world which never really existed. Spitalfields, as Raphael Samuel suggests, was never the pure Georgian world that its faddists assume. It has always had mixed architectural styles, each era imposing a new layer of peoples and buildings. It would be sheer escapism to hope that the Jewish East End could be preserved as a folk museum, but that all trace of the Jewish presence should disappear, as is presently occurring at an alarmingly quick pace, is an indictment against the Jewish community. The roots of the Jewish community for future generations to explore are being destroyed without thought.[63]

Synagogue buildings, like all other aspects of Jewish history and heritage, are not straightforward monuments to be celebrated. As Judy Glasman illustrates, they represent the battles fought within Anglo-Jewry and the constant fear of the non-Jewish world that operated amonst its elite. Synagogue architecture cannot be understood without wider reference to general society. Equally, the fascinating strategies adopted by Anglo-Jewry in their design of synagogues are an essential part of the history of British architecture. The conservation of synagogue buildings and other structures including as Kadish suggests, graveyards, can easily become an exercise in creating and promoting nostalgia – the bread and butter of the heritage industry. This need not be the case, as Judy Glasman illustrates – the nature of buildings is part of the critical study of history.

IX

The essays in this volume cover a huge chronology and subject range. They are connected in their desire to take the Anglo-Jewish past *seriously* – a plea aimed equally at the Jewish and non-Jewish worlds. The factors that have stopped this happening – the lack of security of British Jewry and the indifference and ignorance of gentile society – have not disappeared. Nevertheless, the contributions in this volume have shown more positive trends in recent times which suggests that

Jewish historical studies (in their broadest sense) in this country may be free to develop with greater freedom than ever before. Ritual murder accusations are still circulating in the Britain of the 1990s yet it is still possible to write the first critical history of Jewish prostitution in this country without self-censorship taking over.[64] In this sense Anglo-Jewish historiography has come of age. In its new mature form there is even less excuse for the general historical world to ignore Jewish history.

The Jewish Heritage in British History: Englishness and Jewishness is designed to chart the development of Jewish historiography and non-Jewish responses to the Jewish heritage. The essays in it are concerned not just with charting the past but with providing alternatives for the future in terms of approach and subject matter. Resources are needed (although they need not be on a massive scale) so that the achievements of a new generation can be maintained and their potential realized. Knowledge of and access to relevant sources is one major problem and to that end a brief directory of relevant museums, archives, libraries and other resources is provided as an appendix to the volume.

To conclude, this volume is designed to show that history and even 'heritage' must now allow for a balanced approach and the inclusion of groups such as women and minorities within their focus of interest. Writers of history and those responsible for museums, art galleries, 'heritage centres' and so on have also to learn *how* to use the new approaches and subject matter in a critical manner. Then, rather than causing splintering and 'ghettoisation', minority studies can actually lead to a more sophisticated, richer and, ultimately, more synthetic view of the past.

NOTES

1. National Curriculum History Working Group (NCHWG), *Final Report* (London, 1990), p.10; comment on the curriculum by David Parker, 'History as Bunk', *The Times Higher Education Supplement*, 1 June 1990.
2. Thatcher quoted by *The Times*, 31 January 1978; Neal Ascherson, 'Why "Heritage" is Right-Wing', *Observer*, 8 Nov. 1987; Hewison in *The Listener*, 26 June 1986.
3. Robert Hewison, *The Heritage Industry: Britain in a Climate of Decline* (London, 1987), pp.10, 43. An important precursor of both Wright and Hewison was E.R. Chamberlin's *Preserving the Past* (London, 1979).
4. Patrick Wright, *On Living in an Old Country: The National Past In Contemporary Britain* (London, 1985), pp.125–6.
5. Geoff Dench, *Minorities in the Open Society: Prisoners of Ambivalence* (London,

1986); Paul Gilroy, *There Ain't No Black in the Union Jack* (London, 1987); Thatcher in *The Times*, 31 Jan. 1978.
6. Huw Richards, profile of Cannadine in *The Times Higher Education Supplement*, 7 June 1991; David Cannadine, 'Cousinhood', *London Review of Books*, 27 July 1989.
7. J.M. Roberts, *A History of the World* (London, 1976) and quoted by Stephen Bates, '1066, 1485, 1588, 1939 and all that', *The Guardian*, 13 March 1990.
8. NCHWG, *Final Report*, pp.1,52–3.
9. *Observer*, 11 Nov. 1990 and 18 Aug. 1991.
10. Thatcher quoted in the *Sunday Times*, 22 May 1988.
11. Waldemar Januszczak, 'Romancing the Grime', *The Guardian*, 2 Sept. 1987.
12. Sylvia Collicot, letter to *The Guardian*, 5 Sept. 1987.
13. Graham Coster, 'Another Country', *Weekend Guardian*, 1–2 June 1991.
14. Peter Fryer, *Staying Power: The History of Black People in Britain* (London, 1984), pp.1, 24–5, 72–7; F.Shyllon, *Black Slaves in Britain* (London, 1974).
15. Stuart Millson, letter to *Weekend Guardian*, 8–9 June 1991.
16. Ferdinand Dennis, *Behind the Frontlines: Journey into Afro-Britain* (London, 1988), p.17. Change has taken place at the Maritime museum – see letter of Richard Foster of National Museums and Galleries on Merseyside to *The Guardian*, 1 Sept. 1987; Tony Kushner, 'The Holocaust in British Society and Culture', *Contemporary Record*, Vol. 5, No. 2 (Autumn 1991); Roberts quoted in *The Guardian*, 13 March 1990.
17. Gilroy, op. cit. The Rushdie Affair in particular has exposed the dual and contradictory pressures operating on minorities in Britain in terms of rejection and demands to assimilate. See R. Webster, *A Brief History of Blasphemy: Liberalism, Censorship and 'The Satanic Verses'* (Southwold, 1990).
18. Sylvia Collicot, *Connections: Haringey Local–National–World Links* (London, 1986), p.7; London Borough of Waltham Forest, 'A Future for Our Past' (1991).
19. Elton quoted in *Times Educational Supplement*, 17 Sept. 1986.
20. NCHWG, *Final Report*, p.17.
21. Ibid., pp.40–41,48–9,60–61,64–65,96–7; idem., p.32 for the curriculum instructions concerning information.
22. Ibid., pp.32, 184; Stephen Bates, 'School Libraries Shelve Fall of Empire', *The Guardian*, 19 Dec. 1990. David Parker, 'History as Bunk' on the compromises offered by the authors of the *Final Report*.
23. Dennis, op. cit., p.206. A survey by the London Museums Service found that visiting was strongly race–related with 'whites' more than twice as likely to go to a museum than Afro-Caribbeans who 'felt the museums contained nothing about their own histories'. See Maev Kennedy in *The Guardian*, 1 April 1991 for the report.
24. David Cannadine, 'The Past in the Present' in Lesley Smith (ed.), *The Making of Britain: Echoes of Greatness* (London, 1988), p.19.
25. Raphael Samuel, 'History's Battle For a New Past', *The Guardian*, 21 Jan. 1989.
26. Catherine Lowe, 'Gay Studies Come Out of the Academic Closet', *Observer*, 31 March 1991.
27. Chaim Bermant, *The Cousinhood: The Anglo-Jewish Gentry* (London, 1971), particularly Chapter 12. See also the comments of W. Rubinstein, 'The Decline of the Jewish Influence in Britain: Jews Among Top British Wealth Holders, 1857–1969', *Jewish Social Studies*, Vol.XXXIV (Jan. 1972), p.76. For earlier buildings see Malcolm Brown, 'Anglo-Jewish Country Houses from the Resettlement to 1800', *JHSE Transactions*, Vol.28 (1981–2), pp.20–38.
28. John Vincent (ed.), *The Crawford Papers: The Journals of David Lindsay* (Manchester, 1984), pp.62, 67, 268, 280–81, 528; Stephen Doree, 'The Sassoons of Trent

Park' in Jewish Research Group of the Edmonton Hundred Historical Society (ed.), *Heritage*, Vol.1 (London, 1982) no page numbers; Bermant, op. cit.; pp.123, 361 for social disdain of the 'Cousinhood'.

29. For Nicolson and Crawford see Tony Kushner, 'Beyond the Pale? British Reactions to Nazi Anti–Semitism, 1933–39', in Tony Kushner and Ken Lunn (eds.), *The Politics of Marginality: Race, the Radical Right and Minorities in Twentieth Century Britain* (London, 1990), pp.143–60; J. Vincent, *The Crawford Papers* and 'An Acceptable Level of Antisemitism', *Times Higher Educational Supplement*, 16 Nov. 1979; Martin Wiener, *English Culture and the Decline of the Industrial Spirit 1850–1980* (Harmondsworth, 1985), p.107.

30. Curtin at the American Historical Association, 1983, quoted by *The Chronicle of Higher Education*, 4 Jan. 1984.

31. Williams in *The Jewish Quarterly*, Vol.35 (Spring 1989), p.67; Jonathan Clark, 'A Patriot for Me', *The Guardian*, 18 July 1989.

32. See, for example, Kenneth Morgan, *The People's Peace: British History 1945–1989* (Oxford, 1990), pp.202–4, 283–7 and 466.

33. David Cannadine, *The Decline and Fall of the British Aristocracy* (London, 1990), p.91.

34. C. Bermant, *The Cousinhood*; Stephen Doree, 'The Sassoons of Trent Park'.

35. Lord Boothby, *Boothby* (London, 1978), p.71 quoted by Doree and Bermant, *The Cousinhood*, pp.233–4.

36. Lionel Kochan, *The Jew and His History* (London, 1977), p.11. See also Michael Meyer, *Ideas of Jewish History* (New York, 1974), pp.xii, 22, 25.

37. Dan Cohn-Sherbok, *The Jewish Heritage* (Oxford, 1988).

38. See Tony Kushner, 'A History of Jewish Archives in the United Kingdom' *Archives* (forthcoming); L. Gartner, *The Jewish Immigrant in England, 1870–1914* (London, 1960), p.10.

39. E.H. Carr, *What is History?* (Harmondsworth, 1980), p.44.; see Cesarani, contribution in this volume, for the Anti-Demolition Movement and the articles by Glasman and Kadish on the *chevroth*.

40. In the United States a heated and generally unconstructive debate about 'multicultural' education (and particularly history) is continuing. See Lucy Hodges, 'A Darker View of History', *The Guardian*, 23 April 1991 and *Time Magazine*, 8 July 1991. I would suggest that both 'sides' have put too much attention on what is studied rather than the *way* history is approached.

41. Cesarani, contribution to this volume, p.36.

42. John Hooper Harvey, *The Plantagenets* (London, 1972 edition, originally 1948), p.120; Matthew-Paul Linday, Magdalene College, Cambridge, letter to *Jewish Chronicle*, 1 Feb. 1985; Colin Richmond, contribution to this volume, p.56.

43. David Stocker, 'The Shrine of Little St Hugh', in *Conference Transactions of the British Archaelogical Association*, Vol. VIII (London, 1986), pp.109–17.

44. V.D. Lipman, *The Jews of Medieval Norwich* (London, 1967), p.56 and Richmond, contribution to this volume, p.54 for Langmuir and Thomas.

45. Gavin Langmuir, 'The Knight's tale of Young Hugh of Lincoln', *Speculum*, Vol.47 (1972), pp. 459–82.

46. See J.W.F. Hill, *Medieval Lincoln* (Cambridge, 1948), pp.231–2 and the bizarre comments of J.B. Priestley, *English Journey* (London, 1934), pp.365–6.

47. *Jewish Chronicle*, 26 Oct. 1990 for the description on the shrine; Cecil Roth, *Medieval Lincoln Jewry and Its Synagogue* (London, 1934), pp. vii–ix, 11–14,27; *Jewish Chronicle*, 29 June 1934.

48. For controversy about John Hooper Harvey's *The Plantagenets*, see *Jewish Chronicle*, 16, 23, 30 Nov. and 14 Dec. 1984; the Manchester Jewish Museum has oral testimony of a non-Jew living in a Jewish area who as a child born in 1911

refused to go in a Jewish house. He had heard of Christian children and 'their being garrotted' in the homes of Jews. In the Second World War the ritual murder accusation was revived against Jewish evacuees – see Jewish Women in London Group, *Generations of Memories* (London, 1989), p.90; letter to Victor Gollancz, 4 December 1962 in the Gollancz papers, Warwick University, 157/3/PR/19/7; for Lincoln cathedral see *Jewish Chronicle*, 10 March 1990.

49. Letter of Dr David Jacobson to *Jewish Chronicle*, 25 Dec. 1987.

50. For the York commemoration see *Jewish Chronicle*, 23 March 1990 and *1190–1990 Clifford's Tower Commemoration Programme and Handbook* (York, 1990); Channel 4, 'All the King's Jews', 31 Oct. 1991. For the Lincoln tours see *Jewish Chronicle*, 9 May 1986.

51. *Jewish Chronicle*, 29 June 1934; Cesarani, contribution to this volume, p.36.

52. Cecil Roth, *Archives of the United Synagogue: Report and Catalogue* (London, 1930), pp.9–11. These archives are now housed at the Greater London Record Office.

53. Katz, contribution to this volume, p.61; Roth, *Archives of the United Synagogue*, p.7.

54. V.D. Lipman (ed.), *Three Centuries of Anglo-Jewish History* (London, 1961).

55. Geoffrey Alderman, 'British Jewry', *Times Higher Educational Supplement*, 26 Oct. 1990.

56. See, for example, V.D. Lipman, *A Century of Social Service, 1859–1959: The Jewish Board of Guardians* (London, 1959).

57. The suggestion to create a lectureship in Anglo-Jewish history was rejected by Norman Bentwich – see the minutes of the Tercentenary Executive Committee, 20 Sept. 1955 in AJA 49/20, University of Southampton archives.

58. Marks, contribution to this volume, p.110.

59. Jewish Museum's Acquisitions Policy Statement, 1986. Its long-hoped for move is covered in *Jewish Chronicle*, 14 June 1991; Bill Williams in *Jewish Chronicle*, 30 March 1984.

60. Bill Williams, 'Local Jewish History: Where Do We Go From Here?', in S. Lipman and V.D. Lipman (eds.), *Jewish Life in Britain 1962–1977* (London, 1981), p.95.

61. Audrey Linkman and Bill Williams, 'Recovering the People's Past: the archive rescue programme of Manchester Studies', *History Workshop*, No 8 (Autumn 1979), pp.111–26 and Rickie Burman, 'Participating in the Past? Oral History and Community History in the Work of Manchester Studies', *International Journal of Oral History*, Vol. 5 no 2 (June 1984), pp.114–24 for the background of those involved in projects, which eventually led to the formation of the Manchester Jewish Museum; Bill Williams, contribution to this volume, p.114.

62. J.M. Richards (ed.), *The Bombed Buildings of Britain: A Record of Architectural Casualties: 1940–41* (London, 1942), p.3; Cecil Roth, *The Great Synagogue London* (London, 1950), p.viii; A.B. Levy, *East End Story* (London, 1950), *passim*.

63. Raphael Samuels, 'The Pathos of Conservation', in Mark Girouard *et al.* (eds.), *The Saving of Spitalfields* (London, 1989), p.162.

64. See Lara Marks, 'Jewish Women and Jewish Prostitutes in the East End of London', *The Jewish Quarterly*, Vol.34, No.2 (1987), pp.6–10.

Dual Heritage or Duel of Heritages? Englishness and Jewishness in the Heritage Industry

DAVID CESARANI

The construction of an Anglo-Jewish heritage in the 1890s was part of the struggle against exclusionary tendencies in English culture and politics. Continuing efforts to meld Anglo-Jewish with English heritage from the 1900s to the 1940s were influenced by the imperative of communal defence and resulted in a distorted historiography along with a selective approach to the preservation of archives and monuments.

Nostalgia isn't what it used to be. Although a longing and reverence for the past has always been a part of human society and culture, at some times more intense than at others, only recently has it become the object of commercial exploitation. Economic forces, abetted by public policy, have propelled the past into the market-place and massively broadened its social impact. This phenomenon has been the subject of critical scrutiny by range of commentators, notably Patrick Wright in *On Living in an Old Country* (1985) and Robert Hewison in *The Heritage Industry* (1987). They have shown the instrumental use of the past for commercial and political objectives and stressed the conservatism inherent in heritage as defined by a small circle of entrepreneurs, conservationists and partrons of the arts. They have also pointed out that heritage constructs a mythological national unity and homogenity that excludes or marginalizes minorities. As Patrick Wright has written, 'The nation is not seen as a heterogenous society that makes its own history as it moves forward, however chaotically, in the future. Instead, it is portrayed as an *already achieved* and timeless historical identity which demands only appropriate reverence and protection in the present.'[1]

Wright and Hewison see the desire to reconstitute an artificially concocted, freeze-dried history as a response to the crisis of national identity and economic decline. However, the heritage industry has been in existence for far longer than they conceive and over this time its function has been more varied. The construction and projection of Englishness has been going on since the 1880s, exemplified, as Paul Greenhalgh has shown, in the British contributions to the Expositions Universelles, Great Exhibitions and World Fairs.[2] The 'invention of tradition' in the late nineteenth century posed a challenge to minorities in British society not unlike that set by the heritage industry today, a challenge that reflected the relations between the majority and the minority at the time.[3] While Wright and Hewison acutely analyse the interaction between present needs and the interpretation of the past, they neglect the contemporaneous dynamic existing between minorities and majorities which at any one time feeds into the depiction of their historical relationship.

Anglo-Jewry began to construct its heritage in the late 1880s, when the crystallization of 'Englishness' was already well under way. The Anglo-Jewish heritage was thrown together in response to a number of pressures: the mass immigration of East European Jews, anti-alienism and a strengthening of anti-Jewish currents in politics, society and culture. Above all, it was assembled to prevent English Jews being extruded from the definition of Englishness which was in the process of elaboration. From the 1890s onwards, the construction of an Anglo-Jewish heritage was not merely an exercise in the establishment and perpetuation of Jewish values: it was also part of a continuing struggle with the taxonomy of Englishness. Anglo-Jewish history was part of the weaponry deployed by English Jews in the struggle against exclusionary tendencies in English culture and politics. Indeed, Anglo-Jewish historiography has for most of its existence been overdetermined by these strategic ends: it has been part of communal defence. Jewish heritage was defined in relation to both the Jewish past and the non-Jewish present. But the attempt to define and meld Anglo-Jewish heritage and English heritage produced a paradoxical and debased progeny.

I

The first Jews to research and publish Anglo-Jewish history in a systematic way and to draw attention to the sources and artefacts of Jewish history were Myer Davis and James Piciotto in the 1870s.[4] Before then the Anglo-Jewish past had been chronicled in a haphazard and prejudiced way for the most part by non-Jews and converts. Davis and Piccioto wished to rectify this lacunae and were stimulated to action by the publication of English historical documents which revealed in their interstices glimpses of Jewish life in England in the Middle Ages and the seventeenth century.[5] Research was spurred on by political events. During the Eastern Crisis of 1876–79, prominent British historians, notably Goldwin Smith and Edward Freeman, assailed Disraeli for his anti-Russian and pro-Turkish foreign policy because, they claimed, he was motivated by hebraic sympathies (as well as concern for Rothschild investments in Turkey), rather than the national interest. In the course of several articles, Smith buttressed his arguments that the Jews were clannish and obssesed with money by drawing on the history of the Jews in medieval England. Israel Davis and Asher Myers, respectively proprietor and editor of the *Jewish Chronicle*, both men of a scholarly and historical inclination, were appalled by these assertions and angry that Jews were almost helpless to rebutt them. In October 1881, the *Jewish Chronicle* complained that Jews were losing the argument by default:

> The burden of proving the claims of its ancestors to the respect of the modern nations of Europe falls primarily on the shoulders of its own members. Nevertheless, the Jews of England have signally failed to recognise this responsibility. They have made no attempt worthy of the cause to utilise the masses of documentary material relating to the English Jews of the middle ages which have within late years been freely placed at the disposal of historical studies.[6]

The *Jewish Chronicle* proposed to remedy this by publishing research on Anglo-Jewish history: indeed, Israel Davis had already made a number of contributions in this field.[7]

The evolution of Anglo-Jewish history must also be seen in the light of the development of English history as a discipline and the delineation of English heritage. The School of History at Oxford opened its doors in 1871, while history emerged into the tripos at Cambridge in the following year. In 1886, the *English Historical Review* was established as the vehicle for professional historians who were crucial to the process of defining heritage.[8] The construction of heritage as a conscious preoccupation may be dated from 1877, with the founding of the Society for the Protection of Ancient Buildings. This was followed by the setting up of the National Trust in 1895. Organizations devoted to preservation and conservation were then founded steadily from the

1920s onwards.[9] It is notable that the first Anglo-Jewish conservation movement, the Anti-Demolition League, emerged within this framework. The League was set up in 1886 after the elders of the Spanish and Portuguese Synagogue resolved to demolish the old structure at Bevis Marks (opened in 1701) and build a new one. The successful attempt to prevent this demolition was conducted by several figures who were soon afterwards engaged in the creation of the first exhibition devoted to the Anglo-Jewish past.[10]

In 1886 Sir Isidore Spielman, the impressario of art exhibitions, had the idea that Anglo-Jewry should mark the jubilee of Queen Victoria with an exhibition of Jewish history and religious artefacts from the 50 years of Jewish life in England since the Queen's accession to the throne. He took this idea to his friend Lucien Wolf, a journalist and amateur scholar who had long been interested in Anglo-Jewish records. The proposal won the keen support of the *Jewish Chronicle* whose editor, Asher Myers, played a large part in the preparations. One of his editorials underlined the importance vested in the project: 'The proposed exhibition will do much to familiarise the public with a portion of the life-story of the Jews of this country. It will be a means of disseminating information about the past of the Anglo-Jewish community which has hitherto been known only to a few ...'.[11] The proposal came to fruition with a varied and wide-ranging exhibition in the Albert Hall during 1887, accompanied by a series of lectures on Anglo-Jewish historical subjects. It was a record of prejudices lived down through 'honest conduct', of social progress made by the Jews, of the contribution which they had made to English life – in other words, an unalloyed expression of gratitude to England that the Jews were allowed to live as citizens in that country.[12] Many years later, Sir Isidore recalled that

> It showed to the outside world, which appeared to regard Jewish worship and all things Jewish as a kind of close freemasonry or secret society, what Judaism really is and what the people really are. [It] ... did something ... towards the education of our non-Jewish friends for the formation of a more correct estimate of us and our religion. They saw clearly that there is nothing to hide.[13]

In the run-up to the exhibition and in its aftermath, suggestions were made for the establishment of a permanent society devoted to Anglo-Jewish history. Yet the Jewish Historical Society of England (JHSE) was not established until 1893 – more than five years after the Anglo-

Jewish Exhibition. By this time, the need for such a body to correct misinterpretations of the Jews was felt to be urgent. Reviewing the prospectus for the Society in September 1893, the *Jewish Chronicle* commented: 'The Jew is deeply concerned that his Christian fellow-citizens should know the history of his race. Then alone will the Jews' position be realised, and his rights to the world's consideration vindicated; his faults will be explained, and possibly condoned, his virtues admitted and perchance admired.' It is quite clear that the Jewish Historical Society of England was founded with Jewish defence in mind. In fact, so deep was the apologetic strain that the *Jewish Chronicle* felt obliged to actually justify why a separate *Jewish* historical society should exist at all. It did so by arguing that Jews could best express their love of England, their gratitude to their country and their patriotism through the study of the Jews in England: 'Thus the English Jew must feel that he owes a duty his country. He must do for Englishmen that portion of English work which he, the Jew, can do best.'[14]

If the impetus for the foundation of the society can be traced to fear of anti-Semitism, so may at least some of reasons for its delay. In 1912, Lucien Wolf recalled that there was 'formidible opposition' to the founding of the society. Sir Isidore Spielman later explained some of the motives for the resistance to an open exploration of Anglo-Jewish heritage. Despite his deep involvement with the Anglo-Jewish Exhibition in 1887, he wanted nothing at all to do with a Jewish historical society. For ten years after it came into existence, he ignored it completely. Only in 1903 did he consent to become involved in its work, agreeing to serve for a year as its President. In his inaugural address to the society he accounted for his ten-years silence on matters of Anglo-Jewish history: 'It arose from the fears I first entertained with others, when the Society was first founded, that the history of the Jews in this country – the early history at least – might prove to be but a history of money-lending.'[15]

Sir Isidore's apprehension, while not necessarily justified, was not wholly unfounded either. His brother Marion was engaged in writing a history of *Punch* and through him he was no doubt only too well aware of the insidious pervasiveness of the caricature of the Jew as money-lender. Throughout the 1890s and 1900s there was a protracted campaign against money-lending, culminating in a Parliamentary statute. The agitation was marked by a series of well-publicized court actions in which Jews were prominent as creditors. Any historical evidence which bolstered the claim that Jews were, and always had been, money-dealers could be used as evidence in this often vicious crusade.[16]

II

Lucien Wolf, in his 'Plea for Anglo-Jewish History' his address as the society's first President, argued that Anglo-Jewish history was an integral part of England's domestic and overseas history. Above all, Anglo-Jewish history demonstrated the empathy, even the symbiosis, between Jewish Englishmen and Christian Englishmen who both centred their beliefs, religious and political, on the Old Testament. Wolf and the others who defined the Anglo-Jewish heritage asserted passionately that the study of history could reinforce Jewish pride and help secure Jewish continuity. But they insisted that alongside any internal function it might perform, Anglo-Jewish history was also intended to show the rootedness of Jews in English society, their contribution to English life and their patriotism.[17]

This preoccupation was intimately linked to currents in English society and politics. We have seen that the pioneers of Anglo-Jewish history in 1887 were driven on by the need to explain Anglo-Jewry to the majority society, to justify its existence in this country and to illustrate how English Jews manifested their gratitude through their contribution to all aspects of English life. This desire became ever more intense as mass immigration in the 1890s and 1900s led to a souring of popular feeling towards the Jews. The 'anti-alien' agitation was sustained throughout the 1890s, but it failed to have much political impact while the Liberals were in power between 1892 and 1895, and while the Tory government of 1895–1900 was loath to engage in a protectionist measure. This altered after 1900. Increased Jewish immigration, heightened national chauvinism generated by the Boer War and the election in 1900 of a cadre of Tory MPs for East End seats who were pledged to end free immigration meant that the writing was on the wall. The government conceded a Royal Commission which inquired into alien immigration during 1902–3. A bill was introduced unsuccessfully in 1904 and successfully in 1905. The Aliens Act came into force in January 1906; it was the legislation which Anglo-Jewry dreaded, since it was aimed primarily at Jews and stigmatized the whole Jewish population. The Act could well be interpreted as vindicating the anti-alien propaganda that accused the Jews of clannish-ness, displacing English men and women from their jobs and homes, destroying the English Sunday and imposing an alien culture on the poverty-stricken working class districts of London, Leeds, Manchester and Glasgow.[18]

During the struggle over the Aliens Act, Anglo-Jewry did all it could to propitiate the objections of the majority society by making the immigrants acceptable, proving their worthfulness and advertising their patriotism. Jewish polemicists also pointed out that the story of Anglo-Jewry was itself an illustration of how louche immigrants could turn into pillars of society. Would the English have wanted to exclude the Rothschilds, Montefiores, Goldsmids, Salomons just because they were 'aliens'? Anglo-Jewish history was, thus, pressed into service in the defence of open immigration.

In 1894, the JHSE organised a major heritage event to celebrate 'Resettlement Day'– the anniversary of the return to England in 1655. Resettlement Day assumed ritual status over the next ten years, marked in ever more expansive and lavish fashion, reaching a climax in February 1906 with the two hundred and fiftieth anniversary celebration of the Whitehall Conference of 1656.[19] Surely it was less than a coincidence that at a time when there was a powerful movement to *prevent* Jewish immigration, English Jews were pointing to Cromwell who allowed them *back* into England? The Whitehall Conference of 1656 was notable partly because the opponents of Jewish immigration – like William Prynne – failed to carry the day. The anniversary celebration in 1906 was held barely two months after the Aliens Act came into force. Again, was it just coincidental that the organizers of the banquet invited the former Conservative Prime Minister, Arthur Balfour, who had forced the Act through Parliament in 1905?[20]

Resettlement Day was something of a cult in the 1890s and 1900s, but the story has retained a fascination for Anglo-Jewish scholarship to this day. In fact, until quite recently, there has been surprisingly little deviation from the historiographical model set out in the early *Transactions* of the Jewish Historical Society: the unrelenting focus on the readmission, the resettlement and emancipation. The construction of the Anglo-Jewish past since the 1880s remained locked within this framework because of an unremitting pressure from the majority society. In the 1900s it took the form of anti-alienism, in the 1910s riots in South Wales and the Marconi Scandal. The First World War was a period of ferocious chauvinism accompanied by attacks on foreign-born Jews that did not abate in the post-war years. Of the 1930s and

1940s, it is unnecessary to do more than mention Mosley and the spectre of Hitler. Even after 1945, tension created by the struggle in Palestine narrowed the room for the free expression of all possible strands of Jewish life.

As a consequence of this continuous pressure on the Jews, an unwritten code evolved that directed researchers away from anything that was unpleasant, tainted with criminality, or discordant with the dominant political trends of the day. The construction of the Anglo-Jewish past, its heritage, was to stress the rootedness of Jews in English society and their positive contribution to politics, culture and the economy. The discussion of anti-semitism was to be avoided because to raise it as an issue risked the appearance of ingratitude. The readmission, the community of the resettlement and the emancipation period offered the perfect synthesis of Jewish and English heritage: they melded together the story of the Jews with the notion of progress towards a liberal society, the glorious national institute of Parliament, and the careers of statesmen such as Cromwell, Disraeli and Gladstone, heroic and quintessentially English figures.

III

Cecil Roth, the pivotal figure in Anglo-Jewish historical studies from the 1930s to 1960s, ensured the continuity of this tradition almost to our own day. Roth was constantly engaged in writing history as communal defence. During the 1930s and 1940s he produced a stream of apologetic works demonstrating the Jewish contribution to English arts and science, politics and the economy, and the defence of the country.[21] He explicitly defined this function of Anglo-Jewish heritage during these critical years in his Presidential Address to the JHSE in October 1936. Speaking to the society less than three weeks after the 'Battle of Cable Street', Roth observed that the attack on the Jews had 'altered from religion to race; and its justification, from theology to history'. Since anti-semites drew on history to support their claims that Jews were an alien, malign influence on European society it was up to Jewish history to 'answer argument with argument, slander with refutation, allegation with fact'. He concluded with a summons to Anglo-Jewish history:

> The anti-Semites of today, under Hitler's inspiration have thrown down the challenge to Jewish history. Jewish history can

well afford to take up that challenge; and in this country it is for us, the Jewish Historical Society of England, to take the lead. It is not a question of antiquarian recreation, as is so often associated popularly with our activities, but of a fundamental, essential service to the Jewish cause and to the Community at large.[22]

This injunction has persistly overshadowed Anglo-Jewish historiography. For years there was almost nothing in books or exhibitions that referred to poor Jews, unsuccessful Jews, Jews engaged in crime or prostitution, Jews who deserted their wives, 'bolshe Jews' – that is to say, Jewish political radicals, trades unionists, communists, anarchists – Jews who did *not* want to fight in the First World War, Yiddish culture, traditional Judaism (labelled scornfully as 'ultra-orthodoxy') or anything that smacked of Jewish separatism and the petty as well as important divisions within Jewish society in England – the repression, exclusion, snobbery practised by Jews against Jews.[23] This edited heritage reached its apogee in the 1956 Exhibition of the Tercentenary of the Resettlement of the Jews in England.[24]

Of course, reducing Anglo-Jewish historiography before 1960 merely to apologetics would be quite wrong and would misrepresent the complexity of the undertaking. In one very important sense, the early Anglo-Jewish historians simply reflected the unquestioning patriotism and adulation of English institutions characteristic of F.W. Maitland, William Stubbs, J.B. Seeley, J.R. Green, Edward Freeman – the great Victorian historians later debunked for their racist and imperialist preconceptions.[25] Jewish historians may have bent over backwards to identify with England and English culture; but the history they produced as a consequence was an integral part of the historiography of the time. Anglo-Jewish history has always reflected the trends within English historiography. Indeed, it has been the changing nature of English history writing that supplies a key to understanding the break with the older tradition of Anglo-Jewish historiography. Although the inhibitions imposed on Jewish historians remained as forceful as ever, society in Britain changed massively in the century following the founding of the Anglo-Jewish Historical Society. Each phase in the process of transformation was reflected in English historiography and found an Anglo-Jewish echo, although usually at a much later date. The story of the welfare state, the labour movement, socialism, immigration, feminism, regionalism entered into mainstream English history. Gradually, these themes infiltrated

into Anglo-Jewish history and have all been manifested in studies of
Jewish welfare bodies, Jewish radicals, the settlement of East European immigrants, the experience of Jewish women and centres of
Jewish settlement outside London and beyond the borders England.
Indeed in the case of oral history, the pioneering work of Bill Williams
and the Manchester Studies Unit at the Polytechnic may even be said
to have led the field from written Anglo-Jewish studies.[26]

The Celebration of the Jewish East End in 1987 was an acute
reflection of the shift away from the celebration of success. Here was a
meditation on the place of the Jewish experience set alongside that of
other immigrant groups whose contemporary situation had become a
focus of profound concern.[27] Yet it has not supplanted the older
tradition. In 1987, there was a good deal of interest in Jewish Historical
circles in the possibility, ultimately unfulfilled, that the Jewish
Museum might be housed in Cromwell House – clearly a throw-back to
an earlier tradition.[28] When Manchester Jewry organized a celebration
of its bicentenary in 1988, the major event took place in the grounds of
Chatsworth House – home of the Duke of Devonshire. The Duke is a
firm and generous friend of Israel, but otherwise there was no reason
for the choice of location other then the desire to identify with rural,
aristocratic English heritage in its classic form.[29]

IV

It is an ironic insight into dual heritages that, at several key moments,
Jews have served valiantly in the definition of English heritage. Imre
Kirafly was the doyen of the international exhibitions staged by
England between 1890 and 1920 and made a distinctive contribution to
the isolation and elevation of the Anglo-Saxon race over other, lesser
species of homo sapien. A Hungarian Jew by birth, Kirafly was to the
imaginistic projection of the English race what Disraeli was to its
concrete extension abroad. Paul Greenhalgh comments that

> It was as though his Jewish origins, in a country which was part of
> an unstable empire, had filtered through to the very core of his
> psychological make-up, to surface in a manic involvement with
> the empire of his adopted home. He had made himself part of a
> stable, powerful nation by lauding it in a way it had never been
> lauded before. By 1914, he was more responsible perhaps than

anyone for the vivid and vulgar understanding the British population had of its foreign territories.[30]

Sir Isidore Spielman, the man who created the Anglo-Jewish Exhibi-
tion of 1887, was chairman of the Royal Commission supervising the
British Pavillion in Paris in 1900. He filled the pavillion with William
Morris furnishings illuminated by light falling through Edward Burne-
Jones stained-glass windows. According to Greenhalgh, 'The choice of
architectural style and interior decor guaranteed a vision of aristocratic
England in existence long before the industrial revolution.' This is the
heritage that is still purveyed by Laura Ashley, *Country Life* and the
National Trust. Spielman and his brother Marion were also formative
influences on the display of fine art at the 1908 Franco-British Exhibition. Greenhalgh observes that on this occasion 'They attempted to
generate nationalist ideas for a modern British art ... [focussing on the
Pre-Raphaelites] ... who, they proposed, showed genuine English
characteristics in their style and moral approach'.[31]

So it was that some Jews collaborated in the definition of an English
heritage – imperial, aristrocratic, rural – that excluded them. The
historical project of others, Jewish historians who cleaved to this
mythic representation, only distorted attempts to elaborate a genuine
Anglo-Jewish heritage. Consequently, that which is authentically
precious has been neglected, while that which is a synthetic creation, a
hybrid of two distinct and actually conflicting cultures, has been
jealously guarded. That is the difference between celebrating the
Jewish heritage in Tower Hamlets and in the grounds of a stately
home.

NOTES

1. Quoted in Robert Hewison, *The Heritage Industry* (London, 1987), p.141.
2. Paul Greenhalgh, *Expositions Universelles, Great Exhibitions and World Fairs,
   1851–1939* (Manchester, 1988), Ch.5.
3. See E.J. Hobsbawm and Terrence Ranger (ed.), *The Invention of Tradition*
   (London, 1984).
4. This account draws heavily on Revd S. Levy, 'Anglo-Jewish Historiography',
   Presidential Address to the JHSE, 9 Dec. 1907, *TJHSE*, 6 (1905–11), pp.1–20.
5. The Public Record Act was passed in 1858; the PRO building was completed
   between 1851 and 1861 and a room opened for researchers in 1866. The publication
   of Calenders of State papers, Chronicles and Memorials began 1856–57. The first
   Commission on Historical Manuscripts was convened in 1869, the second in 1882.

Ironically, Sir Francis Palgrave, first Keeper of the Rolls was of Jewish origin. See Phillipa Levine, *The Amateur and the Professional. Antiquarians, Historians and Archeologists in Victorian England, 1838–1886* (Cambridge, 1986), Ch.5.

6. *JC*, 21 Oct. 1881, p.3.
7. *JC*, 26 Nov. 1880, pp.10–11; 10 Dec. 1880, p.4.
8. Levine, *The Amateur and the Professional*, Ch.6.
9. Hewison, *The Heritage Industry*, p.26.
10. They included the Haham Moses Gaster, Lucien Wolf, Leopold Greenberg: *JC*, 5 Feb. 1886, p.11; 12 Feb. 1886, p.5; 19 Feb. 1886, pp.7, 11; 6 March 1891, p.11; 27 March 1891, p.5.
11. *JC*, 2 July 1886, pp.8–9.
12. *JC*, 8 April 1887, pp.9–10.
13. Sir Isidore Spielman, Presidential Address to the JHSE, 9 Feb. 1903, *TJHSE*, Vol.5 (1902–5), p.47.
14. *JC*, 29 Sept. 1893, pp.11–12; 9 June 1893, pp.5–6, 8–9.
15. Sir Isidore Spielman, Presidential Address, 9 Feb. 1903, *TJHSE*, Vol.5 (1902–5), p.44.
16. On the campaign against money-lending, see *JC*, 26 July 1889, 9–10; 23 January 1891, pp.13–14; 17 March 1893, p.13; 13 April 1894, pp.13–14; 4 May 1894, pp.13–14; 6 March 1896, pp.15–16; House of Commons Select Committee on money-lending, *JC*, 9 July 1897, 14 and 30 July 1897, 13, 18 March 1898, p.19; on money-lending bill, *JC*, 9 March 1900, p.18.
17. Wolf, 'Origin of the Jewish Historical Society of England', pp.6–7.
18. Israel Finestein, 'Jewish Immigration in British Party Politics' in A. Newman (ed.), *Immigration and Settlement* (London, 1971); John Garrard, *The English and Immigration* (Lonon, 1971); Bernard Gainer, *The Alien Invasion* (London, 1972).
19. *TJHSE*, 5 (1902–5), pp.275–300.
20. He did not attend, but did send a letter emphatically affirming that there was no 'Jewish Question' in England because 'the Jews have themselves shown themselves entirely worthy of the rights and privileges which they enjoy as citizens of this country'. Ibid., pp.278–9. See also *JC*, 21 April 1899, pp.17–18 on the Cromwell anniversary.
21. *The Jew as British Citizen* (London, 1936); 'The Challenge to Jewish History: Some Contributions to English Jewish Life', *TJHSE*, 14 (1940); *The Jewish Contribution to Civilization* (London, 1943); 'Jews in the Defence of Britain', *TJHSE*, 15 (1939–45).
22. Cecil Roth, Presidential Address to the JHSE, 20 October 1936, published in pamplet form as *The Jew as British Citizen* (London, 1936).
23. American and non-Jewish historians were free from these inhibitions: for example, see the work of Todd Endelman, *The Jews of Georgian England 1714–1830* (Philadelphia, PA, 1979) and idem., 'The Checkered Career of King; A Study in Anglo-Jewish History', *AJSR*, 7–8 (1982–83), pp.69–100; Edward J. Bristow *Prostitution and Prejudice: The Jewish Fight against White Slavery 1870–1939* (Oxford, 1982) and L. Gartner, 'Anglo-Jewry and the Jewish International Traffic in Prostitution 1885–1914', *AJSR*, 7–8 (1982–3), pp.129–78; Bill Williams, *The Making of Manchester Jewry, 1740–1875* (Manchester, 1976); Jerry White, *Rothschild Buildings* (London, 1980).
24. The catalogue of the exhibition was published by the Jewish Historical Society of England, London, 1956.
25. See J. W. Burrow, *A Liberal Descent, Victorian Historians and the English Past* (Cambridge, 1981); Robert Colls and Philip Dodd (ed.), *Englishness: Politics and Culture 1880–1920* (London, 1986).
26. See editor's introduction to David Cesarani (ed.), *Making of Modern Anglo-Jewry*

(Oxford, 1990), pp.3–5.
27. See Catalogue of the Celebration of the Jewish East End and press discussion, for example, John Cunningham, *Guardian*, 17 July 1987 and Tony Kushner's contribution in this volume.
28. News stories, *JC*, 10 July and 14 Aug. 1987.
29. Entry on Anglo-Jewry, *Encyclopedia Judaica Yearbook*, 1986–88.
30. Greenhalgh, *Expositions Universelles, Great Exhibitions and World Fairs*, p.93.
31. Ibid., pp.212–13.

Englishness and Medieval Anglo-Jewry

COLIN RICHMOND

'Englishness and Medieval Anglo-Jewry' is a discussion of (and reflection on) the manner in which English historians have dealt with, or omitted to deal with, the history of medieval English Jewry. It examines, in particular, the ritual murder charges at Norwich in 1144 and Lincoln in 1255, the York massacre of 1190, the government's exploitation of the Jews, the gentry's hatred of them, and their expulsion from England in 1290 by Edward I. In the course of the article aspects of 'Englishness' which relate to Jews are presented; these Anglo-Saxon attitudes, it is suggested, are so deeply embedded as to be well-nigh unconscious; they are undoubtedly negligent.

I frequently ask myself: what would a Jewish history of Europe be like? Sitting in the Botanical Gardens at Oxford one summer's day recently I pondered what such a history of England would consist of. What would it say about this beautiful place for example: its honey-coloured stone walls, the goldfish among the water-lilies, the immaculate lawns? Beyond the green water of the Isis, on which a punt was being indolently poled along, a cricket match was in progress: middle-aged men in garishly-coloured caps trundled after the ball on Magdalen School field. A slow bowler (rarest of sights) was hit for six, and the silence was scarcely broken by that particularly English sound of summer: random applause from pavilion and deck-chairs. This side of the river a family of foreign tourists (Spanish? Italian? Greek?) watched uncomprehendingly. Over the trees Magdalen College tower rose (as one might say) timelessly, while Merton College clock struck the quarter-hour: it was 4.15 and I was due to take tea in Magdalen cloister. Here, as any Englishman was bound to think, was Grant-chester. I *was* thinking that. I was also thinking that here until 1290 had been the cemetery of the Jewish community of Oxford, and (more-over) that the cemetery had occupied the other side of the road as well as this until 1231, when the pious Henry III granted it as a building site to the hospital of St John the Baptist, which itself gave way to Magdalen College in the fifteenth century.[1]

I had not learned these facts from *Medieval Oxford* by the Reverend H.E. Salter, Fellow of Magdalen College and doyen of the historians of medieval Oxford. Jews feature neither in the index of that book, published in 1936 by the Oxford Historical Society, nor (so far as I can detect) in its 150 pages of text. The information came from Cecil Roth's *The Jews of Medieval Oxford*, published by the same society in 1951. The moral is obvious. It would require no elaboration were it not for its utter neglect by English historians and because of my failure to comprehend it in the question I pondered in the Botanical Gardens: what would a Jewish history of England consist of? The moral is this: why does it have to be a history of the Jews in medieval Oxford which discusses the Jews of Oxford in the Middle Ages? They were not unimportant (whatever that means); quite the contrary – on any measurement of 'importance', whether social, economic, political, cultural, or intellectual, for 200 years the Jewish community of Oxford was important. Were this simply a matter of 'out of sight utterly out of mind' this article might be unnecessary. History, however, is more than Heritage; indeed, this case demonstrates that it has to be un-swervingly anti-Heritage, for it is precisely those aspects of the English past which are out of sight that have to be kept in mind. 'Have to be' if history is not to succumb to myth, as well as to that invidious conven-tion, more racialist (I fear) than nationalist, that Jewish history is only for Jews. Do not Frenchmen write about the history of England, Englishmen about Polish history? Jewish history permeates European history; its absence from the history of Oxford and England tells us at once a great deal about Englishness.

Have things changed since 1936? It may be thought that they have. Professor Barrie Dobson is an Englishman who not only has written about medieval English Jewry, but has become President of the Jewish Historical Society of England. He has said that 'at the end of the twentieth century it often seems that the treatment of their Jewish minorities by Edward I, Philip the Fair, and *los reyes catolicos*, much as those monarchs would have been disconcerted by the thought, is more 'relevant' to our own problems than any other feature of their respec-tive reigns'.[2] Gavin Langmuir, a non-Jewish American, is more speci-fic: 'To explain what Hitler had done, scholars found they had to rewrite sections of earlier history.'[3] In other words it has become essential to re-cycle the past if the *Shoah* is not to slip entirely into that historical limbo which is half-Heritage (it is happening, it is happening) and half-Entertainment (it has happened, it has happened). One cause of the *Shoah* was that non-Jewish historians ignored the Jews, as – to take what seems so trivial an instance but is not – H.E. Salter ignored them in writing the history of medieval Oxford. A masterly non-Jewish historian in the course of mourning a majestic Jewish one has put that ignorance into crystalline perspective: 'This refusal to see permanent value in the particularity of the Jews had left Christian countries morally impotent, when the Nazis proposed annihilation as the alternative to absorption'.[4]

Oh, but that did not happen here – might be an Englishmen's answer. Oh, but it would have – has to be the response of historians of twentieth-century England. There is, therefore, no excuse for those English historians who have not changed their ways, who write as if the *Shoah* had not happened. Take Edward I, the English king whom Barrie Dobson singled out and who was a pioneering anti-Semite when he expelled the Jews from the kingdom of England in 1290: he was the first European ruler to make his state permanently *Judenrein*. He, or one of his civil servants, was a pioneer in small things as in great. 'The fatal step', as Cecil Roth describes it, 'was taken on 18 July 1290 by an act of the king in his Council. It happened to be (as was long after remembered with awe) the fast of the ninth of Ab, anniversary of manifold disasters for the Jewish people, from the destruction of Jerusalem onwards.'[5] That neutral phrase, 'it happened to be', may have been carefully chosen, for Professor Roth, even though writing without our knowledge of the Nazi habit of deliberately selecting the Holy Days of Judaism on which to initiate atrocities against Jews, must have suspected that Edward I knew (or was reminded) what day it was on 18 July 1290. English historians ought to remember (with a good deal more awe than they have done hitherto) not only the vindictiveness Edward displayed, but also the political connection he was making, when he chose the fast of the ninth of Ab.

Edward knew what he was doing on 18 July 1290. This is evident from his close association with the construction of the shrine to Little St Hugh in Lincoln cathedral in the first half of the 1290s. As David Stocker has shown,[6] the shrine was of a design similar to that of the Eleanor Crosses, notably the cross at Waltham: they shared the same contractor, sculptor and master-mason. The shrine, he suggests,

'belongs to a group of Edward I's projects which bring with them

an element of political propaganda ... Edward clearly wanted
the new shrine to be associated with the Crown; not only was he
the sole monarch recorded as giving alms at the shrine, but it
appears he may have provided expertise from the royal workshops to create this monument, which may even have been
intended to remind pilgrims of the Eleanor Crosses. To reinforce
the connection between the saint and the Crown, the royal arms
were prominently displayed ... Edward had a strong interest in
emphasising both the alleged criminality of the English Jewry
and the Crown's position as a principal defender of the English
Christians. Edward's apparently enthusiastic support for the
shrine of Little St Hugh suited this royal purpose very well.

Such demonstrable enthusiasm might lead one to believe that a
Jewish policy was close to Edward's bigoted heart, that the king placed
himself, in the words of Paul Hyams, 'at the head of anti-Jewish forces,
which were not necessarily any stronger in numbers than a century
earlier'.[7] Yet, even the expulsion itself is fleetingly dealt with in
Michael Prestwich's Edward the First, published in 1988. In a text of
567 pages the Jews get less than three. It is also evident that, however
pressing were the financial circumstances, it was Edward's 'sincere
religious bigotry'[8] which impelled him to expel the Jews in 1290.
Despite this, in a paper by Professor Prestwich entitled 'The Piety of
Edward I', there is no mention of the Expulsion. One's suspicions that
these omissions are more than simple negligence are deepened by
some of the little Professor Prestwich has to say on Jewish topics in
Edward the First. He writes, for example, that (and the italics are
mine) 'there were stories of ritual child-murder and torture, which,
although they now appear groundless on the basis of the recorded
evidence, were generally believed', and that 'the expulsion itself went
surprisingly smoothly, and was not the occasion for massacres, as it
might well have been'.[9]
   This reminds me of the evening I was at the heart of Englishness. In
Shakespeare's schoolroom at Stratford-on-Avon I had given a lecture
on the Expulsion and was answering questions and listening to comments; one of the latter was to the effect that the Expulsion had been
undertaken and conducted in a comparatively humane manner, and I
was to realize (was the implication of the tone of the communication)
that this was a reason for self-congratulation. There was no indication
that the speaker was aware the Expulsion might not have taken place.

What confronted me in that most English of English locales was the terrible and terrifying habit of viewing the past as inevitable. Moreover, when historians write about Edward I in the way Professor Prestwich has, the *Shoah* will disappear into the pre-determined as the Expulsion has done, for as historians our approach to both is bound to be identical.

I am not (as we shall see) singling out Professor Prestwich. Edward I, on the other hand, deserves picking on. It must be a measure of Englishness that he is recognized as the Hammer of the Welsh and Scots, but has no such reputation where the Jews are concerned, despite perpetrating 'the largest ever massacre of English Jews'.[10] This was the notorious coin-clipping affair of 1278; on a charge of filing the edges of England's silver pennies the heads of every Jewish household were arrested and imprisoned in the Tower of London; after hanging 269 of them (along with a mere 29 Christians) Edward got over £16,000 from the sale of their forfeited property. This was the gamekeeper turned poacher with a vengeance. Philip the Fair was no innovator when he turned on the Jews and Templars in France a generation later. How remarkable that the English king who is remembered for his legislation had no greater regard for legality than Adolf Hitler.

Or, possibly, than his father. This, however, may be unfair to Henry III. It is true, as Gavin Langmuir has pointed out,[11] that when Henry III had 19 Jews of Lincoln hanged in 1255 for the alleged murder of Little St Hugh he was the first major authority in Europe to order executions for so-called ritual murder: Henry too was a pioneer. Yet, we must assume Henry was genuinely scandalized by the story extracted under torture from the Jew Copin; thereafter he duly (and dutifully) applied the law to those guilty of a heinous crime. This case, which 'entered into the folk-lore of the English people',[12] was also cause and consequence of what Robert Stacey has called a 'Watershed in Anglo-Jewish Relations',[13] when in the middle years of the thirteenth century victimization of the Jews by King, Church, and Top People plumbed new depths. An historian, Matthew Paris, was on hand to chronicle and explain the 'new themes' of anti-Semitism: 'magic, murder, and excrement'.[14] Yet, we are told by Professor Richard Vaughan, 'Matthew, to his credit had no very deep-seated prejudices against the Jews, perhaps because of his sympathy for them as victims of royal extortion'.[15] Here is the sympathetic Matthew:[16]

> Though miserable, they [the Jews] deserved no commiseration, for they were proved to have been guilty of forgery, both of money and seals. And if we are silent about other crimes, we have decided to include one of them in this book, in order that their wickedness may be better known to more people. There was a certain quite rich Jew, Abraham by name but not in faith, who lived and had property at Berkhamstead and Wallingford ... In order to dishonour Christ the more, this Jew bought a nicely carved and painted statue of the blessed Virgin, as usual nursing her son at her bosom. This image the Jew set up in his latrine and ... he inflicted a most filthy and unmentionable thing on it, daily and nightly, and ordered his wife to do the same.

It is necessary to grasp that to a thirteenth-century mind a religious image was not the simple representation it would be to a twentieth-century one, in order to appreciate the disgust a fastitidious monk would have felt when told this story. Can a historian afford such credulity? Moreover, does not credulity in a historian exactly coincide with his prejudices, shallow or deep? I do not think Professor Vaughan can get away with his Matthew Paris any more than Professor Prestwich can with his Edward I.

Nothing of this is to be found in the large volumes on the reign of Henry III by Sir Maurice Powicke. That gentlest of historians and most sensitive of men was writing during and just after the Second World War; his sympathetic understanding of the plight of the English Jewry in the thirteenth century, especially at the hands of royal tax-collectors, is evident in a number of passages. He has not one word on Little St Hugh. It is almost as if a Christian, English gentleman, of which Powicke was a near perfect example, did not speak of such things. On Powicke's part we may talk of innocence not ignorance; on the part of so many others it was (and is) that ignorance which, because it is of the ostrich variety, will not save them from condemnation at the bar of History.

Powicke certainly made no bones about Simon de Montfort: Simon 'hated Jews'.[17] He does not deal with what have been called the 'savage anti-Semitic riots' in London of April 1264, when over 500 Jews were killed and robbed, beyond a neutral 'the Jews were attacked'; but we should not expect him to: he was not writing about Simon.[18] David Carpenter recently has been – in what is likely to become a widely read and influential article.[19] The Jews do not feature. There is every reason that they should, because Dr Carpenter's theme is that Simon was an enthusiastic bigot who knew how to appeal to (and manipulate) the instincts of the English political nation, not excluding the baser ones. Simon was zealous for political reform: so were many of 'the knights, gentry and those below them in the counties of England'. He seemed to desire reform in the Church: 'reform-minded ecclesiastics' rallied to him. 'Equally significant was Simon's skill in exploiting the question of the aliens': here, at last, I anticipated a sentence on the way in which Simon's anti-Semitism endeared him to knights and gentlemen, those *buzones* or big-wigs of the English provinces, whose hatred of the Jews was even sharper than that of the civil servants at Westminster – the latter, after all, took advantage of the indebtedness of the former to Jewish financiers. There was no such sentence. An opportunity had been missed. We are bound to ask: why? Why such forgetfulness? Why is it that something which stares one historian in the face escapes the attention of another?

Simon de Montfort, apart from initiating pogroms in English cities, was among the first of those who had the authority to do so to expel Jews from an English town. Simon was granted the earldom of Leicester in August 1231; this included lordship of the town of Leicester; by the end of the year the Jews had gone. Simon's charter of 1253 making Leicester *Judenrein* for all time survives in the borough archives:[20] 'Know ... that I, for the good of my soul, and the souls of my ancestors have granted ... that no Jew or Jewess, in my time or in the time of any of my heirs to the end of the world, shall within the liberty of the town of Leicester, inhabit or remain or obtain a residence.' This is the authentic voice of the Founder of Parliament, a man who 'is much commemorated in Leicester – a square, a street, and a concert hall are named after him, his statue adorns the Clock Tower'. So writes Professor Jack Simmons in his popular history of Leicester, published in 1974.[21] His only other comment is that 'the town's deepest cause of gratitude to Simon de Montfort is negative: that he did not involve it in the turmoils of the close of his life'. Jews (and their expulsion) are not mentioned.

According to Matthew Paris, Simon's 'father confessor' was Robert Grosseteste. Sir Richard Southern subtitled his study *Robert Grosseteste*, published in 1986, 'The Growth of an English Mind in Medieval Europe'. Professor Southern confronts head-on Grosseteste's attitude towards the Jews; the passage in which he does so commands even greater admiration as one senses in reading it how hard Professor

Southern found it to write: he has never been an historian to lack
courage.[22] In 1231 Grosseteste was archdeacon of Leicester; the Jews
of that town after their expulsion in that year went to Winchester: 'they
were welcomed on her land by the Countess of Winchester. But
Grosseteste, not content with having got rid of the Jews from his own
archdeaconry, sent the Countess a letter of bitter reproof and condemnation of her hospitality.' After summarizing the letter, Professor
Southern comments: 'I have softened rather than exaggerated the
violence of Grosseteste's words, which extend to four pages of print.'
He continues:

> Here we see Grosseteste in an unfavourable light ... It is
> unfavourable to him, because it shows that in an area of conduct
> where brutality was the rule, he was prepared to go to even
> greater lengths of brutality, because he took the principles on
> which it was based more seriously than most men. He thought
> with more energy, with more fierce commitment, and with a
> more urgent desire to give practical expression to his thoughts
> than most men in high positions, who had worked their way to
> the top by many compromises. Grosseteste had risen almost by a
> single bound. He had had no lessons in keeping silent. He was a
> man of the people, and he spoke with a peasant's violence and
> passion to those above him as well as those beneath.

Grosseteste had been born about 1170, almost certainly in a village
near Bury St Edmunds. Until 1230 his life was 'a struggle appropriate
to a poor man without a patron'; his long and tough route to high office
– he became bishop of Lincoln in 1235 – followed (and this is Professor
Southern's highly original conclusion) an entirely English education:
Grosseteste never attended the schools of France. It was just this
'provincial career' which made Grosseteste the intellectual giant of his
time. His great mind was not like other great thirteenth-century minds.
He was original and complicated; he was impatient of academic
constraints; intellectually he was both reckless and broad; he went
back to the sources; in life he followed the Gospels; he had a prophetic
clarity of vision which enabled him to tell the pope to his face that what
was wrong with Christendom was the Papacy; he was a cheerful man
who loved music and a moral fanatic who wanted compulsory Christianity; he was 'one of the most independent and vigorous Englishmen
of the Middle Ages – a medieval Dr Johnson in his powers of mind and

personality'. Because they had rejected the Incarnation he hated the Jews. That such an Englishman, so principled an Englishman, so English an Englishman hated Jews (and with so brutal a hatred), explains a good deal – perhaps all we need to know– about the precocity of English anti-Semitism.

Yet, not quite all: there may be a connection to make which Professor Southern does not. It is the Bury St Edmunds connection. Anti-Jewish feeling among the monks at Bury was a consequence of their ambition to build and to adorn their abbey in the grandest (and most expensive) style; no doubt they believed themselves to be glorifying God and honouring St Edmund by doing so; in order to do so they had to borrow from God's murderers; the outcome of this paradox was an animosity fuelled by guilt and self-contempt. The notorious Bury St Edmund's ivory cross is a product of that tension. Its inscriptions, as Elizabeth Claridge has written

> don't mince words. 'The synagogue falls after vain and stupid effort', reads one part of a Latin hexameter; and elsewhere, 'The Jews laugh at the Death Agony of God'. The words inscribed on the Cross at Calvary are reputed to have read 'Jesus of Nazareth, King of the Jews', but even this sarcastic reference was too much for the ivory cross artist. His inscription reads 'Jesus of Nazareth, King of Confessors'.[23]

In 1181 the monks were involved in a ritual-murder accusation against the Jews of the town. In the following year Samson was elected abbot. This middle-aged ex-schoolmaster, like Grosseteste a country-boy in origin but from Norfolk not Suffolk and unlike him in that he had studied in Paris, set about freeing the monastery from debt. On Palm Sunday 1190 57 Jews were killed in the town by crusaders. Shortly afterwards Abbot Samson petitoned the Crown for permission to expel the Jews who remained: 'there cannot have been many', notes Cecil Roth. Permission was granted and the Jews of Bury were dispersed. Jocelin of Brakelond, the Bury chronicler, observed dryly: 'The recovery of the manor of Mildenhall for eleven hundred paltry marks of silver, and the expulsion of the jews from the town of St Edmund, and the foundation of the new hospital of Babwell are all proofs of the Abbot's excellence'.[24] Grosseteste grew up in the 1170s next door to Bury; in 1181 he was ten or twelve; by 1190 he was a schoolmaster himself in Lincoln, but presumably he heard of Samson's expulsion of the Jews from his old 'home town'. Was he influenced by any of this? Did he, for example, recall Samson's 'excellence' in 1231? Professor Southern believes 'he may himself have been the instigator of their [the Jews] expulsion from Leicester by Earl Simon'. Samson, ever since Thomas Carlyle made him famous, has been thought of as a type of Englishman: rightly so. Perhaps, therefore, one extraordinary Englishman made a formative impression upon another.

The massacre at Bury in March 1190 inevitably brings us to York and the eve of the 'Great Sabbath' before Passover 4950. There is, however, no need to dwell on that particular massacre and mass-suicide: Professor Barrie Dobson has written an account which is a minor classic. 'The Dead have no voice of their own', but in Professor Dobson the York Jews of 1190, whose bones 800 years later lie beneath a supermarket carpark, have a historian who has done them justice – all an historian is able to do.[25] None the less, three observations are worth making. First, while we should not be surprised that Rabbi Yom-Tob has not entered any pantheon of English heroes, it is significant that Richard Malebisse did not become a household name for evil like king John, the sheriff of Nottingham, or Guy Fawkes. Secondly, it should be noted that not only were no converts made (or rather, such was the mentality of the crusaders, no prisoners taken), but also that there was no trial of the murderous rebels,[26] nor did the archbishop of York condemn the atrocities. Even though archbishop Geoffrey was the half-brother of the king, the failure of the English Church *ever* to condemn either the excesses of rioters or the exactions of the state (where the Jews were concerned) should be stressed, as this dereliction lays bare the moral ambivalence of the Roman Church's attitude towards and programme for the Jews. Thirdly, in the words of Professor Dobson, 'the York massacre was not only a tragedy but an influential tragedy: it helped to promote the closest relationship between state and Jewry yet seen in western Europe and to bring about a decisive transformation in the constitutional position of the medieval English Jews'.[27] How typical it was that the consequence of a tragedy (on such a scale, in England's second city) was more and, therefore, worse government for the Jews.

It is one of the truisms of English history that England has been tightly and closely governed since the tenth century, first from Winchester and subsequently from Westminster. The Norman Conquest altered little in that regard. It is also generally held that this has been to the advantage of Englishmen and women. That is one of those pernicious myths that rulers put about in order that the ruled may be quietly governed. One way in which we are enabled to see that it is myth is the history of the Jews in England: there England's rulers are revealed to be without clothes; naked and unashamed they go about to despoil their subjects in order to benefit themselves. Is this not why the Jewish History of England is not taught in schools – because it is a type of anti-history as perceived by those who finally determine National Curricula? I write in anger as well as sorrow.

The result of the tragedy at York was 'the compulsory registration of all Jewish bonds and chattels in a few fixed urban centres, the critical step in the complete reorganization of royal control over the English Jewry', that is the establishment of the Exchequer of the Jews.[28] It is, therefore, yet another paradox of Jewish history (which being saddled with so many one has to learn to think in them in order to understand it) that what began as 'a financial conspiracy' of the Yorkshire gentry and ended for them as 'a murderous [and entirely successful] business affair', should be for English Jews the beginning of the process which was to destroy them.[29] Their destruction was not to come about by the forces of popular anti-Semitism, but by the agency of that authority which was their chief protector: the government. What a familiar ring that has to it for the post-Auschwitz generation. From the mid-1190s kings of England had the means to tax their Jews to extinction; they did not hesitate to do so. Hubert Walter, Archbishop of Canterbury and Chancellor of England in the 1190s, was a bureaucratic genius: he made the essential first moves towards a final solution of the Jewish 'problem' in England.

Where the kings of England are concerned rapacity is a word which comes almost naturally to mind. King John and the Bristol tallage of 1210 is a remarkable example of the ruthlessness of that monarch as well as of how government may be transformed into its opposite. Sir James Holt also showed us (as long ago as 1961) how rapacious were the English baronage of the late twelfth and early thirteenth centuries – for land, for wardships, for widows. It is, therefore, sad (not to say astounding) to discover the following sentence in *The Northerners*:[30]

> In re-examining the problem of *debita Judeorum* he [John] was entering treacherous country full of ugly scenes and vistas, of pogroms, cheating, traffic in mortgages, and dispossession, a country in which baron and knight were involved in an obscure and unwholesome conflict with the rapacity of the Jew, the

> acquisitiveness of monastic houses, and the interest of the King
> as the residuary legatee to whom, in the end, the profits of
> usurious transactions descended

It is unnecessary to italicize the phrase 'the rapacity of the Jew': no
emphasis is required to identify the chaff among the grain. We are
bound to inquire: what was Professor Holt thinking of? If he is to be
caught nodding all the worse; dropped casually such a phrase is even
more revealing of a frame of mind. Unconscious Anglo-Saxon attitudes (if that is what are on view) make for bad history. That is the
case here. It was a king consumed by the desire to recover Normandy
and lords and gentlemen driven by the compulsive itch of acquisition
who were rapacious. Jewish financiers, who were no more than one
Jew in a hundred,[31] provided the means by which the rapacity of others
was accomplished. From 1980 to 1984 Professor Sir James Holt was
President of the Royal Historical Society of England.

Anglo-Saxon attitudes are also to be detected in accounts of Magna
Carta. The sins in this instance are ones of omission. I am not
competent to challenge Professor Holt's dismissal of the anti-Jewish
clauses 10 and 11 as 'superficial',[32] but I am sure it should not have been
left to Cecil Roth to reveal that 'when London was occupied on 17 May
1215, the Jewry was the first objective of the [baronial] insurgents. It
was ruthlessly sacked, the houses being demolished and the stone used
to repair the City walls.' It is Cecil Roth also who points out a
difference the loss of Normandy made which is unnoticed by English
historians: 'To the Jews the consequences were no less momentous
than to the country at large. They, too, were henceforth cut off to a
considerable extent from the great centres on the Continent.'[33] If the
loss of Normandy was the start of that long process by which 'Little
Englanders' came into being, it must also have quickened the demise
of English Jewry. Increasingly isolated from intellectual contact in
France and Germany the community turned in upon itself; there is
evidence of contact with the German *Hasidic* movement of the early
thirteenth century, but it amounts to very little.[34] In addition, financial
business was circumscribed once it became more difficult to make and
maintain continental connections. The loss of Normandy was truly
England's loss.

One matter cannot be avoided. It is an English 'first' which is the
most shameful of them all. Between Norwich in 1144 and Kielce in
1946 there is an unbroken thread of ritual murder charges. The

'inventor' of the first of these and of the 'sacrificial' boy-victim, St William of Norwich, was Thomas of Monmouth, a Benedictine monk; one presumes he was English and not Welsh. Gavin Langmuir writes:[35]

> We may feel reasonably sure that the fantasy that Jews ritually murdered Christians by crucifixion was created and contributed to Western culture by Thomas of Monmouth about 1150 ... He did not alter the course of battles, politics, or the economy. He solved no philosophical or theological problems. He was not even noteworthy for the holiness of his life or promotion to monastic office. Yet with substantial help from an otherwise unknown converted Jew [Theobald of Cambridge], he created a myth that ... caused, directly and indirectly, far more deaths than William's murderer could ever have dreamt of committing ... Those deadly consequences should not blind us, however, to the creative imagination with which Thomas manipulated religious symbols and his perception of events in his environment in order to ... mould the religiosity of others to support his own. For Thomas was more concerned to strengthen his own Christian cosmos than to destroy Jews.

The last sentence apart, the latter portion of this quotation has to remind us – and it may be Professor Langmuir's intention to do so – of Adolf Hitler. Both these monsters must make the historian of today pause, for we are too ready to de-individualize history. Gibbon would have been better able to find a place for them. Nor are we yet prepared to give due weight to fantasy, the irrational, and myth as powers to move mankind, especially Western mankind. Here we have still much to learn from Gershom Scholem. A single Englishman was the sole begettor of a lie which had more life in it than most truths have; that lie led to terrible and untold suffering. I do not think, however, that Englishness, the Englishness of Thomas himself, or of the people of Norwich and East Anglia (such as it was), is relevant: this lie could have had its origin in almost any city or town of twelfth-century Europe: man and moment – with a great deal of heaving and shoving from the man – coincided at Norwich in the 1140s. Where responsibility is involved, what may be far more relevant was a visit to Northern France in 1171 of William Turbe, an English monk who spent all his life at Norwich, who was an enthusiast for the cult of St William, and who was bishop of Norwich from 1146 to 1174: the second ritual-murder accusation occurred at Blois in Spring 1171;

more than 30 Jews were burned by order of the Count of Blois on 26 May 1171.[36]

William Turbe, as Dom David Knowles describes him, was 'a man of learning in the monastic literary tradition'.[37] Being learned in that tradition did not prevent one being bigoted and credulous; quite the opposite: a reading, for instance, of *The Dialogue of Miracles* by Caesarius of Heisterbach, written about 1230, opens the window wide on medieval monastic culture. A monk was prone to believe anything; he was particularly ready to believe the worst about Jews (women, and his fellow monks).[38] The Friars thought they knew more, and they undoubtedly did; their greater knowledge made them even more zealous to make Christians of everyone: ordinary men (and women), heretics, pagans, and Jews. They could be very deliberately provocative, like zealots before and after them, founding their houses bang in the middle of urban Jewish communities – as at Oxford and Cambridge: in Cambridge the Franciscans set themselves up in a former synagogue.[39] In the twelfth century many monks were bishops; in the thirteenth a number of friars were. The unexceptional point I am seeking to make is that the anti-Semitic notions of the English people had their origins in the religious culture of monks and friars. Moreover, they were violent men, at any rate in their language – and it was by their words that they communicated their ideas to ordinary folk. This is Richard of Devizes, a Benedictine monk, on the massacres of March 1190:[40]

> On that same coronation day, at about the hour of that solemnity in which the Son was immolated to the Father, they began in the city of London to immolate the Jews to their father, the Devil. It took them so long to celebrate this mystery that the holocaust was barely completed on the second day. The other towns and cities of the country emulated the faith of the Londoners, and with equal devotion they dispatched their bloodsuckers bloodily to hell ... Winchester alone spared its worms.

Here is the familiar temptation intellectuals perenially fall for: the pornography of bad language. When the ideologues speak like this synagogues burn.

In England they did not. Kings had to pull them down. After all, ordinary people are far less gullible than intellectuals; the anti-Semitic notions of monks and friars had far less impact than historians (those credulous intellectuals) tell us they had. At Winchester, Northamp-

ton, Hereford, Canterbury, and in other English towns in the thirteenth century[41] Christians and Jews rubbed along as neighbours; no
doubt they would have continued to do so were it not for the intervention of their spiritual, social, and political 'betters'. It is there that the
blame has to be lodged: with those who maintained that to be a
Christian you had to hate Jews. We should not mistake the message.
The identity of Christendom and of Christians was the issue; the more
Christian one was the more potent one's anti-Semitism. Once rulers
got the message then there was no hope for the Jews: a Christian king
had to rule a Christian kingdom. Edward I had got the message.

There is, none the less, another issue. If by 1290 being Christian
meant being anti-Jewish, did being anti-Jewish mean being English?
The Expulsion has been said to have been a 'popular' measure. What
may be meant by this is that it was done to please the parliamentary
classes, who in summer 1290 granted the taxes Edward had asked them
for.[42] The only people in England in 1290 who may have regarded
themselves as English were those parliamentary classes: the king, his
bishops, his clerical bureaucrats, the judges, the barons, the knights,
urban businessmen. These, I venture to suggest, were anti-Semites. It
is, in other words, and entirely as one would expect, the governing elite
who first equate Englishness with non-Jewishness.

Jews disappeared from England in 1290; 'the Jew' did not. In wall-
paintings, as at Chalgrove in Oxfordshire and in St Stephen's Chapel,
Westminster, or in wall-tiles, like those at Tring, now in the British and
Victoria and Albert Museums, he could have been seen. He was also
visible on stage – in the Croxton (or Babwell) 'Play of the Sacrament'
as well as in Passion plays; one company of players called themselves
'the Jeweis de Abyndon'; they performed interludes at Christmas 1427
for the five-year old Henry VI.[43] There was also a handful of 'real'
Jews, converted ones anyway, who lived in the Domus Conversorum
in London. Michael Adler published a poignant paper about them in
1939.[44] Working in the Public Record Office, which is on the site of the
Domus Conversorum, and looking through the Wardens' accounts,
which run in an unbroken sequence to 1609, is to know at first hand
what Englishness is. That continuity, on which the English pride
themselves, is evident in these neatly written account rolls in their trim
white-leather pouches, reminiscent of whited sepulcres because there
is no life within them. The salaries of the warden, two chaplains, and a
clerk after the mid-fourteenth century invariably come to three or four
times what it costs to keep two or three converted 'foreign' Jews. The

institution that survives long past its active life, no longer serving its original purpose: that is very English – think of parliament, the monarchy, the Church of England.

Yet, very English too is the idiosyncracy of the Domus Conversorum in the first place: 'England is the only country where a king founded a home for converts.'[45] Henry III established the house in 1232. His son, Edward I, did an equally English thing, when in the 1280s, for the upkeep of the Domus Conversorum, he established a poll tax of 3d a head on the Jews of England who refused conversion. The collectors of the tax were the chaplains themselves, usually converts; the dispatch of William le Convers to gather the tax in his own former community at Oxford shows the nasty logic of which English government is capable: the predictable assault duly occurred.[46] With this incident we get close to the moral ambivalence which is at the root of so much that is regarded as typically English. When the *Daily Telegraph* tells us that 'Raffles must be accounted one of the most powerful myth figures of popular fiction', we have to sit up and listen. Yet, Raffles, 'a public-school man of the best sort', an elegant Clubman, and 'the finest slow bowler of his time', was a common thief. This is the gentleman who is the hero of the English reading classes. In the story, 'A Costume Piece', the reader is left in no uncertainty as to Raffles' attitude towards Reuben Rosenthall of St John's Wood. The genteel anti-Semitism of the uniquely English Raffles has a very long history – the longest in Europe.

One last thing is a thought from Poland, from a Polish masterpiece, *The Beautiful Mrs Seidenman* by Andrzej Szczypiorski; the thought concerns the Poles of Warsaw: they were 'unaware that they were maimed, for without the Jews they are no longer the Poles they once were and should have remained for ever'. Might this be said of the English after 1290?

NOTES

1. Cecil Roth, *The Jews of Medieval Oxford*, Oxford Historical Society, 1951, pp.107–8.
2. In a note distributed to members of the Ecclesiastical History Society, of which President Professor Dobson was President in 1991; the note was an introduction to the Society's annual conference, whose theme was 'Christianity and Judaism'.
3. *History, Religion, and Antisemitism* (1990), p.351.

4. Professor Peter Brown's obituary of Professor Arnaldo Momigliano, *Proceedings of the British Academy*, Vol.lxxiv (1988), p.434.
5. *A History of the Jews in England* (Third edition, Oxford, 1964), p.85.
6. 'The Shrine of Little St Hugh', *Transactions of the British Archaeological Association Conference*, Vol. viii (1986), pp.109–117; the quotation is from p.115.
7. 'The Jewish Minority in Medieval England, 1066–1290', *Journal of Jewish Studies*, Vol. xxv (1974), p.293.
8. Ibid., p.288.
9. Professor Prestwich's paper 'The Piety of Edward I' is to be found in W.M. Ormrod (ed.), *England in the Thirteenth Century* (Harlaxton, 1985); the quotations are from his *Edward I* (1988), pp.345 and 346.
10. Archie Baron, 'Hidden Exodus', *The Listener*, 1 November 1990.
11. 'The Knight's Tale of Young Hugh of Lincoln', *Speculum*, Vol. xlvii (1972), p.479.
12. Cecil Roth, *A History of the Jews in England*, p.57.
13. '1240–60: A Watershed in Anglo-Jewish Relations?', *Historical Research*, Vol. lxi (1988), pp.135–150.
14. Ibid., pp.149–150.
15. *Matthew Paris* (1958), p.143.
16. Richard Vaughan (ed. and trans.), *Chronicles of Matthew Paris* (Gloucester, 1984), pp.214–15.
17. *Henry the Third and the Lord Edward* (Oxford, 1947), Vol.ii, p.447.
18. Ibid., p.461; the phrase 'savage anti-Semitic riots' comes from Gwyn A. Williams, *Medieval London. From Commune to Capital* (1963), pp.217 and 224. Dr Huw Ridgeway has kindly supplied me with a reference to another, hitherto unrecorded, anti-Jewish (as well as anti-government) incident: 'on about 6 May 1260, during an abortive rising led by Simon de Montfort and the Lord Edward, the Wardrobe of the Jewry at the Exchequer, Westminster, was broken into and records stolen [London, Public Record Office, E.159/33, m.10]'.
19. 'Simon de Montfort: The First Leader of a Political Movement in English History', *History*, Vol.lxxvi (1991), pp.3–23.
20. S.Levy, 'Notes on Leicester Jewry', *Transactions of the Jewish Historical Society of England*, Vol. v (1902–5), p.39.
21. *Past and Present*, Vol.i, *Ancient Borough to 1860* (Leicester, 1974), p.25.
22. The passage, 'The Jews of Leicester', is on pp.244–9.
23. For the cross, see Norman Scarfe, 'The Bury St Edmunds Cross', *Proceedings of the Suffolk Institute of Archaeology*, Vol.xxxiii (1974), pp.75–85 and references there. Elizabeth Claridge wrote a column beside a picture of the cross in a *Sunday Times Colour Supplement*; I have mislaid the date, but it is likely to be of, or before, 1974.
24. H.E. Butler (ed.), *The Chronicle of Jocelin of Brakelond* (1949), p.45; Cecil Roth, *The Jews of Medieval England*, p.25.
25. *The Jews of Medieval York and the Massacre of March 1190*, Borthwick Papers No. 45 (York, 1974). The quotation is from Gordon J. Horwitz, *In the Shadow of Death. Living Outside the Gates of Mauthausen* (London, 1991), p.180.
26. Or do I misunderstand the workings of late twelfth-century English law in such matters, as there were fines (*The Jews of Medieval York*, pp.33–4)?
27. Ibid., p.30.
28. Ibid.
29. The phrases are from the 'Timewatch' programme, 'All the King's Jews', written and produced by Archie Baron, and shown on BBC 2 on 31 Oct. 1990.
30. On p.165.
31. See, for example, V.D. Lipman, 'The Anatomy of Medieval Anglo-Jewry', *Transactions of the Jewish Historical Society of England*, Vol.xxi (1968), pp.64–77.
32. *Magna Carta* (Cambridge, 1965), p.233.

33. Cecil Roth, *The Jews of Medieval England*, pp.34 and 36.
34. Ibid., p.118; V.D. Lipman, *The Jews of Medieval Norwich* (London, 1967), pp.148–9, for Joseph the Hasid of Bungay; Cecil Roth, 'Elijah of London, the most illustrious English Jew of the Middle Ages', *Transactions of the Jewish Historical Society of England*, Vol.xv (1939–45), pp.52–3. There may, of course, be more than meets the eye.
35. 'Thomas of Monmouth: Detector of Ritual Murder', *Speculum*, Vol.lix (1984), pp.842 and 844–5.
36. The bishop's journey was mentioned in the 'Timewatch' programme, cited in note 29; I have not (so far) found the source for it.
37. *The Episcopal Colleagues of Archbishop Thomas Becket* (Cambridge, 1951), p.32.
38. Although, it should be said, the Carthusian St Hugh, bishop of Lincoln, suppressed at Northampton a cult to a Christian looter killed by another Christian looter during the anti-Jewish rioting in the town of March 1190: D.L. Douie and H. Farmer (eds.), *The Life of St Hugh of Lincoln* (1962), Vol. ii, pp.17 and 201.
39. John Moorman, *The Grey Friars in Cambridge, 1225–1538* (Cambridge, 1952), p.8.
40. J.T. Appleby (ed. and trans.), *The Chronicle of Richard of Devizes* (London, 1963), pp.3–4.
41. Michael Adler, 'Benedict the Gildsman of Winchester', *Transactions of the Jewish Historical Society of England, Miscellanies in Honour of E.A. Adler* (London, 1942), pp.1–8; A.J. Collins, 'The Northampton Jewry and its Cemetery in the Thirteenth Century', *Transactions of the Jewish Historical Society of England*, Vol.15 (1939–45), pp.151–64; Cecil Roth, *The Jews of Medieval England*, p.77; Michael Adler, 'The Jews of Medieval Canterbury' in his *Jews of Medieval England* (London, 1939), pp.49–103.
42. Maurice Powicke, *The Thirteenth Century* (Oxford, 1962), p.513.
43. W.K. Tydeman, *The Medieval Theatre* (London, 1978), pp.218–9. For the 'Play of the Sacrament', see Norman Davis (ed.), *Non-Cycle Plays and Fragments* (Early English Text Society, Supplementary Text No. 1) (1970), pp.lxx–lxxxv and 58–89. If the play is to be associated with Babwell rather than Croxton (near Thetford), then we return to the Bury St Edmunds' connection: Babwell is a mile from that town.
44. 'The History of the Domus Conversorum', in *Jews of Medieval England*, pp. 277–379.
45. Ibid., p.281.
46. Ibid., p.301; V.D. Lipman, 'The Anatomy of Medieval Anglo-Jewry', *Transactions of the Jewish Society of England*, Vol.xxi (1962–7), p.64.

The Marginalization of Early Modern Anglo-Jewish History

DAVID S. KATZ

The history of early modern Anglo-Jewry has suffered from a dual disability: English historians often pass over Jewish themes, while at the same time Anglo-Jewish historiography has been excessively patriotic, conservative, and 'Whig', that is, ends-oriented, the 'End of Anglo-Jewish History' being Emancipation. These tendencies can be illustrated by examining three specific examples: (1) a 'Christian' subject whose 'Jewish' component has been left out (Newton's theology); (2) a 'Jewish' subject whose 'Christian' aspect has been excised (Spinoza and the Quakers); and (3) a 'neutral' subject which has been misunderstood through lack of co-operation between gentile and Jewish historians (Anglo-Jewry and the Glorious Revolution).

Complaints by historians about the 'marginalization' or 'neglect' of their own specialized subjects inevitably have a somewhat pathetic quality about them. Accusations about a 'conspiracy of silence' are more likely than not liable to provoke Oscar Wilde's famous advice to join it. In historiography, it is too often the case that where there is no smoke, there is no fire. Historians of Anglo-Jewry are famous for their self-mortification. It is depressing, and even degrading, to see how often English historians pass over Jewish and Hebrew themes when discussing the Reformation or millenarianism, or to find that the standard work on English witchcraft and magic lacks the word 'kabbalah' in the index. At one level, at least, historians of Anglo-Jewry have only themselves to blame for this lack of force. Jews in England never experienced any *Haskalah* ('Enlightenment') movement, nor did they suffer the sort of tireless physical persecution that was the lot of the Jews on the Continent. The historian of Anglo-Jewry who works within the framework of departments of Jewish history often has a dormant inferiority complex when faced with his colleagues who study and chronicle the history of the Jews in the full flowering of Hebraic culture in Germany or Eastern Europe. Another reason for the low-key nature of Anglo-Jewish history lies in the extremely cautious character of the historians themselves. Mostly gifted amateurs rather than university teachers, they have been clergymen, businessmen, lawyers, and civil servants, who saw the writing of Anglo-Jewish history as an act of testimony, reflecting their dual wish to praise their people and their country. Almost any subject that was liable to place the Jewish community in a negative light was self-censored, and any twist of interpretation which might spark gentile anger was banished and buried.

As a result, Anglo-Jewish historiography has always been patriotic, conservative and Whig, that is, ends-oriented, written with one eye on the final destination of the history train, the End of Anglo-Jewish History – 'Emancipation', that minor alteration in the oath of office which allowed Baron de Rothschild to take his seat in the House of Commons on 26 July 1858 and never utter a word thereafter. It is a fact that no major historians of pre-Emancipation Anglo-Jewry have yet emerged who are English-born Jews writing about their own community. The late Cecil Roth's refusal to specialize on the history of Anglo-Jewry, and his tendency to abandon scholarly conventions, resulted in his many books and articles in the field being full of mistakes, undocumented assertions, and numerous gaps. Roth's determination to praise 'the Jewish contribution to civilization' led him to emphasize the 'positive' elements in both Jewish and English history, and pursuing this goal he was even willing to distort a text and substantially alter its meaning. But Roth was a pioneer who worked very largely during the blackest era of Jewish history, when it seemed that the very last thing the Jews needed was avoidable criticism from within, supplying genuine arguments to even more genuine anti-Semites. To attack Roth now would be pointless, but it is simultaneously enlightening and disheartening that in the 20-odd years since his death no native son or daughter has replaced him. Nearly all the professional historical works on pre-Emancipation Anglo-Jewry have been the products of research by Americans, Israelis, and gentiles.

At the same time that professional Jewish historians have shied away from Anglo-Jewry, so too have mainstream English historians consistently demonstrated a blind spot about Jewish themes. Partly this has been because the subject remains inaccessible, obscured behind a veil of exotic Oriental languages and a battery of unfamiliar practices. If Jewish historians avoid negative themes, English historians eschew Jewish subjects altogether, even at the expense of coherence and comprehensiveness. Very often the cause of neglect is not to be found in any deep-seated fear of Jews and their themes, but rather because no easily available work was to hand. Until the publication of Professor Jonathan Israel's masterly book on *European Jewry in the Age of Mercantilism*, gentile scholars could pass over early modern Jewish subjects with impunity.[1] Certainly there were books that might be found, but the name of Oxford University Press rang in their ears far louder than those of Graetz, Baron, or even Yerushalmi and Kaplan. One is already beginning to see the effects in general historiography of a book like Israel's, that synthesizes the existing secondary literature and puts it into a form which adheres to all of the standards of modern scholarship. In the recent past there have been some historians who admitted the problem. Dr R.J.W. Evans, for example, states quite openly in his gripping biography of Rudolf II that here was a man whose interest in kabbalah was deep and almost obsessive, but that since this entire subject is beyond the abilities of the author, it must be left behind. But Evans makes a point of identifying this lacuna for the reader's benefit, and informs him that a complete understanding of the mind of Rudolf II would have to include a discussion of the Jewish background as well.[2]

This marginalization of Anglo-Jewish history, not only by gentile historians but by Jewish scholars as well, can best be illustrated by taking three specific examples from the early modern period, illustrating in turn: (1) a 'Christian' subject whose 'Jewish' component has been left out; (2) a 'Jewish' subject whose 'Christian' aspect has been excised; and (3) a 'neutral' subject which has been misunderstood through lack of co-operation between gentile and Jewish historians.

I

The life and work of Sir Isaac Newton provides us with the best example of the first syndrome. The importance of Newton in the history of science is axiomatic, but it is now becoming clear that the picture we have been given of the great pioneer has been sanitized so as to present him as a scientist who managed early on to free himself from the shackles of religion and dogma and thereby to reach scientific breakthroughs in a number of key fields. Newton has been traditionally presented as a clear-headed scientist whose interest in religion came late, during the period of his physical and mental decline, and that therefore we can easily disregard his metaphysics and millenarianism as unimportant to understanding his work as a whole. Newton's religion is therefore at best the irrelevant hobby of a tragically near-senile formerly great scientist.[3]

In fact, more than half of what Newton wrote was concerned with theology and alchemy, and these manuscripts have never been printed. On Newton's death, the papers were offered to the Royal Society, of which he had been president for the past 24 years, but that body rejected them, finding them inconsistent with the man in whose name they now acted. These manuscripts eventually were inherited in the 1930s by the earl of Portsmouth, who again offered them to the Royal Society, which once more turned them down. After Cambridge University, where Newton had been professor, declined to take them, the papers were offered for auction at Sotheby's in 1936. The Newton manuscripts were divided there between John Maynard Keynes, who bought mostly alchemical texts, and Professor A.S. Yahuda, who purchased most of the theological papers. Yahuda was a Palestinian Jew who had taught Arabic at Heidelberg, fled to England, and found refuge in the United States in 1940 through the help of his friend Albert Einstein. Yahuda was a great collector, and the Newton papers, kept in 41 boxes, formed only part of his mammoth library. Yahuda and Einstein tried to interest Harvard, Yale or Princeton in housing Newton's theological manuscripts, but all declined, and the entire collection remained with Yahuda at home in New Haven. Finally, Yahuda willed the collection to the National Library in Israel, but his family contested the legacy and the Newton theological manuscripts were not available to scholars until 1972.[4]

In a general way, the reasons for this consistent rejection of Newton's true philosophical orientation are clear. Newton was and still is understood as the man who postulated a universe which operates on the basis of laws, and this rational man had no business in meddling with biblical chronology or the true dimensions of the Second Temple. But in a deeper sense, the fact that Newton regarded Jewish history as more important than science caused unrest in the Royal Society of the early eighteenth century, as it would continue to do there two centuries later. Yet by expunging Newton's theology from his world-view, historians falsified even Newton's science as it was understood by Newton himself.

In Newton's eyes, what he had done was to provide the final and conclusive proof for the existence of God, and that on the basis of scientific observation rather than philosophical speculation. This was the result of his view of gravitation, a non-mechanistic force which was capable of acting across a vacuum, and which operated not only in this world, but in space as well according to a group of well-defined principles. Indeed, it was Newton's description of gravitation which so incensed his contemporaries, who saw it as a magical, almost occult power, which if accepted might open the way to attributing to the world whatever unknown qualities one wished. From the point of view of the Cartesians, whose mechanistic world-view was replaced by the Newtonian synthesis, Newton's theory had to be rejected because it was bad science. Newton, however, argued that his system conclusively demonstrated the existence of God, because gravitation did not work perfectly. Motion 'is much more apt to be lost than got and is always upon the decay', he explained. Indeed, 'a continual miracle is needed to prevent the sun and fixed stars from rushing together through gravity'. Newton's God was not a vague First Cause or a Divine Watchmaker, but rather a living figure active in this world, whose intervention was necessary if the laws of nature which He himself created were to function. In short, Newton provided the scientific proof for the existence of God, and saw this as the main function of his science.

Newton's theological research was meant to flesh out this conception of the workings of God in the world. The Second Temple was for Newton a microcosm of God's plan for the universe, and the key to understanding it. The cubit was the divine unit of world construction, and Newton invested a good deal of time and energy trying to determine its true length, with special reference to the Great Pyramid of Egypt and other sources. It was in this context that Newton turned to Maimonides for information, as the font of Jewish wisdom. Newton's almost unbridled interest in Maimonides has led Professor Richard H. Popkin, the foremost historian of philosophy, to suggest that perhaps instead of seeing Newton as merely an anti-trinitarian Arian, we should understand him as a Christian follower of Maimonides, and very close to the acceptance of the Jewish unitary theory of God.[5] Frank E. Manuel, one of the few scholars to have interested himself in Newton's theology, suggested that any monotheistic culture will have an internal drive to seek the single unitary, unifying principle, and this is what Newton's laws provided: a conception of world order deeply satisfying on a spiritual as well as on a scientific level.[6]

Clearly then, any even cursory examination of Isaac Newton's vast collection of theological writings, with his massive commentaries on Daniel and the prophecies, his work on church history, his biblical studies, and his colossal chronologies, reveals that religion was central for his work, and that to understand Newton in his own context we need to address ourselves to these issues. Newton's Jewish scholarship was profound, both on the purely biblical level and with regard to the commentaries, and anyone attempting to fathom these writings must be at home with both the Hebrew language and with the Jewish tradition. Despite these truths which are almost axiomatic, little has been done even now on the entire question of Newton's theology. The writings remain unpublished, and only recently has an effort been made to organize, catalogue, and finally publish what Newton considered to be his most important work. Apart from Professors Popkin and Manuel, and more recently by Professor James E. Force, Whiston's biographer, little synthesis of this material has been attempted. Even Professor Richard Westfall, whose massive biography of Newton remains the standard work, somewhat underplays the theological background, and remains fundamentally unconvinced that there is a necessary connection between Newton the scientist and Newton the theologian.[7]

This blind spot in Newtonian studies, one of the major growth industries in the history of science, is only slowly being corrected, and is a prime example of one variety of marginalization suffered by Jewish history and culture in Britain itself.

II

The second species of marginalization is characterized by a Jewish subject in which the Christian element has been left out. In this way, much of the wider relevance is omitted and even its universality. The best example of this phenomenon in early modern English history is the case of Spinoza. Little hard information exists about Spinoza's life: even the reasons for his excommunication on 27 July 1656 are unclear. What is now certain is that Spinoza was in contact with English Quaker circles in the years after his excommunication, from the spring of 1657 to the autumn of 1658, in the period before he left Amsterdam in 1660 for Rijnsburg, the village near Leiden where he lived afterwards. As is well-known, the Quaker leader Margaret Fell wrote two pamphlets addressed to the Jews during this time[8] and her husband George Fox wrote works persuading them to convert somewhat later.[9] Margaret Fell was especially anxious to have her work translated into Hebrew, and corresponded with fellow Quakers Samuel Fisher and John Stubbs on this important matter.[10] William Caton wrote to Margaret Fell from Amsterdam in October 1656, reporting that the Jews there 'are hungering for' her book, warning that 'in one of their houses we had three or four houres discourse with some of them, and a good principle in ye Conscience they owned in wordes, but they could scarce endure to here Christ mentioned'.[11] He soon wrote to her again and reported that her book to the Jews had been translated, presumably into Dutch, in preparation for its translation into Hebrew.[12] That Dutch translation was done by William Ames, who himself wrote to Fell in April 1657 regarding the prospective translator of her work into Hebrew:

> theare is a Jew at amsterdam that by the Jews is cast out (as he himselfe and others sayeth) because he owneth no other teacher but the light and he sent for me and J spoke toe him and he was pretty tender and doth owne all that is spoken; and he sayde tow read of moses and the prophets without was nothing tow him except he Came toe know it within: and soe the name of Christ it is like he doth owne: J gave order that one of the duch Copyes of thy book should be giuen toe him and he sent me word he would Come toe oure meeting but in the mean time J was Imprisoned.[13]

Caton confirmed 'that there are some Among them that would willingly become Christians, but that they fear intollerable persecution, and that especially from their brethren'.[14] Pending the translation of Fell's pamphlet into Hebrew, Caton also had 'seuen or eight score of them deliuered to them at their synagouge, some to the Rabbyes, and some to the Doctors'.[15] In November, Caton could write to Fell reporting 'that J haue bene with A Jew and have shewed him thy booke, & haue asked him what Languadge would bee the fittest for them hee told mee porteegees or Hebrew, for if it were in Hebrew they might understand it at Jerusalem or in almost any other place of the world'. Most importantly, 'he hath undertaken to translate it for us, he being expert in seuerall Languadges'.[16]

At some point during this period, a decision seems to have been made not only to have the Jew translate Fell's *Loving Salutation*, but also to have him relieve Samuel Fisher, whose attempt to translate her book to Menasseh ben Israel into Hebrew seems to have failed. 'Some moueinges there is in him towardes the jewes', it was reported of Fisher from his home in Kent, 'which will bee fulfilled in the Lordes time'.[17] Clearly the translation of Fell's pamphlet could not be delayed that long. It may also be that Menasseh's death in September 1657 gave that book an untimely association. By March 1658, Caton was writing to Margaret Fell as if the Jew had taken on both translations:

> As touching thy booke (titulated A Loving Salutation), I have gotten it once translated in Duch, because the Jew that is to translate it into Hebrew, could not translate it out of English; He hath it now, and is translating of it, like he hath done the other, which Samuel Fisher and John Stubbs have taken along with them: the Jew that translates it, remaines very friendly in his way.

Caton also reported that

> Sam. Fisher was in their Synagogue at Amsterdam and among them at Rotterdam; they were pretty moderate towards him: (I meane they did not abuse him) but assented to much of that which he spoke: he had some discourse with two or three of their Doctors in private at Amsterdam, and they seemed to owne in words the substance of that which he declared: but they were in bondage as people of other formes are.[18]

The translation of Fell's *Loving Salutation* was completed within two months, for in May 1658 William Caton wrote that he 'gott them from the presse and the same day that J came from thence J gott about 170 of them dispersed Among the Jewes who willingly & greedyly receiued them, (they being in the Hebrew tongue) J purpossed to haue brought halfe A hundred of them with mee to England but J dispossed of them in Zealand their being seuerall Jewes'.[19] In October, Ames would be writing to George Fox reporting that he had gotten his book translated into Dutch as well, 'because he who is toe translate it into Hebrew cannot understand english, and I have spoke with one who hath been a Jew toe translate it intoe Hebrew'. Ames was writing to Fox to suggest that he consider having the book translated into Yiddish instead, 'since I have understood that the Common people of the Jewes cannot speak Hebrew'.[20]

There has been much speculation over the years as to the identity of the anonymous Jewish translator of Margaret Fell's work.[21] As of April 1657, when Ames wrote his letter to Fell, there were four Jews who had been excommunicated from the synagogue in Amsterdam, or accused of heretical beliefs: Uriel da Costa, Baruch Spinoza, Juan de Prado, and Daniel Ribera. Of these four, only Spinoza, excommunicated on 27 July 1656, could have been Ames's 'Jew at amsterdam that by the Jews is cast out'.[22] Spinoza seems to have been introduced to William Ames by Peter Serrarius, the professional millenarian and tireless intermediary.[23] That Spinoza was in contact and in sympathy with the Quakers during this period seems fairly certain, and it may be that his claim that there is 'no other teacher but the light' may have led him to recognize similar beliefs among the English Quakers in Amsterdam. The attraction was strong enough for Spinoza himself to have sent for Ames, as was reported in the Quaker's letter of April 1657.[24] Spinoza continued his contacts with Englishmen, even after his Quaker period ended about 1658. In 1661, Henry Oldenburg, later secretary of the Royal Society, sought him out at Rijnsburg.[25] Four years later, Oldenburg would write to Spinoza asking for more information regarding the activities of Shabtai Sevi, the Jewish false messiah whose appearance threw European Jewry into a turmoil of indecision.[26]

The fact that Spinoza was in contact with English Quakers, and indeed, that his first publication was a Hebrew translation of a Quaker tract, is itself startling and begins to put flesh on the bare bones of Spinoza's biography, much of which was invented by his supporters. In more recent years, the research (once again) of Professor Richard H. Popkin has suggested that Spinoza was influenced by the Quakers in an even more fundamental way. According to Popkin, Spinoza's great *Tractatus Theologico-Politicus*, usually regarded as the starting point of modern biblical criticism, was very heavily influenced by an earlier Quaker work by the aforementioned Samuel Fisher, *The Rustick's Alarm to the Rabbies*. The comparisons and coincidences between the two texts certainly suggest a good deal of intellectual interaction, at the very least.[27]

Spinoza's Christian connections have been suppressed partly because, as with Newton, they do not fit in with the role we expect Spinoza to play in modern history. A new book on Spinoza by Professor Y. Yovel, for example, suggests that Spinoza may be the first secular Jew, and with this in mind, close connections with religious enthusiasts would hardly be fitting. Spinoza's philosophy is developed within a framework of Marrano life, despite the fact that Spinoza himself was born in Amsterdam, and had as little connection with marranism as the child of Holocaust survivors has with Nazism. A Quaker connection for Spinoza, proven beyond any reasonable doubt in the archives of the Friends' House Library in London, is dismissed as unworthy of discussion by Yovel, and then only in a footnote. Yovel presents as his clinching argument the fact that Spinoza did not know English, but we have already seen that this lack is fully documented in the Quaker letters.[28]

The consigning of 'Jewish' subjects to an historiographical ghetto, then, is another type of marginalization which has plagued Anglo-Jewish history. Spinoza should be a part of the English experience, and by extension related to the English Jews with whom the Quakers themselves were involved in London and Amsterdam. But this entry is denied, to the poverty of all concerned.

III

The third variety of marginalization which I have defined is perhaps the saddest: when an historical event is misunderstood by both the Jewish and the general historians simply because they have been working separately rather than in tandem. A very good example of this can be seen in the treatment by both varieties of historian when confronted with the period of the Glorious Revolution. 'The succeeding Reign of King *James* the second, being deservedly very short, afforts us, likewise, but a very short Portion of *Jewish* History', ruled D'Blossiers Tovey, the eighteenth-century historian of Anglo-Jewry 50 years later.[29] The duration of James's reign is not held in doubt, but brief though it may have been, it was characterized by several rather powerful attacks on the Jewish presence in England.

Clearly the accession of a new king was a golden opportunity for those who saw Jewish merchants as a threat to the livelihoods of their English competitors. A scheme for remedying this danger was devised at the end of October 1685 by the brothers Beaumont, Thomas and Carleton, and its progress provides an unusually striking case in which apparent issues of principle concerning the Jews were so often resolved so as to serve other interests entirely. The Carletons took refuge in Queen Elizabeth's act of 1581 'to retain the Queen Majesty's subjects in their due obedience', by which all recusants were obliged to pay an increased monthly fine of twenty pounds.[30] This provision was meant to be a threat to English Catholics, and was not uniformly enforced, but it served as the legal prop for the issuing of writs against 48 Jews on the charge of recusancy. Indeed, '38 of the principal Jews were taken off the Exchange and obliged to give bail'. The reaction of the Mahamad, the governing body of the Sephardi congregation, was swift and in accordance with past methods: they made a direct appeal to the king. The petition was signed by three leading members, Joseph Henriques, Abraham de Oliveira, and Aron Pacheco. The Jews reminded the new king of his brother's previous declaration of protection in 1664, and reaffirmed their own loyalty to king and country. Yet now they were attacked 'in your Majesties Court of King's Bench att the Suit of one Thomas Beaumont on the Exchange' as part of a plan 'sett up and managed by his Brother one Carleton, Beaumont an Attorney [of] the Said Court designing to gett great Summes of money from your Petitioners'. The Mahamad pointed out that the entire affair would be to the 'great Scandell and prejudice of their Creditt and Reputation both here and abroad', and would thereby be to the mutual disadvantage of the king and his Jewish residents, 'their Chief dealings being in Merchandizing the major and better part of whome by Such their Said trading having paid and Still paying Considerable Somes of money yearly to and for your and his Late Majesties Customes'. The Jews suggested that the king was unaware of these proceedings, and thereby begged him 'to order that the Said Thomas Beaumont And Carleton Beaumont be Conveened to appeare before your Majesty' to answer for their unjustified disturbance of the religious and commercial peace of the realm.[31]

The Jews' petition was presented at court by Henry Mordaunt, the second earl of Peterborough, that rebellious noble who 40 years before had led an ineffectual uprising against Parliament in the second civil war. This essential support did not, of course, come gratis, and the Mahamad was forced the make the free gift, as it were, of 200 guineas to the earl in return for his services.[32] But it was certainly value for money: the earl of Peterborough was present in the Privy Council on 13 November 1685, when James II gave his royal order 'that his Ma^tyes: Attorney Generall, do stopp all the sayd Proceedings att Law against the Pet^rs: His Ma^tyes: Intention being that they should not be troubled, upon this account, but quietly enjoy the free exercise of their Religion, whilst they behave themselves dutifully and obediently to his Government'.[33] Strangely, the king's order does not seem to have had the desired effect immediately, and when three weeks later it was 'Reported that the two Beaumonts, who are prosecutors, would not surcease their suite', James II gave a further order in council to the Lord Chief Justice of the King's Bench, Sir Edward Herbert, 'to send for Beaumont the Atturney and examine him touching his behaviour in this affaire'. Herbert did exactly that on 9 December 1685, and summoned Carleton Beaumont to his chambers, whereupon these proceedings against the Jews were finally quashed.[34]

King James II thus gave the Jews of England what amounted to a Declaration of Indulgence, at the very time when the entire issue of his suspending and dispensing powers was becoming extremely controversial, and a year and a half before he granted the same rights to all other non-Anglicans. Certainly it was a strange piece of timing, even if the case in question originated neither at Court nor in synagogue. Bishop Burnet recalled the year 1685 as one most dangerous to all non-Catholics:

> This year, of which I am now writing, must ever be remembered, as the most fatal to the Protestant Religion. In February, a King of England declared himself a Papist. In June, Charles the Elector Palatine dying without issue, the Electoral dignity went to the House of Newburgh, a most bigotted Popish family. In October, the King of France recalled and vacated the Edict of Nantes. And in December, the Duke of Savoy being brought to it, not only by the persuasions, but even by the threatnings of the Court of France, recalled the Edict that his father had granted to the Vaudois. So it must be confessed, that this was a very critical year. And I have ever reckoned this the fifth great crisis of the Protestant Religion.[35]

So too did Macaulay note that 'Through many years the autumn of 1685 was remembered by the Nonconformists as a time of misery and terror'.[36] Not only was Judge Jeffreys hard at work in his Bloody Assizes, in the aftermath of the defeat of Monmouth's Rebellion, but during the summer and autumn of that year, James extended to England the practice used in Ireland of dispensing from the Test Act officers of the Roman Catholic religion. The revocation of the Edict of Nantes by Louis XIV on 18 October 1685 seemed somehow to be part of a very sinister international plan for the eradication of Protestantism.

Let us look again at the chronology. After Monmouth's capture at the beginning of July 1685, Parliament was prorogued until 4 August, and then further adjourned until 9 November. It was during this period, when the Beaumonts were plotting against the Jews, that James filled the officers' lists with Roman Catholics, and he fully expected that he would have to defend himself and the entire issue of the use of his dispensing powers when Parliament reconvened. James opened Parliament on 9 November 1685, congratulating the nation for defeating Monmouth's Rebellion, but making the point that now more than ever the nation needed a strong military, and as regards the newly-appointed Catholic officers, warned that 'after having had the benefit of their services in such a time of need and danger I will neither expose them to disgrace nor myself to the want of them if there should be another rebellion to make them necessary to me'. The debate on Parliament's response to James II's address opened in the House of Commons on 12 November, with the evident aim of thereby conveying to the king their displeasure with his use of the dispensing power. The following day, our day, 13 November, the House defeated by one vote a proposal that supply be voted before dealing with the question of the appointment of Catholic officers in the army. The House thereby resolved on 14 November that the commissions were illegal and in violation of the Test Act. But James had already decided to act decisively and without delay. On 20 November 1685, the king summoned both Houses and informed them without any explanation that he had decided to prorogue Parliament until 10 February 1686.[37] By this sudden decision, James II lost the parliamentary grant of £700,000 which had been approved, but he had made the point that the use of his dispensing power was not a proper subject for debate.[38]

It is therefore against the background of the parliamentary debate on the use of the royal dispensing power in the appointment of Roman Catholic army officers that James II's extraordinary decision in favour of Jewish residence needs to be seen. Even more striking, the very day of his Order in Council, 13 November 1685, was the day on which pre-debate tension over the dispensing power reached its pitch in Parliament. In that division the Court lost a vital vote on the question of supply, which had become inextricably linked with the recent events in the army. Professor W.A. Speck has described this moment as 'a crucial loss of control'. When James issued his Order at the Privy Council, therefore, he was not only affirming the right of Jews to continue to live peaceably in his realm, but defiantly demonstrating that his dispensing and suspending powers might apply in situations unrelated to Roman Catholic officers in the army, and was an inalienable royal right which could not be altered by the parliamentary interference which was expected the next morning. His reaffirmation of that decision on 9 December, after Parliament had already been prorogued, was a decisive ratification of the principle he had expressed the previous month.

The intimate connection between the King's Order in Council regarding the Jews, and the parliamentary debates over his use of the dispensing power is thus an essential element in understanding the policy of James II towards them. It is saddening to realize that Jewish historians have failed to make this link, and have placed his decision exclusively in the realm of evolving English attitudes towards the Jews within their midst. So too have historians of the Glorious Revolution been unaware of this document and its significance. Certainly the king's actions were not related only to the political exigencies of the moment, but it is true that the Beaumont brothers and their case landed in his lap at precisely the moment when he needed it. No doubt the Beaumonts themselves reckoned that the king would relish the chance to enforce anti-Catholic legislation on non-Catholics and thereby harmlessly champion the validity of statute law. Instead, James used the opportunity to reaffirm his use of the dispensing and suspending powers, and as far as we know, Parliament raised no objections in this instance. Their problem was with Roman Catholics, not with Jews, who had no desire to become officers in the army nor ministers of state. They were strangers, albeit of a peculiar variety, whose legal status, it was acknowledged, ought best to be dealt with in another framework entirely. By means of this ambiguity, then, the Jews were permitted to enjoy their royal privileges, the last occasion on which it was necessary to have the king's protection given them in writing. The Jews were also beneficiaries of James's Declarations of Indulgence issued in 1687 and 1688, which were sufficiently vague so as to include them as well.[39] The events preceding the Glorious Revolution, then, give us a good example of how both Jewish and general historians have missed the point.

'It is singular that few enlightened and wealthy communities know so little of their own early history, as the Jews of Great Britain', lamented James Picciotto, in his pioneering history of Anglo-Jewry published in 1875, 'Yet few races indeed present more vicissitudes for description, or possess records offering a more interesting and extended field for investigation.' One of the explanations for this sorry state of affairs, he thought, was that 'the archives of the older Synagogues, which are treasures of curious information, remained until the present time buried in obscurity, their very existence being scarcely known.' The end result was that 'to the vast majority of even the Jews themselves these books were as hidden and impenetrable as the Vedas or the Zend Avesta.'[40]

The three varieties of marginalization described above grow out of Picciotto's complaint. General historians can hardly be faulted for not looking for a Jewish angle to every event in English history. The joke about the student who writes on 'The Elephant and the Jewish Question' reflects, after all, a Jewish obsession. Jewish historians, on the other hand, are entirely to blame here for their own blindness, and for the perceived need to see the Jewish people wherever they may live as part of a continuous historical quilt. Like anthropologists writing on a wide variety of cultures, historians of Jewish England meet with historians of Jewish France and Jewish Germany, and look for common features rather than trying to integrate Jewish history into the surrounding culture. Certainly this does not hold true for all writing in Jewish history, but it is undeniable that the standard of acceptability tends to be somewhat lower in this field than in others. Much work in Jewish history never reaches a wider audience and thereby is spared truly critical attention, published as it is in specialized periodicals which are often even displayed in separate reading rooms in university libraries. This self-ghettoization has accelerated inherent tendencies towards the marginalization of Jewish history, and the development of the historiographical myth that the progress of the Jews can be viewed as an independent whole. In England the problem is intensified by the lack of interest and even respect for historical documents evidenced by religious leaders more concerned (perhaps justifiably) with communal questions, anti-semitism, and the State of Israel, and by the gradual disappearance of senior university positions in the field.

Picciotto declared that although his book was 'written by a Jew for Jews, the author trusts that Christians, whose faith was founded by members of the Jewish race, will find in these chapters, in addition to that which is entirely new, much that may be of interest also to them.'[41] Picciotto's words in some ways might serve as a goal for all of Jewish historiography, aiming for a utopian era in which Anglo-Jewish history might itself be emancipated and given equal rights and expression.

NOTES

1. J.I.Israel, *European Jewry in the Age of Mercantilism, 1550–1750* (Oxford, 1985).
2. R.J.W. Evans, *Rudolf II and His World* (Oxford, 1973).
3. Traces of this attitude can even be found in the standard biography of Newton, R.S. Westfall, *Never at Rest* (Cambridge, 1980). Newton's religion is hardly mentioned in G.E. Christianson, *In the Presence of the Creator: Isaac Newton and his Times* (New York and London, 1984).
4. See generally R.S. Westfall, 'Newton's Theological Manuscripts', in Z. Bechler (ed.), *Contemporary Newtonian Research* (Dordrecht, 1987), pp.129–43; J.E. Force and R.H. Popkin, *Essays on the Context, Nature, and Influence of Isaac Newton's Theology* (Dordrecht, 1990); and R.H. Popkin, *The Third Force in Seventeenth-Century Thought* (Leiden, 1992).
5. For more on these subjects, see the excellent analysis in Force & Popkin, *Newton's Theology*.
6. F.E. Manuel, 'Three Scientists in Search of God' in his *The Changing of the Gods* (Hanover & London, 1983), pp.1–26, and the other extraordinary essays printed in this book. See also Manuel's other works, *Isaac Newton Historian* (Cambridge, 1963); and *The Religion of Isaac Newton* (Oxford, 1974).
7. See Westfall, 'Manuscripts', p.139.
8. [Margaret Fell], *For Manasseth Ben Israel. The Call of the Jewes out of Babylon* (London, 1656); idem, *A Loving Salutation to the ... Jewes* (London, 1656). Her later works to the Jews are: *A Call to the Universal Seed of God* (London, 1664); *A Call unto the Seed of Israel* (London, 1668); and *The Daughter of Sion Awakened* (London, 1677). See generally, I. Ross, *Margaret Fell: Mother of Quakerism* (London, 1949).
9. George Fox, *A Declaration to the Iews For them to Read Over* (London, 1661); idem, *An Epistle ... To the Jews and Turks* (London, 1673); idem, *A Looking-Glass for the Jews* (Philadelphia, PA, 1784).
10. Fell to Fisher, Mar. 1656: Friends' House Library, London, MS Spence III, p.37; Fell to Stubbs, [?1656], ibid., pp.38–40.
11. Caton to Fell, 29 Oct. 1656: Frs. Hse. Lib., MS Caton III, p.25.
12. Same to same, undated: Frs. Hse. Lib., MS Caton III, p.13. Presumably the pamphlet under discusion was Fell's address to Menasseh ben Israel, which was translated into Dutch by William Ames, according to William Sewel, *The History of the ... Quakers* (London, 1722), ii. 624. The book appeared as *en Manasse ben Israel, Den roep der Joden uyt Babylonien* (n.p., 1657).
13. Ames to Fell, 17 April 1657, from Utrecht: Frs. Hse. Lib., MS Swarthmore 4/28r (Transcr. i. 71–4).
14. Caton to Fell, 5 June 1657: Frs. Hse. Lib., MS Caton III, p.35.
15. Same to same, 26 June 1657: Frs. Hse. Lib., MS Caton III, p.38.
16. Same to same, 18 Nov. 1657, from Amsterdam: Frs. Hse. Lib., MS Caton III, p. 48.
17. Stubbs to Fell, 7 Sept. 1657: Frs. Hse. Lib., MS Abraham III, case 17: Stubbs reported that her books to the Jews had already been translated into Latin.
18. Caton to Fell, 15 March 1657–8, from Leiden: Frs. Hse. Lib., MS Caton III, p.507.
19. Same to same, 21 May 1658: Frs. Hse. Lib., MS Caton III, p. 50. A copy of Fell's *Loving Salutation* in Hebrew, שאלת שלום באהבה , is in the Frs. Hse. Lib., Tracts Vol. 1133, 38. The translation is followed by a letter in Hebrew by Samuel Fisher, 'to all the House of Jacob at all corners of the earth', Tract 38a. This pamphlet has now been published in a modern edition by R.H. Popkin and M.S. Singer as *Spinoza's Earliest Publication?* (Assen/Maastricht, 1987), with an introduction and commentary.
20. Ames to Fox, 14 Oct. 1658: Frs. Hse. Lib., MS Barclay.
21. That this translator was Spinoza was asserted by H.G. Crosfield, *Margaret Fox of*

Swarthmoor (London, 1913), p.50n.; W.I. Hull, *The Rise of Quakerism in Amster-dam 1655–1665* (Swarthmore, 1938), p.205; Ross, *Fell*, p. 94; D. Carrington, 'Quakers and Jews', *Jewish Chronicle Spec. Supp.: Tercentenary of the Settlement of the Jews in the Brit. Isles 1656–1956* (27 Jan. 1956), p.46; H.J. Cadbury, 'Spinoza and a Quaker Document of 1657', *Med. & Ren. Stud.* (1943), pp.130–33; idem, ed., *The Swarthmore Documents in America* (London, 1940), p.7; L. Feuer, *Spinoza and the Rise of Liberalism* (Boston, 1958), p.49; L. Roth, 'Hebraists and Non-Hebraists of the Seventeenth Century', *Jnl. Sem. Stud.,* vi (1961), 211; J. van den Berg, 'Quaker and Chiliast: The Contrary Thoughts of William Ames and Petrus Serrarius', in R. Buick Knox (ed.), *Reformation, Conformity and Dissent: Essays in Honour of Geoffrey Nuttall* (London, 1977), pp.182–3. Most recently, Prof. R.H. Popkin has re-examined all of the available evidence concerning Spinoza's Quaker connections and has placed it in the context of the work of Serrarius and other millenarians of the period: see his 'Spinoza, the Quakers and the Millenarians, 1656–1658', *Manuscrito,* vi (1982), pp.113–33; idem, 'Spinoza's Relations with the Quakers in Amsterdam', *Quaker History,* lxxiii (1984), pp.14–28; idem, 'Spinoza and Samuel Fisher', *Philosophia,* xv (1985), pp.219–36; idem and Singer, *Spinoza's Earliest Publication?*

22. Uriel da Costa died in 1640; Juan de Prado was excommunicated on 4 Feb. 1658, although expelled the previous May; and Daniel Ribera was still employed by the Jewish community on 14 Feb. 1657 and was still making contributions on 21 Sept. 1657: I.S. Revah, *Spinoza et Juan Prado* (The Hague, 1959), pp.23–5, 28, 29–30; idem, 'Aux Origines de la rupture spinozienne: nouveaux documents sur l'incroyance dans la communaute Judeo-Portugaise d'Amsterdam a l'epoque de l'excommunication de Spinoza', *Rev. Etud. Juives,* 4th ser., cxxiii (1964), pp.359–431, especially pp.371–3. See generally the masterful book by Yosef Kaplan, *From Christianity to Judaism: The Story of Isaac Orobio de Castro* (Oxford, 1989).

23. According to van den Berg, 'Quaker and Chiliast', p.183. See now E.G.E. van der Wall, *De Mystieke Chiliast Petrus Serrarius (1600–1669) en zijn Wereld* (Leiden, 1987), forthcoming in English as well.

24. See text of letter above.

25. Oldenburg to Spinoza, 16 Aug. 1661: A.R. and M.B. Hall (ed.), *Correspondence of Henry Oldenburg,* (Madison, WI., 1965–), ii. pp.414–15.

26. Same to same, 8 Dec. 1665: ibid., ii, pp.633–7; A. Wolf (ed.), *Correspondence of Spinoza* (London, 1928), pp.214–17. Spinoza's reply to Oldenburg, if there was one, is now lost.

27. Compare Samuel Fisher, *The Rustick's Alarm to the Rabbies* (London, 1660) with Spinoza's *Tractatus Theologico-Politicus* (Hamburg, 1670), either in the translation by R.H.M. Elwes first published in 1883 and repr. (New York, 1951) or in the new one by Samuel Shirley (Leiden, 1989), with an introduction by B.S. Gregory incorporating Popkin's views. For Popkin, see 'Spinoza, the Quakers and the Millenarians'; idem, 'Spinoza's Relations with the Quakers'; idem, 'Spinoza and Samuel Fisher'; idem and Singer, *Spinoza's Earliest Publication?*

28. Y. Yovel, *Spinoza and Other Heretics* (Princeton, NJ, 1989), Vol.i: 'The Marrano of Reason'. Yovel is reviewed by Popkin in *The New Republic,* 21 May 1990, pp.35–41, an enlarged version of which appears, with footnotes, in his book of collected essays, *The Third Force.*

29. D'Blossiers Tovey, *Anglia Judaica: or the History and Antiquities of the Jews in England* (Oxford, 1738), p.287. See now D.S. Katz, 'The Jews of England and 1688', in O. P. Grell *et al.* (eds.), *From Persecution to Toleration* (Oxford, 1991), pp.217–49.

30. 23 Eliz. l, c. 1: repr. *The Tudor Constitution,* ed. G.R. Elton (Cambridge, 1972),

p.423.
31. Span. and Port. Jews Cong., London, MS 641: also repr. in L.D. Barnett (ed.), *Bevis Marks Records, I* (Oxford, 1940), pp.13–14; newsletter to John Squire of Newcastle, 3 Nov. 1685: *Cal. S.P. Dom., Feb.–Dec. 1685*, #1856 (pp.374–5).
32. Records of the Mahamad, as reported in A.M. Hyamson, *The Sephardim of England* (London, 1951), pp.56–7. C. Roth, *A History of the Jews in England* (3rd edn., Oxford, 1964), p.183, gives the sum as three hundred pounds, for some reason.
33. James II, Privy Council order, 13 Nov. 1685: Span and Port. Jews Cong., London, MS 344 1c: photograph in Barnett (ed.), *Bevis Marks Records, I*, plate v, between pp.14–15; cf. p.15.
34. James II, Privy Council order, 4 Dec. 1685; note by Herbert, 9 Dec. 1685: Span. and Port. Jews Cong., London, MS 344 1d: photograph in ibid., plate vi, opp. p.15. When the final reckoning was made, the congregation discovered that their defence had cost them £288 8s. 6d., paid for by a special *Finta* which brought in £286 14s. 0d.: ibid., p.15n.
35. Gilbert Burnet, *History of His Own Time* (3rd edn., London, 1724–34), ii, pp.344–5.
36. T.B. Macaulay, *History of England* (Everyman edn., London, 1906), i, p.501. Generally, see now W.A. Speck, *Reluctant Revolutionaries: Englishmen and the Revolution of 1688* (Oxford, 1988), pp.51–62.
37. Anchitell Grey, *Debates of the House of Commons from the Year 1687 to the Year 1694* (London, 1763), viii, pp.353–69: the Parliament in fact never sat again.
38. Ibid., pp.366–7. Generally on the debates in November, see R.E. Boyer, *English Declarations of Indulgence 1687 and 1688* (The Hague, 1968), pp.36–42; Macaulay, *History*, i, pp.514–28; Speck, *Revolutionaries*, p.59.
39. Declaration of Indulgence, 4 April 1687, which James issued, among other reasons, 'for the increase of trade and encouragement of strangers': J.P. Kenyon (ed.), *The Stuart Constitution* (Cambridge, 1969), pp.410–13. The Declaration of Indulgence of April 1688 was nearly identical. James's religious policy in regard to persecuted minorities has been re-examined in R.D. Gwynn, 'James II in Light of his Treatment of Huguenot Refugees in England, 1685–1686', *Eng. Hist. Rev.*, xcii (1977), pp.820–33.
40. James Picciotto, *Sketches of Anglo-Jewish History* (ed. I. Finestein) (London, 1956), p.xiii.
41. Ibid., p.xiv.

The End of the 'Anglo-Jewish Progress Show': Representations of the Jewish East End, 1887–1987

TONY KUSHNER

In 1887 the Anglo-Jewish Exhibition at the Albert Hall ignored the experience of the East End. In contrast in 1987 the Jewish East End was 'celebrated' with a series of remarkable exhibitions and events across the capital. This article explores how the lives of Jews in immigrant areas have been represented in Anglo-Jewish heritage and historiography over this hundred year period. It suggests that only recently have East European immigrants been dealt with in a balanced and comprehensive manner by historians and others. Nevertheless, the article also points out that there is a new danger where bias may occur not, as was previously the case, through embarrassment but due to distortion caused by a looking back with nostalgia.

The East End of London has represented much more than a geographical entity in modern British history. The area, with its imprecise borders has become a symbol of the 'state of the nation' – of social questions, poverty and physical deterioration, the threat of revolution and unrest, the blitz and Britain 'taking it', of ethnic pluralism and racial intolerance. The East End has been forgotten and then 'rediscovered' and reinvented. In the process, myth and reality have become intertwined making the writing of East End history all the more difficult. Both left and right have used and abused the past of the East End and, in the process, exposed the dangerous area where critical history becomes an uncensorious 'heritage'. Already, to many, the East End has become a historical 'theme park' yet the area continues to be occupied – indeed it was one of the few whose size of population is actually growing in the capital. To those who still inhabit the East End, poverty, racism, sweated labour, the housing crisis, the lack of schools and social facilities are of more pressing concern than 'heritage' preservation. The writing of East End history and the creation of its heritage provide a series of dilemmas both of a practical and theoretical nature.[1]

One of the most endearing, or alternatively (depending on one's perspective) repulsive, features of the East End is its taking in of successive immigrant groups and its concomitant blatant multi-cultural nature. There is tremendous potential for distortion in this specific aspect of its history. On the one hand, *celebration* of the East End immigrant past and present may lead to the ignoring of less savoury features including the area's traditions of racial and ethnocentric intolerance. On the other, stress on its poverty and racism has been and continues to be used to justify immigration control or 'colour-blind' policies on a local and national level. *Jewish* history of the East End presents its own particular problems. In the late nineteenth and early twentieth centuries, when Anglo-Jewish historiography was established, East End Jews were at best an embarrassment to the established community. The programmes instituted by upper and middle class Jews (including anglicization, dispersal and even removal of the poor, foreign Jews) were designed to take away attention from the new arrivals. It was in a general background of anti-alienism, as David Cesarani suggests elsewhere in this volume, that the first Anglo-Jewish history was written. It attempted to show the rootedness of the Jews of Britain by focusing on the medieval and early modern periods and thus it is not surprising that the early practitioners shied away from studying the teeming contemporary Yiddish culture of the East End. What is more remarkable, however, is how long it took for the Jewish East End to be historicized and how much of the record was lost before it was subject to detailed scrutiny.[2]

More recently, Jewish embarrassment about the East End has largely, though, as we shall see, not totally, disappeared. It has given way to a rediscovery of roots, of Jews returning to the East End 'looking for the street they lived in, or ... retracing their ancestors' history'. Previously there had been a danger that Jewish East End history was subject to distortion through self-censorship; there is now a parallel danger of history being warped through nostalgia – a 'chicken soup with everything' approach. This article focuses on the changing representations of the Jewish East End from the first Jewish historical exhibition in 1887 through to the Celebration of the Jewish East End in 1987. Through an exploration of the development of historical heritage by Jews in Britain over the past one hundred years, especially in the form of national exhibitions, it analyses whether the 1987 Celebration marked the historiographical coming of age of Anglo-Jewry.[3]

I

The 1887 Anglo-Jewish Exhibition in the Albert Hall coincided with the publication of John Burnett's report to the Board of Trade on sweated labour. The report suggested that alien Jewish immigrants were at the root of the sweating system in the East End tailoring trade. The report and a response to it – *Denial From the East End* – appeared in the Tercentary of the Resettlement of the Jews in the British Isles celebration in 1956 at the Victoria and Albert Museum: 'Anglo-Jewish Art and History'. The 1956 exhibition also included an engraving of the Soup Kitchen for Poor Jews in the East End; posters from the Jewish Tailors' Strike and other material from the Jewish trade union movement; anarchist and socialist Yiddish newspapers from the period of mass immigration and other items portraying East End Jewish life before 1914. Even had they been available, it would have been inconceivable for such items to be represented amongst the 2,600 exhibits at the Albert Hall in 1887.[4]

Prior to the Anglo-Jewish Historical Exhibition, strict guidelines had been produced of 'Objects Admissable' for consideration. Strong preference was indicated in the classified scheme for 'Relics and Records ... of the Expulsion and Pre-Expulsion Periods'. Where the post-resettlement period featured it was in carefully prescribed form: 'Letters and autographs of Distinguished Persons'; 'Lists and mementoes of Jews, celebrated in Anglo-Jewish History'; 'Records of Jews (not now living) who have received Honours in the British Empire'; 'Portraits and prints of members of representative Jewish Families'. As Cesarani suggests, the exhibition was part of the defensive strategy of elite Anglo-Jewry at a time when the position of all Jews in British society was being questioned. Historical items were being called upon to play their part in the armoury of Anglo-Jewry against attacks, especially the alleged unEnglishness of the community – foreign born and native. The exhibition organisers made clear their desire 'to promote a knowledge of Anglo-Jewish history; to create a deeper interest in its records and relics, and to aid in their preservation.'[5]

The survival and appearance of the Yiddish East End items in the 1956 Tercentenary celebration owed little or nothing to the sentiments expressed by the organizers of the Anglo-Jewish Historical Exhibition 70 years earlier. It would be left to the left to exceptional individuals in the immigrant community and their children to preserve aspects of a heritage that was beyond the scope of the first Anglo-Jewish historians. In a remarkably progressive and far-sighted inaugural Presidential lecture launching the Jewish Historical Society in 1893, Lucien Wolf defended the pursuit of Anglo-Jewish history. Wolf acknowledged that in terms of world Jewish history, Anglo-Jewry had not produced any 'great men'. Nevertheless, in what was to be a prediction of the recent achievements of Jewish social history, Wolf categorically stated that even if Anglo-Jewry had produced such men 'it would be no proof that our history was more important than the histories of the French and German communities'.[6]

Nevertheless, there were distinct limitations to Wolf's vision. The men (and only men) he had in mind and their history were *medieval*. Wolf's concern for the modern period was purely political – to protect East European Jews through international diplomacy. It was not until after 1945, when the Jewish East had been devastated by blitz and evacuation, that the Jewish Historical Society would even consider its history. The apparatus of 'official' Jewish history and heritage in Britain which had been established by the early 1930s (with the addition of a Museum in Woburn House and library/museum in University College, London), was not concerned with the experience of the Jewish East End.[7]

The East End of the 1930s continued to be a source of concern and embarrassment for middle class Jews. Radical Jewish activities, and especially the clash with homegrown British Fascists threatened those of the West End who feared for their own safety in this decade of rampant and growing political anti-Semitism. The search for invisibility was not conducive to the pursuit of critical history. It was thus up to East End Jewry to produce its own chroniclers and image makers. Poverty, exploitation, anti-Semitism (experienced or feared) – the sheer battle to survive – as well as the mobility of the East End Jewish community were not conducive to the preservation of historical heritage. From the First World War onwards, for many Jews, contrary to contemporary perspectives, the original immigrant settlement areas such as the East End were places to escape from and wipe away from memory: 'You ask Mr Levi or Cohen in Hale or Whitefield, Allwoodedley or Scarcroft, and he will very conveniently forget his back-to-back in Hightown, Strangeways, the Leylands', wrote one opponent of the plan to set up a Manchester Jewish Museum in the 1970s – one which was seeking to concentrate on a portrayal of the immigrant experience.[8]

Despite, or in many cases, *because* of the hardship, the talent of young East End Jews was thrown up before, during and after the First World War. Some, such as the writer John Rodker and the artist Bernard Meninsky, wished to leave their Jewish milieau and concentrate on 'English' society. Others such as David Bomberg, Isaac Rosenberg and Mark Gertler would explore in their work the life and culture of the Jewish East End. Through the newly formed Whitechapel Art Gallery, such artists provided the first representations of Jewish working class life in exhibition form in a series of shows starting from the early 1900s.[9] The East End as a symbol of wider issues also attracted a series of social investigators, journalists and writers. From the reports and writings of Booth, Potter, and Toynbee Hall, and, as late as the 1930s, the second 'Booth' survey and just before the war, Mass-Observation, East End Jewish life was viewed by outsiders. By the Second World War a new generation of working class Jewish novelists such as Simon Blumenfeld, Willy Goldman and Barnett Sheridan were producing radical novels revealing the class divisions, poverty and brutality (as well as the human bravery and warmth) of East End Jewish life.[10]

The historian is thus left with a rich variety of cultural sources – although this is less true of the records and artefacts of everyday Jewish life in the East End from the period of mass immigration through to the demise of the area as a centre of Jewish life. The artistic flowering of the Jewish East End did not extend to the writing of its own history. A. R. Rollin, a radical leader in the world of Jewish clothing trade unions in the 1930s, was a rare individual who believed it was essential to gather material relating to the history of Jewish socialism of the East End and elsewhere before it disappeared without trace. It was Rollin who was to provide the majority of exhibits representing Jewish East End life in the 1956 celebration.[11]

Just 20 items represented immigrant life in Britain beyond 1881 at the Tercentenary exhibition – almost the same number used to explore the period after expulsion in 1290 and before 1655 when, officially, there were no Jews in the country at all. To put this in further perspective, 288 items represented the period from 1656 to 1856. The relative neglect of modern and certainly working class/immigrant life in the 1956 exhibition with its 720 items is clear.[12] Nevertheless, from a perspective of just ten years earlier or even less it would have been almost surprising that the Jewish East End featured at all. In 1946, C.C. Aronsfeld (a young refugee from Nazism and a leading socialist

Zionist with strong historical interests), complained that 'Anglo-Jewish historical research ... has scarcely moved beyond the date of legal emancipation, 1858'. Commenting on the Jewish Historical Society's concentration on the medieval and early modern period he asked 'But what of the rest, what, for example, of the tremendous event of Russian immigration?' Cecil Roth responded that the Society was now devoting 'special attention' to the modern period.[13] A survey of the Society's Transactions suggests that Aronsfeld's concern was well-placed and that Roth was stretching a point. It is true that an important pioneer paper on 'The Beginnings of the Jewish Trade Union Movement in England' was delivered to the Society in 1948, but it was not until 1964 that the next paper was to be published on a theme relating to East European immigration.[14]

II

A clear opportunity to cover mass immigration occurred in 1951 with the 'Anglo-Jewish Exhibition, 1851–1951' which took place at University College, London as part of the 'Festival of Britain'. The Festival itself was designed to show the material progress that had occurred in the century folowing the Great Exhibition. The organizers of the Jewish exhibition were clearly ill at ease dealing with the modern period. Their inclination was to go back further – as the introduction to their catalogue suggests: 'The roots of the present Anglo-Jewish community go deep down – far beyond the century with which we are dealing.' The solution was to emphasize in the exhibition the emancipation of the Jews in Victorian Britain and, subsequently, 'Anglo-Jewry's achievements over the past hundred years and, through these achievements, its contributions to the corporate life of Britain'.[15] The exhibition was, through its stressing of Jewish contributions in areas such as charity, English letters and public life, essentially defensive and apologetic. Indeed, Sidney Salomon who, as Press Officer of the Board of Deputies, was involved in day to day monitoring of antisemitism, was one of the individuals most clearly involved with the 1951 exhibition. Salomon believed that the exhibition 'has afforded enlightenment even to the well-informed, as well as to the less-informed members of the Christian community. For it must always be remembered that ignorance more than prejudice is responsible for much ill-feeling'.[16]

Lord Nathan, opening the exhibition, remarked that it produced 'a family album of Anglo-Jewry'.[17] If this was the case,the organisers had left out the pictures of what they considered to be if not exactly black sheep, then the 'unacceptable' face of modern Anglo-Jewish history. The journal of the Association of Jewish Refugees, perhaps the most acute observer of Anglo-Jewry at this time, was not slow to see the implications of Nathan's metaphor:

> It is perhaps not altogether surprising that in this colourful album, the family dwelt almost entirely on its thoroughly respectable members. The poor relations were treated with discretion, in fact there was hardly any reference to the refugees from Russia, Poland and Germany who increased the Jews of England from 80,000 in the 'eighties to the present 400,000'.[18]

Other critics were to be found who missed any mention of 'the very rich Yiddish and Hebrew literature and press which exerted so great an influence over the past half century'. If for some it was hard to justify the exhibition's 'treatment of the immigrants, for they are of the very substance of the community', for others it was equally hard to explain the concentration on emancipation or the 'need in 1951 to give expression to gratitude for continued emancipation'. This then, as the Glasgow *Daily Record* put it bluntly, was the 'Anglo-Jewish Progress Show'.[19] Ironically, the limitation of that progress was revealed in the insecurity of the Jewish community which led to the blandness and exclusions of the 1951 exhibition. Only in the Art section at the Ben Uri Gallery was a more inclusive approach adopted with the showing of the work of Jewish modernists with close connections to the immigrant areas such as Rosenberg, Epstein, Bomberg and Meninsky. This was the first time such a collection had been attempted on a large scale since an exhibition at the Whitechapel gallery in 1906. The art section was not, however, part of the major exhibition where the section on culture was dominated by references to Siegfried Sassoon and S.L. Bensusan whose 'deep knowledge of the English character and the countryside' proved that Anglo-Jewry had 'absorbed the English way of life'. Emancipation had thus worked and it was unnecessary to dwell on the rough edges of the East End when Anglo-Jewry itself could now 'write[] with ... authority on Essex life'.[20]

III

No sooner had the 1951 exhibition (which even one of its kinder critics had to admit was 'a gallant failure') finished, than preparations began for the Tercentenary Celebrations of the readmission of the Jews. Here the Jewish Historical Society and Anglo-Jewry as a whole was on more secure territory. There was, admittably, a problem of which year to commemorate – 1655, 1656 or 1657 all had historic significances – but once it was decided to accept the middle year, progress could begin. The first meeting of the Tercentenary Committee was held, appropriately, in the oldest surviving synagogue, Bevis Marks, in July 1952. Initial plans were to concentrate on religion which would neatly connect the philosemitism of English Christianity (which provided the positive ideological atmosphere for the readmission to occur) with the definition of Anglo-Jewry as loyal members of British society differentiated only by faith. To mark the happy symbiosis of Britain and its Jews which had occurred since 1656, a pilgrimage to Holland to the tomb of Rabbi Menasseh Ben Israel (who had acted as mediator for the re-admission) was planned along with the striking of a commemorative medallion featuring the Rabbi and Oliver Cromwell. It was a year later that the idea of another exhibition was raised with the formation of a special sub-committee.[21]

Those involved with setting up the Exhibition had close links to the Jewish Historical Society and Jewish Museum. From the start, the organizers were aware of the 1887 exhibition which they saw as their 'true predecessor'. On the one hand, they believed that they were following on a path of progress which started with the Anglo-Jewish Historical Exhibition, led six years later to the foundation of the Historical Society and then the Jewish Museum and Mocatta Library in the 1930s. The 1956 exhibition was to show the fruits of a now mature tree. On the other, those on the Exhibition sub-committee were aware that they could not match the size of 1887 but that in terms of organisation and quality they could provide a more coherent and professional display.[22]

On the surface there were great similarities between the 1887 and 1956 exhibitions. National public buildings with close connections to the royalty (the Albert Hall followed by the Victoria and Albert Museum) were chosen – the latter because there would be little chance of success 'unless it were held in surroundings sufficiently distinguished to give it standing'.[23] Both exhibititions included:

(1) historic items which related to the medieval or early modern period;
(2) items relating to famous Jews in the British Empire;

(3) items of Jewish ritual art of an exclusive nature.

When pressed whether items chosen in 1887 would be excluded from consideration, the secretary of the Exhibition sub-committee, Richard Barnett, indicated that they would not. He added that there would be a section devoted to Hebrew learning and printing. This, in fact, was the only major subject to be included in 1956 that was not represented in the Anglo-Jewish Historical Exhibition.[24] Nevertheless, despite their many superficial resemblances, the two exhibitions were produced in totally different atmospheres. Whilst both exposed the limitations of Anglo-Jewish historiography, the Tercentenary Exhibition revealed an Anglo-Jewish community in a more self-confident and certainly less defensive mood. This diminishing insecurity is even evident when the 1956 exhibition is compared to that of five years earlier. At the time of the latter, memories were only just starting to fade of 'that unhappy period during the withdrawal of the mandatory Power and the establishment of the State of Israel in 1948'.[25] The Whiggish nature and aims of the 1956 exhibition were blatant – to 'demonstrat[e] the progress of three centuries in Anglo-Jewish life'. Lord Samuel, opening the event, referred to the three hundred years as representing progress from 'toleration through emancipation to fraternity'. Anglo-Jewry of 1956 had made it and the hiccup of the immediate post-war years was over; the great British-Jewish partnership could continue in full and open friendship.[26]

The constant references to British acceptance of Jews (and the expressions of gratitude that brought forth), itself indicate that the self-confidence exhibited by Anglo-Jewry as it reflected on its own history, had its limitations. Nevertheless, the Tercentenary event was designed 'to heighten the Anglo-Jewish consciousness' whereas that seventy years earlier was generally for non-Jewish consumption at a time when the security of the Jews in Britain was in doubt.[27] The Tercentenary exhibition was thus less contrived and a greater freedom of expression became possible. In this process, the family album of Anglo-Jewry grew a little in scope, enabling for the first time consideration of the immigrant Jews of the East End.

As has been shown, the section of the exhibition devoted to the East European immigrants was tiny but their very inclusion was significant. There was enough confidence to include the anarchists, trade unionists and socialists of the East End. Moreover, the organizers had the audacity to suggest that these radical groups too were part of the path of progress followed by Anglo-Jewry – definitely short-lived but effective organizations which, along with Jewish social welfare organisations, combatted 'exploitation'.[28]

'Who was exploiting whom?', was a question well beyond the scope of the exhibition organizers, but they still felt that 'Jewish Trade Union[s] should be represented'.[29] Yet the handful of such items chosen could never represent more than a tokenist attempt to portray the immigrant experience. Complaints concerning the neglect of East European culture had followed the 1951 exhibition but were now even more prominent. The *Jewish Observer and Middle East Review* was particularly scathing suggesting that its 'quaint and amusing' miscellany of objects was all very pleasant

> but as a representative presentation of 300 years of Anglo-Jewry it is full of the most inexplicable omissions ... the long, eventful East End episode with its teeming immigrants and its powerful Yiddish culture, and the decisive formative effects these have had on Anglo-Jewry, are so scantily presented that they scarcely exist as a feature of the Exhibition at all. This is a sociological blunder.[30]

Blunder or not, the limited attention given to the East European immigrants was no oversight. Barnett, as the leading force in the Tercentenary exhibition was well aware that 'the later 19th and 20th century [were] inadequately represented'. He gave the reason for its relative exclusion that it was too close to be dealt with adequately. More important, however, was Barnett's insistence that the exhibition organizers 'confine ourselves to material of high quality'.[31] Barnett's response to the *Jewish Review*'s comments that the exhibition's failure to depict 'the common man ... the common Jew' are worth quoting at length. They reveal much about the state of Anglo-Jewish historiography in the mid-twentieth century:

> This may sound well on paper, but a moment's thought shows the hollowness of the criticism. The characteristic of the ordi[nary] person is that there is neither anything striking 'artistic', historical or curious about him. There is then nothing about him which you can exhibit that people will be interested to look at ... The organisers of the Exhibition ... set themselves against manufacturing exhibits except in the fewest cases ... trades or firms

usually do not possess anything which can be dignified with the name of an exhibit.[32]

Instead, the organizers from the start concentrated on 'high' art material and especially 'ritual objects and general antiquities of Anglo-Jewish interest (the bulk being material from Bevis Marks, the Hambro and Great Synagogues)'.[33] Nevertheless, the smugness and self-satisfaction illustrated in the Terecentenary Celebration had its critics: 'The Exhibition has a good story to tell. Unfortunately, it does not tell it.'[34] The cultural and historical elites of Anglo-Jewry in 1956 were content with comments of the Duke of Edinburgh at the Tercentenary banquet on the importance of British tolerance: Jews and Gentiles in Britain had 'come through so many years without a stain on their honour. Intolerance on the one hand and provocation on the other have often tried to make an appearance, but the good sense of both communities has always kept them in check.'

The Jews' 'success in fitting itself into the life of the adopted country' meant that they were rarely provocative and thus non-Jews could be truly tolerant. A British Zionist journal poured scorn on this updated emancipation contract, but it would take a new generation of Anglo-Jewry to move on to provide a critique in terms of historiography.[35] The 1956 Exhibition was aimed at celebrating the happy partnership of Britain and the Jews – not at exposing an informal pre-marital contract demanding good behaviour from the minority itself. Contemporary anti-Semitism in Britain was not ignored by the Exhibition, yet by using a telegram from Julius Streicher to Oswald Mosley: 'I value the message', and a book by William Joyce, the ex-Mosleyite, published in Germany during the war, the essential foreign and 'unEnglish' inspiration of British anti-Semites was emphasized. Where indeed, as the *Jewish Observer and Middle East Review* put it, were Chesterton and Belloc? Instead the Celebration presented this pastoral vision of Anglo-Jewry:

'Adorned with English roses shines the tent
Of Israel, pitched in pastures doubly green
From living streams of Thames and Jordan blent'[36]

The exhibition organizers had in fact hoped to stage a pageant of Anglo-Jewish history in one of the Rothschilds' stately homes, although in the end they had to settle for a garden party in Lambeth

Palace.[37] Max Beloff in a *Jewish Chronicle* centenary supplement regarded Chesterton and Belloc and later Mosley as foreign inspired – failing as imports because they were 'alien to the fundamentals of British thought or behaviour'. Significantly Beloff was strong in his attack on those Jews who had provided a provocation to the normally tolerant British, and particularly those 'Jews, [who] to their shame, were taking a prominent part in the Communist movement' in the 1930s. These 'were only a handful of outcasts' and thus British Fascism was given no encouragement. Whilst the 1956 Exhibition recorded, in a minor way, the existence of Jewish socialists in the 1880s, it was inconceivable that it would have dealt with contemporary radicals. Anglo-Jewish progress should have ensured their extinction.[38]

IV

The gaps left in terms of Anglo-Jewish historiography by the 1956 Celebration were thus immense. The critic who noticed the absence of the 'ordinary man' was correct – but even he forgot about the absence of the 'ordinary woman'. In terms of Jewish women's history, the only progress made from 1887 to 1956 was the latter inclusion of pictorial images of some of the wives and daughters of the Jewish magnates.[39] It was also clear that the 'Commemoration of the end of exile for Jews from Britain seems to have underlined the exile of the provinces from Anglo-Jewry. A visitor to the London exhibition in this Tercentenary year cannot learn that Jews exist in Manchester even to-day.' Manchester then proceeded to hold its own tercentenary programme which matched London's for its elitism and narrow focus.[40] In short, Anglo-Jewry was not ready in 1956 for a synthetic approach to its history and heritage which would have included all of the United Kingdom, men and women, children and adults, rich and poor, foreign unassimilated and British born, and, decisively, 'respectable' and 'unrespectable'. Ultimately, the Tercentenary exhibition, whilst not designed so much to appease the Christian world as was the case in 1887, still did not want to cause offence or give ammunition to antisemites. It presented Anglo-Jewry as a useful addition to British society, essentially reasonable and if not dull then certainly not dangerous. The Jews of Britain and their history were, in the words of the exhibition organizer 'an interesting novelty'.[41]

In terms of heritage preservation, those behind the 1956 celebrations could see no further than giving proper support to the Jewish

Museum which continued to collect elite artefacts. Even pleas to
promote Anglo-Jewish history in the form of a university position were
rejected on the grounds that the subject was 'parochial'.[42] It is revealing that A.R. Rollin was having to sell off part of his collection of
Jewish radical material at the time of the exhibition. It was at this point
in time that Lloyd Gartner carried out his pioneer study of the
immigrant Jewish East End. He was aware of the loss of material that
was taking place and that there was little knowledge or concern that
this was taking place. Communal neglect post-1945, rather than German bombs in the war, was responsible for the loss of so many
individual and institutional Jewish records and artefacts in the former
immigrant areas. Buildings of historical importance or architectural
merit were also left to deteriorate.[43]

Gartner's work was published in 1960. It had taken an American
schooled in the expanding area of immigrant and ethnic studies in the
United States to reveal the richness and importance of the East
European Jewish experience in Britain. The work, a classic in Jewish
historiography, fell on stony ground. Indeed, Gartner wrote disappointingly in a second edition as late as 1973 that little more of note had
been written after it.[44] British scholars such as Vivian Lipman and
Israel Finestein had begun to open up the area of the 'new community'
in the late 1950s, but there were no native professional Jewish scholars
to develop the subject, nor were general British historians interested in
the Jewish minority. Provincial Jewish history, which Gartner approached only indirectly, developed hardly at all in the 1960s.[45] New
young writers such as Arnold Wesker and Bernard Kops were using
their East End experiences for their literature in the late 1950s and
early 1960s but they had no equivalents in the world of history.[46] As late
as 1981 Bill Fishman wrote that with the exception of the work of the
American, Gartner, the '45 years or so of settlement [before 1914]
have been, until very recently, a vacuum in English and Jewish Social
History'. Only one paper on the Jewish East End appeared in the
Transactions of the Jewish Historical Society in the 1960s and 1970s,
and that by the ageing Rollin. Any change that was going to occur in
the study of Jewish immigration would have to come from outside the
Society.[47]

Fishman himself was the first major British (indeed East End) born
historian to tackle the Jewish East End. In 1975 his brilliant account of
Jewish anarchist life, *East End Jewish Radicals 1875–1914*, was published. The leader of that anarchist movement, Rudolf Rocker, pub-

lished his memoirs in 1956. Given the intellectual climate exposed by the Centenary Celebration of that year it is perhaps hardly surprising that 'it scarcely sold'. Fishman provides his own explanation of why that was and also why change occurred:

> Perhaps the embourgeoisement of a more secure Jewry made it inevitable that the pre-1914 story of Jewish working class radicalism be consigned to oblivion. but a new generation of altruistic youth, Jew and non-Jew, emerged in the '60s, rejecting the acquisitive and competitive *mores* of their parents. In doing so, a minority discarded the old authoritarian shibboleths for an alternative form of communal living, through which, in their terms, they could build on from below to create a truly free, just and equitable society. And in their search for a continuing tradition, they have rescued from obscurity the story of East End Anarchism.[48]

Other reasons can be added to those provided by Fishman. There was a growth of interest in ethnic roots, stimulated by the black movement in America and in terms of British Jewry, the pride emerging from the Israeli 1967 war. Contemporary racism in Britain (and especially the campaign for immigration restriction), prompted the study of the Aliens Question in the East End of London in the 1900s.[49] Compared to the United States, it was a small beginning, but Fishman in particular began the process of archive and building rescue in the East End. He also realized the potential of interviewing survivors from the immigration period though, alas, many had already died, their testimonies lost forever. Fishman, along with amateur enthusiasts such as Monty Richardson, David Jacobs and Harriet Karsh (all involved with Jewish youth and social work), were the basis behind the formation of the Jewish East End Project (JEEP) in the late 1970s.[50] It was also at this stage, as Bill Williams describes elsewhere, that the Jewish studies project at Manchester Polytechnic and the basis for what was to become the Manchester Jewish Museum was set up.[51] Suddenly items of everyday importance, ones that had been rejected in the 1956 Celebration as unworthy of 'the name of an exhibit', were becoming valued by a group of talented historians and enthusiasts and seen to represent aspects of the Jewish experience in Britain – ones previously ignored by historians.

Nevertheless, the battle for acceptance, recognition and, from this, funding, was a hard fought one throughout the 1980s. Williams charts in this volume the indifference and even antipathy of the Jewish community in the Manchester context. Fortunately this did not stop the official opening of the Jewish Museum in 1985. Significantly more help was forthcoming from non-Jewish bodies, partly reflecting a greater commitment to multi-cultural projects at this point in time.[52] In London, progress was, relative to its size, even slower and progress, certainly on the museum front, owed much to the direct stimulation of Manchester. In 1980 JEEP organized a Jewish East End Festival which was attended by over 1,200 people. The event focused 'on the rich Jewish culture that evolved in the East End' and included exhibitions and recreations of Jewish economic, social and cultural life up to 1945. Although on a much smaller scale, this festival was the precursor of the 1987 Jewish East Celebration and a genuine landmark in Anglo-Jewish historiography.[53]

Shortly afterwards a major conference on the 'Jewish East End: 1840–1939' took place. For the first time the Jewish Historical Society was involved although the iniative had come from JEEP again. The conference and festival revealed that Jews of all ages were interested in their recent immigrant past. Moreover, a new generation of historians – Jewish and non-Jewish – were exploring the life of the Jewish East End and other settlement areas.[54] The politics, social, religious and cultural life of the immigrants were analysed as were 'embarrassing' topics such as anti-alienism/anti-Semitism and class conflict in the lives of the immigrants and their children. Yet the flowering of talent and enthusiasm of the early 1980s also exposed the lack of institutional structure that could be developed and exploited. JEEP encouraged and pursued Jewish East End heritage preservation whether in the form of artefacts or oral history recordings, but there was no museum or resource centre to act as a proper repository. In terms of academic positions, Bill Fishman developed East London studies at Queen Mary College and Colin Holmes was forming the basis of what has become known as the 'Sheffield school' of British minority studies at the University there. Through both individuals and the presence of Bill Williams at Manchester and the independent work of Jerry White (a product and leading figure of the History Workshop movement) on everyday Jewish life in an East End tenement block, great stimulus was given to Anglo-Jewish social history.[55] There was still, however, no position devoted to Anglo-Jewish studies at any institute of higher education in Britain and no formal structure for younger researchers to exploit. Neither University College London nor the Yarnton Oxford

Hebrew Postgraduate Centre saw Anglo-Jewish history in any form as something to develop in what were the two major locations for Jewish studies in the United Kingdom.

V

In 1983 the first step was taken in forming an institutional base with the formation of the Museum of the Jewish East End. The connection to the Manchester project was direct – Rickie Burman, the curator, had been one of the key individuals in the development of what was to become the Manchester Jewish Museum.[56] The Museum of the Jewish East End eventually took over the functions of JEEP, including the promotion of research and heritage preservation. The Museum has successfully rescued much archival material, continued the collection of artefacts and photographs and carried out a series of important oral history projects. This work has led to the creation of a permanent and many temporary exhibitions. The latter were to play a vital role in the success of the 1987 celebration. There have been several problems, however, which have not been overcome. First, the Museum is located in a Jewish communal building which, due to its size and layout, has limited the development of the permanent exhibition and important functions and activities. Secondly, recurring financial problems have led to insufficient staffing and other resourcing needs. Thirdly the Museum is located in Finchley and is distant from many of the immigrant areas which its exhibitions cover. Whilst heritage preservation has improved in terms of records, artefacts, oral history and photographs, the physical evidence of the Jewish East End has continued to disappear. The location of the Museum in the East End could have helped to save at least one building and also provided an example to others. Lack of money and, ultimately, the absence of a will on the part of Anglo-Jewry behind that shortage of funding explain this state of affairs.[57]

The Museum of the Jewish East End thus acted as a valuable stimulus to those interested in exploring the immigrant past, but much of the progress subsequently made has been on an informal level. After its brief flirtation with the Jewish East End in the early 1980s, the Jewish Historical Society gave little help. It was at this point that the Jewish Museum in New York, it should be remembered, was 'acknowledg[ing] the significant role of the immigrant experience in shaping the identity of the American Jew today' in a series of important exhibitions (including, ironically, 'The Immigrant Generation: Jewish Artists in Britain 1900–1945').[58] More important in a sense, was grass roots history epitomized by the History Workshop movement and carried out in the Jewish context by individuals such as White and Williams.[59] The 1987 Celebration of the East End was thus a triumph of local and individual initiative rather than coming from any official or institutional basis from within Anglo-Jewry.

VI

The Celebration took place in the summer of 1987 and consisted of 12 exhibitions which took place in the East End itself but also across London in venues ranging from the National Theatre and St Paul's Cathedral to a small flat in Stepney Green and a disused synagogue in Spitalfields. In addition there were live performances of music and theatre as well as films, walking tours and lectures.[60] In size, ambition and range, it far surpassed the show piece exhibitions of 1887 and 1956. What follows is not a detailed account of all the events of the celebration, but an analysis of the approach adopted in the context of Anglo-Jewish historiography and heritage.

The first point to note about the celebration is its lack of reference back to the Tercentenary celebration or the Anglo-Jewish Historical Exhibition. In terms of commemoration, the East End Celebration had a tenuous connection to 1887 – certainly not the exhibition at the Royal Albert Hall, but that 1987, in the words of the celebration coordinator, Helen Carpenter, 'happen[ed] to be the centenary of the Federation of Synagogues, one of the few Jewish organisations still based in the East End'.[61] More important to Carpenter was 'the growth of interest in the social history of the Jews in Britain' in the past few years. Unlike the 1887 exhibition, the Jewish East End Celebration was not designed to appease the ignorant non-Jewish public. Moreover, it was not overly commemorative in function or used to show the rootedness of the Jews of Britain as were the tercentenary events. The defensiveness of both 1887 and 1956 was not a feature of the 1987 celebration, yet the issue of racism was not avoided. Carpenter worked for the Tower Hamlets Environment Trust which had set up a series of projects under the title 'Discover the East End' – including an important exhibition on the Huguenots in 1985. Both the Huguenot exhibition and the 1987 celebration aimed, through the exploration of 'the diverse cultural and social heritage of the East End and its people', to help 'to combat the racism that is prevalent in the East End today towards the Bangladeshis who now live there'.[62] The Jewish East End Celebration was thus part of the development of multi-cultural and anti-racist initiatives which had been sponsored across Britain by local government. It celebrated diversity of culture and acknowledged the force of British intolerance towards minorities in a way that had not been possible just two decades earlier.

The exhibitions, live performances and films revealed an East End previously ignored in Jewish historiography. In particular the world of Yiddish culture, in the form of theatre, music and politics came under scrutiny in the celebration. Here, the most astonishing achievement was the exhibition 'Yiddish Theatre in London' created by David Mazower for the Museum of the Jewish East End and held at the National Theatre. Although surviving until the present day, the Yiddish theatre in London had been largely forgotten – an embarrassment to those who tried to Anglicize the immigrants and not the subject of serious scholarship for later Anglo-Jewish historians. Mazower revealed the range and vitality of Yiddish theatre in Britain up to the early 1950s. Evenings of Yiddish theatre accompanied the celebration throughout the summer of 1987 with a Yiddish Film Season at the National Film Theatre. The complexities, richness and diversity of Yiddish culture, as well as its seedier side and tendency towards sentimentality were explored in these events.[63]

The depth and vitality of the exhibitions owed much to the new, inclusive approaches of social history including the use of oral testimony and photographs and artefacts. Epitomizing this approach was 'Jewish EastEnders: Life in a Stepney Household in the 1920s' researched by Carpenter herself. Following on from the pioneer work of Jerry White, the exhibition posed the question 'What was daily life in a Jewish East End household in the 1920s?' It attempted to provide no easy answers, revealing the range of experiences, the warmth and friendship as well as the hardship and poverty of the Jews of the inter-war East End. Mobility out of the East End was acknowledged but there was recognition that for those still remaining survival was often a struggle.[64] The Jewish East End experience was being celebrated, but without the whiggish assumptions of continuous and universal Jewish progress. Similarly the synagogues of East London and the East London furniture trade were approached in a fresh, critical manner. The former Princelet Street synagogue was the location for a synagogues exhibition which acknowledged religious, ethnic and class conflict in the Jewish community – tensions that affected both the building and design of synagogues and the practice of religion within them.[65] In 'Furnishing the World', the former, defensive approach of Jewish heritage exhibitions of representing the *contribution* of Jews to the British economy was replaced by a more balanced approach – one which accepted the existence of factors such as anti-alienism as well as class struggle between employers and employees in this important East End industry. Moreover, oral history was included to reveal the experiences of workers and trade unionists in different aspects of the furniture trade and not just the captains of industry.[66]

'Furnishing the World' recognized the role of women workers and this theme was further developed in 'Daughters of the Pale' – the first major exhibition devoted to Jewish women in Britain. The exhibition was based on the experiences of daughters of immigrants from Eastern Europe. It was created by the Jewish Women in London Group, who, from 1984, aided by the Greater London Council, carried out an oral history project relating to Jewish women who had settled in Britain or who had been born here. Again, new approaches enabled the inclusion of groups previously ignored in Jewish historiography.[67]

In many ways the Celebration marked the culmination of the efforts of those who had attempted to provide a different representation of Anglo-Jewry since the 1950s and even before. The Whitechapel Art Gallery, which had done so much to promote the immigrant artists, provided an exhibition of the sculpture and drawings of Jacob Epstein; the work of Arnold Wesker and other Jewish East End writers was revived and the path-breaking 'World of Yesterday: Jews in England 1870–1920' (designed by Bill Williams for the Diaspora Museum in Tel Aviv in 1984) was shown again in the remarkable setting of the crypt of St Paul's Cathedral.[68] The Manchester influence was thus still strong even in a celebration devoted to the East End. *The Jewish Quarterly* which had done much to promote the Jewish culture of the East End – when many would have rather forgotten – also played a prominent role in terms of a special edition devoted to the celebration and an evening of Jewish East End writers 'From Zangwill to Berkoff'.[69]

The sheer talent that existed outside establishment Jewish historical circles was thus exposed by the celebration. Several events that could not possibly have been part of an earlier pattern of representations of Jewish heritage took place in 1987. On the one hand, the celebration included 'In England's Green and Pleasant Land' (a 'pageant of Jewish life in England from 1066'), and there was promotion in the celebration programme for the Bevis Marks Association (a successor to the nineteenth century 'Anti-Demolition League') and a historic plaque to Daniel Mendoza was unveiled. On the other, these were relatively isolated tributes to the longevity of Anglo-Jewry and both events took place in the East End.[70] Mendoza made only the one appearance in 1987 whereas in the tercentenary celebrations (just 21 years earlier) he was so prominent that one visitor to the exhibition believed that the impression was given that all eighteenth century Jews were boxers![71]

The 1987 celebration marked an important coming of age in Anglo-Jewish historiography; it enabled the representation of groups such as Jewish prostitutes or anarchists, previously ignored or marginalized in historical writings and exhibitions, and for them to occupy centre stage. The all-encompassing fear of triggering anti-Semitism and the desire to combat it through 'acceptable' images had, at last, been overcome. The dangers of the 'heritage industry', however, are many. Did the celebration avoid the one trap of excluding the unpleasant only to fall into another – providing an idealized and romantic view of the immigrant experience?

In her introduction to the celebration brochure, Helen Carpenter was open in acknowledging one of the sources of inspiration behind the events: 'nostalgia has a part to play. Some, particularly those who know the Jewish East End at first hand, long to recreate, if only for a day or an evening, the spirit of the place as it used to be.' Six years earlier Harriet Karsh had suggested that 'In our fast-paced world JEEP is about slowing down and looking back and learning. Our future is in our Past.'[72] The idea of the past as an unchanging, unproblematic place which has only to be rediscovered in a sanitized form is at the basis of much of the offerings of the heritage industry. The Jewish East End, now safely packaged for most Jews in a world they will never re-enter on a permanent basis, is at particular risk of being distorted today. Inevitably the loving care taken to re-establish the importance of forgotten figures and groups in Anglo-Jewish history in the celebration led to a degree of romanticization. Nevertheless what was remarkable in the celebration was the honesty and lack of nostalgia in the exhibitions and events. This was illustrated in the museum of the Jewish East End's 'Boris: The Studio Photographer 1900–1985'. Boris Bennett 'brought Hollywood to the East End' in his wedding photographs – nearly 150,000 in his lifetime. The exhibition revealed his techniques of providing a form of escapism from the

dreariness of the streets of East London. Any romanticism is shattered
with the revelation that 'it was not unusual for Boris to photograph
thirty weddings on a single Sunday, and, on one occasion, he reached
the record of fifty-six in one day'. The celebration of the Jewish East
End provided the opportunity for much nostalgia; it also represented
East End Jewish life in a hard-hitting way.[73]

VII

What then was the impact of the celebration? Has the history of the
Anglo-Jewish progress school finally been put to rest? Writing in 1987,
Helen Carpenter commented that 'The Jewish East End Celebration
finishes at the end of the summer. It is not intended as a definitive look
at a particular community, but a catalyst for more events to come.'[74]
Carpenter was certainly right to present the celebration as an impressive beginning but not the final word on the subject. Many areas were
opened up in 1987 and needed further exploration. Unfortunately
much of the talent given exposure in the celebration has not been given
the opportunity to develop further. Carpenter and many of those
involved have no positions in the world of Anglo-Jewish heritage and
history; the Museum of the Jewish East End, now the London
Museum of Jewish life, has suffered from its cramped accommodation
and constant financial battles. It has produced some excellent new
exhibitions, reflecting its new title, on the Jews from Nazism and also
post-war arrivals from Aden.[75] Nevertheless, its potential has been
severely hampered by the cut-backs in local authority spending in
recent years. Indeed the assault on multi-cultural and anti-racist
initiatives has made a deep impact on the pursuit of Jewish social
history. The Anglo-Jewish community has not filled the gap and has
yet to see the advantages of promoting the preservation and exploration of its cultural heritage and especially the fascination it provides for
a younger generation.

In terms of academic positions, the future of the Barnett Shine
Fellowship at Queen Mary College, formerly occupied until his retirement by Bill Fishman, hangs in the balance. On a more positive note
both Queen Mary College and the Yarnton Centre at Oxford are
promoting Yiddish studies.[76]

Building preservation, as Sharman Kadish indicates in *Englishness
and Jewishness*, is an area where little progress has taken place. The
East London Synagogue is just one of the most brutal acts of auto-

vandalism committed by Anglo-Jewry in recent years.[77] The Heritage Centre in Princelet Street, location of one of the key exhibitions in 1987, is another illustration of the lack of progress made since the celebration in this sphere. Raphael Samuels has suggested with regard to heritage preservation in Spitalfields, that 'A house is a palimpsest on which successive generations have left their mark'. In terms of the immigrant experience, this is most definely the case with 17–19 Princelet Street. First of all used as a Huguenot house with a later weaving loft, it was taken over and converted into a synagogue in the 1860s and 1870s. In more recent times it has been used to house and educate Bengali families. For nearly a decade attempts have been made to transform the house into a resource centre providing 'a history of immigration in Britain by way of a history of Spitalfields that will help people to identify with their own background and with their British heritage'.[78] Only limited progress has been made on this project at the same time that Ellis Island in the United States has been transformed into a massive history of immigration. Visiting the New York exhibition, Rob Perks, one of the leading British oral historians, 'wondered if £8,000 could be raised in Britain for a museum about immigration, let alone the £80 million raised for Ellis Island'.[79]

The experiences of the Museum of London Jewish Life and the Heritage Centre, Spitalfields, suggest that Perks's pessimism is not misplaced. It is an indictment not just against the Jewish community of Britain and other minorities, but (and in fact more importantly), British society as a whole. In the increasing stridency of English nationalism, it is increasingly difficult to get due recognition of Britain's ethnic diversity and immigrant past.

The Jewish East End Celebration did not provide all the solutions concerning Jewish heritage preservation. For example, buildings connected to Jews or other immigrant and minority groups in the past often now have other functions which may be incompatible with historical usage. Charlie Forman has written with regard to the Heritage Centre project that the Spitalfields Trust (which owns 17–19 Princelet Street) wanted to use the building next to it 'as an extension to the "Minority Study Foundation" next door. As people from ethnic minorities are forced to leave the area it plans a permanent exhibition to show what these people's contribution to the area has been.' Forman's comments are extreme – the absence of one building would not make any noticeable difference to the over-crowding of the area and would be insignificant compared to the loss of housing available to the local Bengalis due to the gentrification that has already taken place. His comments do emphasize the need, however, to avoid treating Spitalfields as no more than a large museum. It is lived in by many thousands of people, including the forgotten Jews who still inhabit the East End, whose day to day problems are ones of exploitation, poverty and racism. The Heritage Centre has to cater for local needs as well.[80]

Nevertheless, the 1987 Celebration showed how British history must become more inclusive and it revealed the way to avoid the dangers of nostalgia and romanticization. Indeed those responsible for the Heritage Centre project have acknowledged that 'the threads that run through the history of Spitalfields and 17–19 Princelet Street are not all good ones' and these sentiments were certainly echoed in the 1987 events.[81] Even the Jewish Historical Society of England was recently able to accept, albeit with some misgivings, a paper by Geoffrey Alderman on Morry Davis, a 'loudmouthed, precocious and intolerant' Jewish East End politician; a man whose activities by the early years of the Second World War were surrounded by 'the smell of bribery, corruption and intimidation' and who later ended up in prison.[82] The idea of including him as *history* would not have occurred to those who created the 1887 and 1956 exhibitions – these representations of Jewish life were in fact designed to hide the very existence of the Morry Davis's of Britain. Without the necessary support for a new generation of Jewish researchers, however, the critical, inclusive approach revealed in 1987 is in danger of being lost. We will not return to the Jewish historical world of 1887 or even that of 1956 in terms of what is covered. Yet there is a real danger that we may do so in our technique if nostalgia gets the upper hand. The history of the Jewish East End and of other immigrant settlement areas is too important to let this occur. This history is not only the rich (but certainly not unproblematical) heritage of the present, it is also the inheritance of future generations – Jews and non-Jews who will depend on the survival of past evidence (as well as critical interpretations of it) to have the chance to create their own identities.

NOTES

1. East End history is still relatively undeveloped. For attempts at an overview see Chaim Bermant, *Point of Arrival: A Study of London's East End* (London, 1975) and Alan Palmer, *East End: Four Centuries of London Life* (London, 1990). Raphael Samuel addresses some of the problems of East End heritage preservation in Mark Girouard *et al.*, *The Saving of Spitalfields* (London, 1989), pp.135–70. For the problems of definition see Raymond Kalman, 'The Jewish East End – Where was It?' in Aubrey Newman (ed.), *The Jewish East End 1840–1939* (London, 1981), pp.3–15.
2. A celebratory approach to Jewish East End history, generally ignoring racism and exploitation, is followed by the Springboard Education Trust. See, for example, their *Memories: the Jewish East End* (London, 1985). For a more critical approach aimed at school education see the work pack produced for the Tower Hamlets Environment Trust 'The Jewish East End'.
3. Susan Ferguson who carries out walking tours of the Jewish East End, quoted in *Jewish Chronicle*, 23 Nov. 1990.
4. *Catalogue of an Exhibition of Anglo-Jewish and History: In Commemoration of the Tercentenary of the Resettlement of the Jews in the British Isles* (London, 1956), pp. 69–70; *Catalogue of the Anglo-Jewish Historical Exhibition 1887* (London, 1887).
5. 'Anglo-Jewish Historical Exhibition: Notice of Exhibition' in AJA 70 for 'Objects Admissable for Exhibition', University of Southampton archive; Cesarani, contribution to this volume.
6. Lucien Wolf, 'A Plea for Anglo-Jewish History', *JHSE Transactions*, Vol.1 (1893–94), p.1.
7. For Wolf's diplomatic career see Eugene Black, *The Social Politics of Anglo-Jewry 1880–1920* (Oxford, 1988), pp.33–5, 305, 325–7, 373–85 and Chimen Abramsky, 'Lucien Wolf's Efforts for the Jewish Communities in Central and Eastern Europe', *JHSE Transactions*, Vol. XXIX (1982–86), pp.281–95; for an overview of archive and heritage preservation in Britain and its ideological underpinnings see Tony Kushner, 'A History of Jewish Archives in the United Kingdom', *Archives* (forthcoming).
8. Lucille Levi, 'Nostalgia or Pain?', *Manchester Jewish Gazette*, 28 Sept. 1979.
9. For the role of the Whitechapel Gallery in exposing Jewish art in the 1900s see letter of S. Cohen to the Gallery, 9 April 1954 in AJA 49/155, University of Southampton archive and Ben Uri Art Gallery, *Anglo-Jewish Exhibition: 1851–1951 Art Section* (London, 1951), p.3. For the immigrant artists see Charles Spencer, 'Anglo-Jewish Artists: the Migrant Generations', *The Jewish Quarterly*, Vol.30, No.4 (Summer 1983), pp.54–9. In 1983 the Jewish Museum in New York produced an exhibition 'The Immigrant Generation: Jewish Artists in Britain 1900–1945'.
10. C. Booth (ed.), *Life and Labour of the People in London* (London, 1889–1903) – which includes Potter's contribution – Vol.III (London, 1893); H. Russell and H.S. Lewis, *The Jew in London* (London, 1901) for Toynbee Hall; H.L. Smith (ed.), *The New Survey of London Life and Labour* (London, 1930–35); Mass-Observation Archive: Topic Collection 'Antisemitism', Box 1. For the new Jewish novelists see Ken Worpole, *Dockers and Detectives* (London, 1983).
11. Rollin's papers are now deposited at the Modern Record Centre, University of Warwick. For his involvement in the 1956 exhibition see AJA 49/62 and 96 in University of Southampton archive.
12. See the *Catalogue*, pp.9–103.
13. C.C. Aronsfeld, 'Anglo-Jewish Research', *Zionist Review*, 31 May 1946 and Roth response, 7 June 1946.
14. Peter Elman, 'The Beginnings of the Jewish Trade Union Movement in England', *JHSE Transactions*, Vol. 17 (1951–52), pp.53–62; A.R. Rollin, 'Russo-Jewish

102 THE JEWISH HERITAGE IN BRITISH HISTORY

Immigrants in England Before 1881', *JHSE Transactions*, Vol. 21 (1962–67), pp.202–13.

15. *Festival of Britain 1951: A Survey of Some of the Aspects of Anglo-Jewish Life Illustrated in the Anglo-Jewish Exhibition* (London, 1951), p.1; *Jewish Chronicle*, 13 July 1951. For the festival itself see Michael Frayn, 'Festival', in Michael Sissons and Philip French (eds.), *Age of Austerity* (Oxford, 1986), pp.307–26.
16. Sidney Salomon, 'The Anglo-Jewish Exhibition', *Jewish Affairs* (Aug. 1951), p.30.
17. Nathan quoted by *Jewish Chronicle*, 13 July 1951.
18. *AJR Information*, Sept. 1951.
19. A. Abrahams, letter to *Jewish Chronicle*, 20 July 1951; *AJR Information*, Sept. 1951; *Daily Record and Mail*, July 1951.
20. For the art exhibition see the catalogue in AJA 36/5, University of Southampton archive; *Festival of Britain*, p.28.
21. Zevi Ze'ev, 'An Estimate of the Anglo-Jewish Exhibition', *Jewish Youth*, September 1951. For the dispute over dates for the tercentenary see the minutes of the Celebration Provisional Committee, 29 July 1952, 20 Jan. 1953 in AJA 49/1 and 6. For the proposed pilgrimage to Holland, see minutes 17 June 1953 in AJA 49/10. The pilgrimage never took place but the medallion was produced. The exhibition sub-committee minutes are in AJA 49/25–34.
22. For the relationship to the 1887 exhibition see the 1956 *Catalogue*, pp.3–4 and Barnett comments in Executive Committee minutes, 18 Oct. 1955, AJA 49/21.
23. Quote from Richard Barnett, notes from conference, 1956, in AJA 49/203.
24. Executive Committee minutes, 18 Oct. 1955 in AJA 49/21.
25. *Festival of Britain 1951*, p.17.
26. In 1952 a sub-committee was set up to find ways of celebrating the tercentenary. The aim of the exhibition was to illustrate the progress made by Anglo-Jewry. See AJA 49/39; Samuel quoted by *Jewish Observer and Middle East Review*, 13 Jan. 1956.
27. 1952 Tercentenary, Sub-Committee, 1952, AJA 49/39. For the insecurity felt by the elite of Anglo-Jewry see David Cesarani, contribution to this volume and Colin Holmes, *Anti-Semitism in British Society, 1876–1939* (London, 1979), Ch. 2.
28. The exhibition's comments on this period are reproduced in its *Catalogue*, p.69.
29. See minutes of the Exhibition Committee, 17 Feb. 1954 in AJA 49/27.
30. *Jewish Observer and Middle East Review*, 13 Jan. 1956.
31. Barnett's unpublished notes on the Exhibition, 1956 in AJA 49/203.
32. Barnett to the editor of the *Jewish Review*, 25 Feb. 1956 in AJA 49/112.
33. Notes from the first meeting of the Exhibition Committee, 5 May 1953 in AJA 49/23.
34. 'The Tercentenary Exhibition: Strange Omissions', *Jewish Observer and Middle East Review*, 13 Jan. 1956.
35. For the Duke of Edinburgh's comments, see *Jewish Chronicle*, 1 June and 7 September 1956. Other official speeches 'praising' the Jewish contribution to British society are reproduced in The Tercentenary Council and the Jewish Chronicle, *Three Hundred Years: A Volume to Commemorate the Tercentenary of the Re-Settlement of the Jews in Great Britain 1656–1956* (London, 1957). For the Zionist critique, see 'Anglo-Jewry in 1956', *Jewish Observer and Middle East Review*, 13 Jan. 1956.
36. For the anti-Semitica, see the *Catalogue*, p.75; *Jewish Observer and Middle East Review*, 13 Jan. 1956; Hugh Harris, 'Thames and Jordan', *Jewish Chronicle Supplement: Tercentenary of British Jewry*, 27 Jan. 1956.
37. 1952 Sub-Committee, 'Cultural Programme', in AJA 49/39. For the Garden Party see *Three Hundred Years*, pp.117–20 and Council of Christians and Jews, *Catalogue of an Exhibition* (London, 1956).
38. Max Beloff, 'From the Other Side', *Jewish Chronicle Supplement*, 27 Jan. 1956. For

an attempt to cover the Jewish socialist experience in Britain without embarrassment see Tony Kushner, 'Jewish Communists in Twentieth-Century Britain: The Zaidman Collection', *Labour History Review*, Vol. 55, No 2 (1990), pp.66–75.

39. The critisism came from Dr Saltman in the *Jewish Review*. For portrayal of the wives of the 'Cousinhood' see the Catalogue, plates 17, 24, 27, 29, 32, 19, 22.
40. 'Whose Tercentenary', *Jewish Telegraph*, 1956 (in AJA 49/203). For the Manchester exhibition see *Jewish Chronicle*, 8 June 1956 and *Three Hundred Years*, pp.131–2.
41. Barnett, notes on exhibition, 1956, in AJA 49/203. 28,800 people saw the exhibition in its eight week run – see its report in AJA 49/48.
42. Thus Barnett's major concern after the Exhibition was the fate of the Great Synagogue silver – see the correspondence in AJA 49/156 and 7. The issue of this silver was revived in 1990 when an attempt was made to take it out of the United Kingdom. See the correspondence in *Jewish Chronicle*, June–Aug. 1990. For the rejection of the lectureship in Anglo-Jewish history see minutes of the Executive Committee, 20 Sept. 1955 in AJA 49/20.
43. Rollin to Barnett, 30 Dec. 1955 in AJA 49/96; Lloyd Gartner, *The Jewish Immigrant in England, 1870–1914* (London, 1960), p.10. Williams and Kadish, contributions to this volume, indicate the loss of buildings in the post-war period.
44. Gartner, *The Jewish Immigrant* (second edition, London, 1973), p.5. For general comment on the development of Anglo-Jewish historiography see Todd Endelman, 'English Jewish History', *Modern Judaism*, Vol.11 (1991), pp.91–109 and Lloyd Gartner, 'Eastern European Jewish Immigrants in England: A Quarter Century's View', *JHSE Transactions*, Vol.XXIX (1982–6), pp.297–309.
45. V.D. Lipman, *A Century of Social Service, 1959–1959: The Jewish Board of Guardians* (London, 1959); Israel Finestein, 'The New Community, 1880–1918', in V.D. Lipman (ed.), *Three Centuries of Anglo-Jewish History* (London, 1961), pp.107–23; Bill Williams, 'Local Jewish History: Where Do We Go From Here?', in S. and V.D. Lipman (eds.), *Jewish Life in Britain 1962–1977* (London, 1981), pp.95–108.
46. Arnold Wesker, *The Wesker Trilogy* (London, 1960); Bernard Kops, *The World is a Wedding* (London, 1963).
47. Bill Fishman, 'Jewish Immigrant Anarchists in East London 1870–1914', in Aubrey Newman, *The Jewish East End*, p.233; A.R.Rollin, 'Russo-Jewish Immigrants'.
48. Bill Fishman, *East End Jewish Radicals 1875–1914* (London, 1975); Rudolf Rocker, *The London Years* (London, 1956); Fishman, 'Jewish Immigrant Anarchists', p.252.
49. John Garrard, *The English and Immigration 1880–1910* (Oxford, 1971); Bernard Gainer, *The Alien Invasion* (London, 1972).
50. See Harriet Karsh, 'The Jewish East End Project', in Newman, *The Jewish East End*, pp.323–6 and Aubrey Newman, 'A Note on Recent Research on the Jewish East End of London', *Jewish Journal of Sociology*, Vol.26–7 (Dec. 1985), pp.135–9.
51. See also A. Linkman and B. Williams, 'Recovering the People's Past: the archive rescue programme of Manchester Studies', *History Workshop*, No. 8 (Autumn 1979), pp.111–26 and Tony Kushner, 'Looking Back With Nostalgia? The Jewish Museums of England', *Immigrants and Minorities*, Vol. 6 (July 1987), pp.200–11.
52. See Wendy Ball and John Solomos (eds.), *Race and Local Politics* (London, 1990).
53. Newman, 'A Note on Recent Research', p.135 and Karsh, 'The Jewish East End Project', p.325.
54. Newman, *The Jewish East End*. The growing interest in the East End was reflected in the success of Bill Fishman's *The Streets of East London* (London, 1979).
55. See, for example, C. Holmes (ed.), *Immigrants and Minorities in British Society* (London, 1978) and the formation of the journal *Immigrants and Minorities* edited by Holmes and Ken Lunn in 1982; Jerry White, *Rothschild Buildings: Life in an East*

End Tenement Block (London, 1980).
56. See R. Burman, 'Participating in the Past? Oral History and Community History in the Work of Manchester Studies', *International Journal of Oral History*, Vol.5, No.2 (June 1984), pp.114–24; Simon Rocker, 'Old Pots and Fish Pans', *Jewish Chronicle*, 19 July 1985 and Liz Sagues, 'East End in East End Road', *Hampstead and Highgate Express*, 10 May 1985 for the origins of the museum.
57. For developments in the museum, see its *Newsletter*, No.1 (Nov. 1985) onwards.
58. Comments of Susan Goodman, Chief Curator, New York Jewish Museum in the preface to the catalogue of an exhibition edited by Kenneth Silver and Romy Golan, *The Circle of Montparnasse* (New York, 1985). The exhibition based on the work of Jewish immigrant artists took place in 1983.
59. History Workshop emerged in the middle 1960s and the journal first appeared in April 1976.
60. The full catalogue of events can be found in *The Jewish East End: A Celebration* [Souvenir Brochure] (London, 1987). For overviews see Victoria Neumark, 'The Long Schlep', *Times Educational Supplement*, 7 Aug. 1987; Matthew Reisz, 'Celebrating the East End's Jewish Heritage', *New York Times*, 7 June 1987; Catherine Bennett, 'In Search of the Jewish Heritage', *Sunday Times*, 29 June 1987 and John Cunningham, 'Eastside Story', *The Guardian*, 17 July 1987.
61. Carpenter in *The Jewish East End: A Celebration*, p.1 and interview with the author, 13 Aug. 1987.
62. Robin Gwynn, *Huguenot Heritage: The History and Contribution of the Huguenots in Britain* (London, 1988); Carpenter, *The Jewish East End: A Celebration*, p.1.
63. David Mazower, *Yiddish Theatre In London* (London, 1987). See Charles Osborne, 'The Theatre That is No More', *Daily Telegraph*, 7 July 1987 and *Jewish Chronicle*, 3 July 1987 for comment on the exhibition. For the autobiography of one of the leading figures in the Yiddish theatre in post-war period see Bernard Mendelovitch, *Memories of London Yiddish Theatre* (Oxford, 1990).
64. Helen Carpenter, *Jewish EastEnders: Life in a Stepney Household in the 1920s* (London, 1987), p.9. See also Simon Rocker, 'East End Snowball', *Jewish Chronicle*, 27 March 1987 for the origins of the exhibition.
65. Gina Glasman, *East End Synagogues* (London, 1987); *Jewish Chronicle*, 19 June and 7 Aug. 1987 and *Jewish Herald*, June/July 1987 for reports on the exhibition.
66. Pat Kirkham, Rodney Mace and Julia Porter, *Furnishing the World: The East London Furniture Trade 1830–1980* (London, 1987) is an excellent publication coming out of the exhibition.
67. For women workers in the furniture trade see Kirkham *et al.*, *Furnishing the World*, pp.82–3, 88–9, 102–5, 119–22; for 'Daughters of the Pale', see the later publication by Jewish Women in London Group, *Generations of Memories* (London, 1989).
68. See *The Jewish Quarterly*, Vol.34, No.2 (1987), p.37 for Jacob Epstein at the Whitechapel Art Gallery; *World of Yesterday: Jews in England 1870–1920* (Tel Aviv, 1984) and *Jewish Chronicle*, 10 July 1987 for its revival.
69. *Jewish Chronicle*, 24 July 1987 and Henry Srebrnik, 'Old-New Literature from Jewish London', *Washington Jewish Week*, 27 Aug. 1987 for the literary events; *The Jewish Quarterly*, Vol.34, No.2 (1987) – 'The Jewish East End'. The *Quarterly* was founded in 1953 and since then has devoted much space to the artistic and literary legacies of the various Jewish immigrations to Britain during the twentieth century.
70. *The Jewish East East End: A Celebration*, pp.13, 16–17.
71. *Jewish Observer and Middle East Review*, 13 Jan. 1956 for the earlier predominance of pugilists.
72. Carpenter in *The Jewish East End: A Celebration*, p.1. In an interview with the author, 13 Aug. 1987, Carpenter re-emphasized the mixture of objectives behind the celebration: 'I wanted a greater awareness of the Jewish heritage among non-

Jews, and it's also a nostalgia thing, an opportunity for Jews to come back, and a platform for anti-racism'; Karsh, 'The Jewish East End Project', p.326.

73. Museum of the Jewish East End, *Boris: The Studio Photographer 1900–1985* (London, 1986), pp.4, 22. The exhibition provided a harder hitting interpretation than an equivalent held in the Manchester Jewish Museum in 1985: 'Jewish Weddings: A Century of Jewish Weddings in Manchester'. For critical comment about the 'Celebration' and the issue of nostalgia see Maurice Kaye in *Jewish Chronicle*, 24 July 1987 and Sam Goldsmith, 'Hamlet Without Ophelia', *Jewish Chronicle*, 9 Oct. 1987.

74. Carpenter in *The Jewish East End: A Celebration*, p.1. Ironically, there was no position in the communal structure for Carpenter herself after the celebration. See *Jewish Chronicle*, 25 Sept. 1987.

75. 'Refugee From Nazism' took place in the Museum in 1988 and 'The Jews of Aden' in 1991.

76. See *Jewish Chronicle*, 1 Sept. 1989 for Devra Kay's work at Queen Mary College and *Times Higher Education Supplement*, 7 Sept. 1990 for Oxford. More generally for the Yiddish revival in Britain see Huw Richards, 'The Language of Survival', *Times Higher Education Supplement*, 8 Dec. 1989.

77. See the contribution of Sharman Kadish in this volume. The Sandys Row Synagogue, the oldest in use in the East End, is now also under threat.

78. Raphael Samuel, 'The Pathos of Conservation', in Mark Girouard, The *Saving of Spitalfields*, p.162; Heritage Centre Spitalfields, 'History of 17–19 Princelet Street'. See also Samuel Melnick, 'Living Heritage: The Princelet Street Project', *Hamour*, Vol. 26, No.2 (1991), pp.16–17.

79. Rob Perks, 'The Ellis Island Immigration Museum', *Oral History*, Vol.19 (Spring 1991), pp.79–80.

80. Charlie Forman, *Spitalfields: A Battle for Land* (London, 1989), p.134.

81. Heritage Centre Spitalfields, 'History of 17–19 Princelet Street'; *Jewish Chronicle*, 12 Oct. 1990 for reflections on the building.

82. Geoffrey Alderman, 'M.H. Davis: the Rise and Fall of a Communal Upstart', *Jewish Historical Studies*, Vol. XXI (1988–90), pp.251, 263–4 – although Alderman does comment that he was advised 'that [Morry Davis'] career ought not to be researched at all' (p.249).

Carers and Servers of the Jewish Community: The Marginalized Heritage of Jewish Women in Britain

LARA MARKS

Jewish women have played a vital role in the heritage of the Jewish community in Britain. Yet while they have been revered as good wives and mothers and held up as good models to non-Jewish women, their history has been obscured by such idealizations and much of their contributions outside the sphere of motherhood has been ignored by historians. This article examines the reasons for this neglect and shows the valuable part Jewish women played not only as wives and mothers but also as single women in a wide range of areas including the family economy, political mobilization, organization of the workplace, education, health, leisure and philanthropic work. It questions the traditional roles Jewish men and women have been expected to play and highlights the complexity of gender and its relationship with class and ethnicity.

In the care of their children the Jewish mothers are a pattern to their Gentile neighbours in the East End. Go and visit the schools in the East End and see the Jewish children. They stand out in marked contrast to other children for brightness and healthy appearance. That is only due to the Jewish mothers.[1]

Such visions of Jewish women as good mothers with their robust children were portrayed by many medical practitioners, voluntary workers and statesmen in late-nineteenth-century England. Praise lavished on Jewish mothers centred on the good care they took of their

The author would like to thank Tony Kushner, Gillian Rose, Hilary Sapire, and Anne Summers for all their invaluable advice on the original manuscript. The study also could not have been completed without the fruitful discussions she had with Michelle Adler, David Feldman, Clive Glazer, and Molly Sutphen.

families and in particular their infants. Jewish mothers were considered to be models to other mothers. They were noted for paying meticulous attention to household chores, for ceasing to work early in pregnancies, and for their breastfeeding habits. Were Jewish women such perfect mothers as these commentators suggested? This is difficult to measure, but the remarkably low rates of infant mortality even among the poorest Jewish community at the turn of the century indicate that Jewish mothers cared for their infants.

Whether Jewish women were good mothers or not is less important than the significance that has been attached to motherhood in the Jewish community and the outside world. This has not only shaped the roles Jewish women have been expected to play but also the way in which their history has been written. Much of this has been influenced by traditional Judaism which asserts that a woman's prime responsibility is to her family and home. Thus women are exempted from all religious tasks which have to be performed at a certain time of day. Women are not counted in *minyans* (the quorum of ten needed for communal prayer) and cannot lead communal prayers.[2] Similarly Jewish women have usually been prevented from reciting the blessings over the Torah, reading from the Torah scroll or studying sacred texts. Traditionally, therefore, women have been restricted in participating in religious and communal decision-making, areas which have been primarily reserved for men.[3] Instead a woman's worth has been measured by her ability to be a good mother. Her role as a good wife and mother has been viewed as the key to the survival of the Jewish family and community.[4]

Yet while they have been exalted as wives and mothers, historically Jewish women have either been taken for granted or regarded as insignificant to the history of the Jewish community in Britain. Even where they have appeared as wives and mothers, their activities and experiences have been marginalized and masked by the idealization of motherhood. The absence of Jewish women in historical research is surprising, given that women constituted a large number of those who migrated and settled in Britain, particularly among those coming from Eastern Europe in the late nineteenth century. In 1871 women made up almost 38 per cent of all the Russian Polish immigrants living in London, and in 1911 they constituted 48 per cent of the total.[5] The percentage of women was higher among Jewish immigrants than many other immigrant groups such as the Italians.

Much of the literature on Jews in Britain has focused on the social, economic and political background of their migration and settlement, but few historians have examined the experience of women in detail or have included gender in their analysis.[6] In the USA, however, a large amount of research has been carried out on Jewish women. One reason for the abundance of such work in the USA and not in Britain is related to the different emphasis that has been attached to ethnicity in each country. This has not only affected the experience of the immigrants and their children but also the history that has been written of them. In the USA where immigrants have constituted a large majority of the population, ethnicity has been regarded as a dominant part of American culture and something to be revered. By contrast, in Britain, the immigrant population has been smaller, and the pressures for immigrants to forget their ethnic identity and conform to precepts set by the English majority have been much greater. This has meant that research on Jews in Britain has tended to emphasize the ways in which they are a part of the British nation and not to distinguish them as a separate group who are important in their own right.[7]

Ethnicity features more prominently in American primary documents than in British ones. Records from hospitals and other welfare institutions, for instance, regularly recorded the ethnic identity of their patients alongside their social and economic circumstances.[8] Thus the American interest in ethnicity has given historians a rich source to work from as well as a greater propensity to pursue research in this field. Some American historians have confused the importance of ethnicity with class and at times glorified ethnicity. None the less the stress laid on ethnicity in the USA has enabled historians to explore its importance in a greater diversity of areas, including that of gender.[9]

In Britain, class rather than ethnic identity is more prominent in people's consciousness. This not only affects people's own perceptions of themselves and where they fit into British society, but also influences historical research on Jewish immigration. Much of the focus of this work has been on issues perceived to be important for understanding class tensions and struggles in areas such as the workplace where the experience and battles of women have been invisible. This has been as apparent in the work of other social and economic historians working on class as well as those concerned with Jewish immigration and settlement.[10]

In recent years, however, the absence of women in historical writing has begun to be addressed through the growth of gender studies which emerged out of the women's movement of the 1960s. This has opened up new questions concerning the traditional roles ascribed to men and women and the dynamics of power between the sexes. Much of the British scholarship in this area has concentrated on the relationship between class and gender and has been less diverse than in America where gender studies are more advanced.[11] While a large literature exists on the experience of working-class and middle-class women in British society and the impact of religion on women's lives,[12] an exploration of ethnicity by researchers working on women's history in general is rarely encountered.[13] This is surprising given the high profile Jewish women had in national campaigns concerning women's rights in the late nineteenth and early twentieth centuries. Their story not only reveals difficulties they suffered as women, but also the disadvantages they experienced as an ethnic and religious minority.

None the less, Jewish women have not been forgotten totally. In 1951 one of the earliest references to Jewish women appeared in the context of their contribution to the advancement of women's education.[14] After this Jewish women rarely appeared in the literature concerning Jewish immigrants in Britain until 1974, when a study of philanthropy among Jews in Manchester illuminated the vital role Jewish women played in establishing sanitary inspection work and health visiting for the Jewish poor.[15]

It was not until the 1980s, however, that gender and women's experience began to be taken seriously in studies on Jewish immigration in Britain. Drawing on a rich collection of oral interviews, Burman has examined the importance of gender and class in the history of Jewish immigrants and their children in Manchester in the late nineteenth and early twentieth centuries, focusing particularly on women's role within the family economy and religious sphere.[16] Work has also appeared on Jewish women's experience of childbirth, infant care, their work patterns and social activities in East London.[17] Studies have also begun to examine the role of Jewish women in social reform and politics within the established Anglo-Jewish community and in the outside world.[18] Much of the research to-date has concentrated either on the experience of the well-settled and established Jews or on that of East European Jewish immigrants. One exception to this is Kushner's examination of the entry of German Jewish women refugees into domestic service in the 1930s and 1940s.[19]

Such studies have opened up new fields of enquiry which need further investigation. Recent research has shown that Jewish women and the issue of gender are not marginal to the heritage of the Jews in

Britain. Jewish women were not only numerically significant but have played a central role in the family economy, workplace and political arena. Tensions within the home, the workplace and the political domain not only reflected class and ethnic divisions but were also heavily influenced by gender. The struggles between men and women had implications for the domestic sphere as well as the wider world.

The challenge for historians is to unite the vast literature on the history of Jews in Britain and on gender, and to show how the issues of class, gender and ethnicity affected not only the settlement and migration patterns of Jews but also the social fabric of British society. Part of the reason for the marginalization of Jewish women has been their under-representation in primary documents and Jewish cultural events such as the Anglo-Jewish Exhibition in 1887.[20] Their history has to be teased from general information. Jewish women have been even more hidden than other women because of their minority status. In order to get information on Jewish women new questions have had to be asked of old material. Some advances in women's history have been made by the recent emergence of oral history which has opened up new directions and illuminated the experience of many whose history was previously obscured. While Jewish woman have been forceful participants in the history of the Jewish community and British society over centuries, this article concentrates on their experiences during the late nineteenth and early twentieth centuries.

Images of Jewish Women and their Marginalization

Much of the history of Jewish women has been shaped by the social concerns of contemporaries and historians. Where Jewish women have been mentioned, they have tended to be portrayed either in idealized or in derogatory forms. It is not a complete exaggeration to say that, in the late nineteenth century when not being praised for motherhood, Jewish women were being cursed for prostitution, reflecting the major anxieties of these years. Arriving at a time of great concern about the strength and future of the empire the East European immigrants became the centre of many social and political debates such as those over the diminishing birth rate, the persistently high infant mortality and the failure of many recruits to pass the fitness tests needed to join the army for the South African War (1899–1902). The mother and prostitute represented the merits and the disgraces of the Jewish community or what British society could become. Weak physique and poverty were preoccupations both among those who feared they would contribute to the physical deterioration of the British nation and among established Jews who feared that anything less than physical and moral perfection and complete respectability would incite anti-Semitism.

Many social reformers and politicians saw good motherhood as the answer to the high infant mortality and physical deterioration.[21] Attention concentrated on the need to educate mothers in proper infant management. This, it was argued, would reduce infant mortality and secure the health of future generations. To this aim health-visiting and schools for mothers were established on an unprecedented level.[22] Drawing on nineteenth-century notions of 'good motherhood' many of these activities were influenced by middle-class ideals of domesticity and the family unit. The Jewish mother and her virtues symbolized the solutions to infant mortality which forbade women from working outside the home, and promoted domesticity, good cooking skills and, above all, lengthy breastfeeding.[23] At a time when the Aliens Act (1905) was just coming into force these stereotypes starkly contrasted the other popular images of the East European Jews which portrayed them as immoral and the bringers of disease.[24] In reality, of course, not all Jewish women conformed to these idealized notions of motherhood. This was particularly the case for unmarried Jewish mothers, and deserted wives, whose presence did not accord with the ideal nuclear family model proposed by the Jewish community or the outside world.[25]

Even more strongly contrasting with the idealized vision of the Jewish mother, however, was the Jewish prostitute. In both the outside world and the Jewish community, the prostitute symbolized the social evils which were undermining the strength of the family and the empire.[26] Jewish prostitutes symbolized immorality and vices the Jewish community preferred to ignore or aimed to reform. Established Jews feared that any Jewish involvement in the trade would not only threaten their respectability but also result in anti-Semitism. As the German-Jewish feminist Bertha Pappenheim expressed it, 'If we admit the existence of the traffic our enemies decry us, if we deny it, they say we are trying to conceal it.'[27] For many Jewish social reformers the Jewish prostitute represented the dislocation of the Jewish community during this period. The economic and social upheaval in

Eastern Europe and the resulting migration of the Jewish community in the late nineteenth century coincided with the establishment of white slavery on a worldwide basis, making many Jewish immigrants vulnerable to the trade. Moreover, Jewish immigrants in East London came into an area where prostitution was already widely prevalent.[28]

Like the mother, the prostitute therefore has held a special place in the history of the Jewish community and British society. The attention lavished on her has raised some interesting questions concerning the status of women and sex in the Jewish community and the outside world. These were most clearly expressed by the Jewish Association for the Protection of Girls and Women (JAPGW) established in London in 1885, to combat the white slave trade.[29] Much of their agitation focused on single women travelling alone or those who were tricked into marriage by a procurer. The JAPGW's premise was that fallen women were innocent victims of the migratory process who needed protection.

Such attitudes failed to understand the choices and conflicts facing these women. Many prostitutes were tricked into the trade by pro-curers, but this did not exclude the reasons others chose to enter the profession. Lacking charitable support and faced with menial exis-tence in the labour market, prostitution could be an attractive alterna-tive to some women. In 1910 one Jewish prostitute in London found that she could earn between £1 and £2 with each client. Sometimes she was able to amass as much as £15 in a day, a sum which surpassed any she could earn in another profession.[30] In 1906 adult women textile workers on average earned 15/5d a week, clothing workers earned 13/6d a week, and those involved in the food and tobacco industries 11/3d.[31] A woman who worked as a tailoress in an East End dress-maker's shop in 1914 only earned 1s a week which by her standards was considered a good wage for an apprentice.[32] Nevertheless, while pros-titution could be seen as lucrative and appealing, the trade had its hazards. Often prostitutes had to face physical threats and hand over at least half or more of their earnings to a 'pimp' and similarly faced the threat of disease, imprisonment and hard labour or deportation.[33] Thus while prostitution could bring its rewards, it also had penalties.

Jewish Women: Active Participants in History

Just as the prostitute can be seen as both a victim and an agent of certain circumstances, so the debate can be extended to Jewish women as a whole. Jewish women have faced constant choices and conflicts in their lives. Stereotypes which portray Jewish women as good mothers or immoral whores have not only obscured the realities of motherhood and prostitution and the daily struggles Jewish women faced in Britain, but have also rendered invisible their activities in a wide range of spheres outside the home. Jewish women were active agents in the making of their own history and the history of those around them not only in the home, but also in the workplace, the synagogue and the political arena. The rest of this article looks at the studies that have been undertaken on women in these different areas.

Much research has appeared on the labour patterns of Jewish East European immigrants arriving at the turn of the century and the political mobilization of these workers,[34] but little has been done on women in this sphere. Instead women have been treated as peripheral to such concerns. One exception to this is Burman's study of Jewish women's role in the household economy in Manchester in the years 1890–1920. She has demonstrated how married Jewish women's work, particularly among the first generation of immigrants, was vital to the economic survival of the family.[35] The immigrants' poverty, especially among the first generation, meant that many married women, as in the general population, were forced to combine the tasks of wife and mother with paid work. Frequent unemployment, illness or the death of the male breadwinner in these families often made the woman's contribution to the family income vital. This was also common among Jewish immigrants who migrated to America at the turn of the century.[36]

Many of these immigrant women were continuing the breadwinning roles they had taken on in Eastern Europe where the male's religious scholarship was prized above his abilities to earn a living. A Jewish woman's worth was measured in particular by her ability to support her husband financially and domestically while he pursued his religious studies. This contrasted with the ideals of middle-class English society which emphasized the role of the mother as caring for her family without working outside the home. In more middle-class families Jewish men and their wives could be supported without the need for the wife to work, but for those less well-off women's work was essential. For these women, work was considered a religious good deed.[37] In this environment men were ideally raised to enter the world of scholastic education, and not the world of business, leaving financial matters to their wives.[38]

Jewish women were therefore not marginal to the family income, yet much of the work they undertook was hidden to the outsider because it was performed around their other domestic duties and childcare. Caring for lodgers or laundry washing, for example, could be combined with other house chores.[39] Those who worked outside the home only did so as a last resort. One area outside the domestic sphere in which Jewish women participated was the sweated labour trade, but even here their work was obscured because it was often carried out in family workshops situated within the home or in close proximity to it. This gave them more of an appearance of remaining within the home than other working mothers.[40]

The extent to which married women participated in paid employment was greatly dependent on the economic circumstances of their family and the labour market where they were living and the sorts of work their husbands were employed in. While many Jewish female textile workers, especially those in the sweated outwork trade, often worked after their marriage, this was less common among those women married to factory or shop workers in other industries. In Hackney, a heavily Jewish district, married women or widows constituted 74 per cent of those women who were employed as outworkers.[41] While migration brought new opportunities, enabling some Jewish married women to refrain from paid work, many women of the first generation could not survive on their husband's earnings alone. In subsequent generations the situation changed and was related to the economic mobility of the Jewish communities. As Jews moved up the social ladder so married women increasingly refrained from paid labour, although this was an uneven process. Coinciding with this disappearance from the wages workforce was the weakening hold many married Jewish women had over the family budget. Increasingly the male breadwinner managed the family economy and dictated what should and should not be spent.[42]

The process by which this change occurred is hard to demonstrate because the work of Jewish women, like that of other women, has not been recorded in official sources. Census material does not include the work of married women after 1881. In 1891 the census labelled housewives 'domestic servants'. Women's part-time or seasonal work was not regarded as important for these enquiries, making the degree of women's participation in the labour market difficult to estimate. Much of the work women carried out in their own homes was not considered 'waged' work, and therefore did not appear in many of the surveys. In addition to this oral testimonies tend to be selective in their accounts of married women's work. Children of immigrants who have been more exposed to English middle-class ideals of female domesticity are less likely to recall their mothers working. For these children, the respectability of their family was less measured by male scholarship than by the way in which a husband could economically maintain his wife and children without them working.[43]

Far more research is needed to understand the patterns of work among Jewish women and the changes in married women's work from the immigrant generation to that of their children. One problem is that the focus of studies so far has been on married women. While this has undermined notions that married women were peripheral to the economic pursuits of the Jewish population, at the same time the emphasis on married women has obscured the role taken by women outside of marriage and motherhood. Little attention has been paid to the economic role played by single Jewish women in England.[44] Glenn's study of Jewish immigrant women's participation in the garment industries and trade unions of New York and Chicago shows that daughters rather than the mothers, fathers or sons were the vital sustainers of the family economy. In 1911 a survey carried out by the Bureau of Labour showed that working daughters earned nearly 40 per cent of the Jewish families' total yearly incomes.[45] Not burdened with the responsibility of the home or the need for religious scholarship immigrant daughters had more flexibility to enter the labour market than other members of the family.[46]

Glenn demonstrates that single Jewish women were not only major contributors to the family income among the immigrant generation, but were also active in changing the conditions under which they worked. Many of their experiences and expectations were shaped by the conditions facing them in America and in Eastern Europe. In America they took advantage of the increasing opportunities of work in the expanding cheap and ready-made garment industry. None the less, such work demanded less skill than the industries of Eastern Europe which Jewish women had previously been employed in. This dissatisfied many Jewish women who were used to more valued and highly-paid work. In America many Jewish women landed up in demeaning and underpaid work which limited their protest, but some were able to unite in trade union activities and to fight to improve their working conditions and occupational mobility.[47]

These Jewish women acted as models for other women involved in work outside the garment industry and challenged the conceptions of passive Jewish immigrant women. Their action was strengthened by their bonds with other women as well as the informal networks at home and the workplace. For these female garment workers the home and workplace were integrally related to the issues they were fighting for. Their struggles drew on the complex inter-relationships between the family economy, the workplace and political sphere. Informal networks of family and work were crucial constituents for these women in turning the whole sphere of work 'upside down' through strikes and other militant action.[48]

No detailed study has appeared on single Jewish women's work patterns or trade union organization in Britain. Recent work by Gordon Kuzmack suggests that Jewish women were less visible in labour struggles in Britain particularly before the First World War. Far more research is needed to understand this phenomenon but one explanation given by Gordon Kuzmack was the conservatism of Jewish male workers in Britain who were 'less inclined towards socialism and unionism' than their American counterparts and like other male British trade unionists unwilling to include women in their campaigns.[49] None the less, while Jewish women might have been less militant than their American sisters, this should not obscure the part played by single women in industries such as the garment trade in Britain where they were numerically visible. It is possible to focus too exclusively on married women and their part in the household economy; too little attention has been paid to the single women whose income was vital to the family's survival and who potentially had more time to strive for a change in working conditions.

Similarly historians need to realize that militancy and conflicts did not only take place within the workplace or just among single women. Housewives in New York and East London neighbourhoods often joined protests over work conditions by calling mass meetings, and organizing rent strikes.[50] More work is also needed on the struggles between men and women within marriage. Ross has shown that in working-class London enormous friction arose between wives and husbands in relationships where either the woman challenged a husband who failed to provide a sufficient family income or where a husband resented a wife not performing her domestic duties properly.[51] Such tensions between Jewish wives and husbands has not been explored, and yet the increasing shift of the Jewish married women away from the waged labour market and into the home must have caused difficulties in the expectations husbands and wives had of each other.

Less hidden than their immigrant working-class sisters, Jewish middle-class women have recently emerged as forceful agents in the history of both the Jewish community and British society. Part of the invisibility of the immigrant working-class Jewish women in trade unions and other militant organizations is countered by the prominent stand taken by some middle-class Anglo-Jewish women in this area, such as Lady Louise Goldsmid who helped raise funds for East London Tailoresses. Despite the conservatism of the established community as a whole in regard to working conditions and relationships between employers and employees, a small number of Jewish women, such as Emily Routledge and May Abraham, were active in the World Trade Union League campaigning against the appalling sweated labour conditions Jewish women faced.[52] With more leisure and status these middle-class women probably had more time and energy than their working-class sisters to struggle in this field.

Aside from their campaigns over work conditions middle-class Jewish women were active on a series of issues. This is testified by a recent comparative study of the Jewish Women's movement in America and Britain which shows that Jewish women participated in a large number of political activities concerning women.[53] They were not only involved in protests to eliminate white slavery, but also the suffragette movement and welfare feminism which called for an extension of social and medical welfare provision for mothers and children.[54] Many of their activities were tied to the new positions women were taking within the synagogue and religious life which extended their traditional charitable roles in communal life to the more public domain of philanthropy.[55]

Perhaps reflecting the institutional and communal bias of historians working on the Jewish community in Britain, most of the work which has appeared on women in philanthropy has reasserted the importance of certain individuals or agencies. Some case records remain from the work that they did, but the experience of the clients of these services has been partially obscured by the aims and goals of those working among them. Despite the limited understanding of the experiences of the clients these women dealt with, the historical scholarship that has appeared on middle-class women's role in philanthropy has shown that Jewish women were not marginal to the history of Jewish communal life and agencies of social reform.

Much of the philanthropic work of Jewish women stemmed from their participation in the Jewish Board of Guardians (JBG). Established in 1859, the JBG was the most cohesive charitable institution in the Jewish community. Its functions were wide, making it distinct from other Boards of Guardians established in Britain under successive Poor Laws.[56] The provision of soup, clothes, apprenticeships, loans for setting up businesses and for further passage to America or South Africa were some of the provisions made by the JBG. While the primary decisions for the dispensation of these services was in the hands of men, women were important visitors to the poor in their own homes, or in hospitals, workhouses, and prisons.[57] As lady visitors, these women educated the newly-arrived immigrants in the importance of hygiene and thrift and acculturated the newcomers to the host society.[58]

One branch in the JBG in which women were particularly visible was in the JAPGW. With its focus on the white slave trade, the JAPGW rapidly developed a wide range of activities which were aimed at helping women. Those active in the organization not only mounted national campaigns to protest against white slavery, but also sent representatives from the 'Gentlemen's Committees' to meet incoming unaccompanied women at the ports and lady visitors to befriend young girls. In addition they established rescue homes for fallen women and unmarried mothers, special shelters to accommodate unaccompanied young Jewish women and hostels to provide lodging for working girls who lacked a home.[59]

In dealing with women who were perceived to have stepped outside the traditional boundaries of wife and mother, the middle-class Jewish women, like non-Jewish women working in this sphere, were also challenging many of the stereotypes attached to them. Their action weakened many of the middle-class notions of domesticity and respectability. This was most apparent in the campaigns against prostitution. Initially middle-class Jewish women were not allowed to perform tasks which would jeopardize their lives and morality. Thus in the JAPGW men were designated the more 'dangerous' tasks of meeting unaccompanied women at the ports where there was the possibility of confrontations with procurers.

A debate within the JAPGW on women's participation in the cases' committee, work mostly allocated to men, reveals the fears that were expressed about women's involvement in curbing prostitution. In 1919 women were admitted to the cases committee, but not without some reservations, because as it was stated 'So many of the ladies did not consider the danger of libel and the limitations of the law, etc., and they would require to learn a great deal.' By 1919, however, it was thought times had changed and 'now even young women spoke of matters without any privacy' whereas in the past they would not have dared to touch certain cases handled by the Gentlemen's Committee.[60] A man was always present to consult on the Jewish women's committees, but women mostly performed the routine work.

Nevertheless, as in the case of non-Jewish women, the action taken by Jewish women in combatting white slavery was productive in that it raised their consciousness and pushed women into the political arena for the first time.[61] By participating in philanthropic work, middle-class Jewish women were breaking down the stereotypes of their own status. Many of the barriers to women's participation in philanthropy had diminished by 1902, as witnessed by the first International Jewish Women's Conference held in London that year. By moving into philanthropy, women stepped out of the private sphere of the home and began to move into the public arena.

These activities not only enhanced the status of middle-class Jewish women, but also challenged wider ideas which confined women's role to that of wife and mother. This was most clearly seen in the work undertaken by the Union of Jewish Women (UJW).[62] Established as a result of the Jewish Women's Conference in London, the UJW was an active campaigner for women's rights within the Jewish community. More importantly it became a major source of help and advice for 'necessitous ladies' seeking employment. Part of the work undertaken by the UJW involved providing loans for women training for suitable professions, such as clerical work and teaching. While many of the professions women were encouraged to take up by the UJW reflected ideas about what constituted acceptable women's work, at the same time the help they provided enabled women to pursue careers which gave them economic independence and extended Jewish women's horizons beyond the traditional roles they had been expected to play.

One of the professions which the UJW was particularly keen to promote was nursing and midwifery which Jewish women were reluctant to enter.[63] The UJW saw nursing and midwifery as professions which not only helped secure economic independence but could also aid women in times of illness and confinement. At a time when families were large and women were expected to bear many children, childbirth was a common experience for Jewish women.[64] For many mothers childbirth implied grave threats to their health and even their life.[65] The availability of Jewish midwives and nurses would therefore have been crucial to these women who often confronted language and cultural barriers when dealing with non-Jewish professionals.

Given the significance attached to motherhood and the joys that are attached to birth in Jewish tradition, it is surprising that childbirth and its potential hazards have been understudied by historians working on Jewish immigration in Britain. Too often childbirth and health generally has been regarded as peripheral to the concerns of these historians.[66] But health is critical for understanding not only the important social and economic circumstances of an immigrant com-munity, but also the ways in which it integrated with the host society to achieve fundamental care at times of life and death, and supplement host institutions. As an event which particularly affects women, child-birth is also an effective subject for measuring how women fare in society when they are at their most vulnerable. For immigrant women childbirth is particularly revealing of the difficulties they encountered as newcomers, coping with language barriers and alien customs.[67] Childbirth not only raises questions about health but also the culture of courtship and marriage and sexual taboos which are areas only just beginning to be explored by historians working on Jews in Britain.[68]

Conclusion

In all the spheres of Jewish life in Britain Jewish women have played an active role in shaping the identity of the community and have been major actors in the world of work, politics and domestic issues. As the bearers of the future generation women have been allotted the primary task of mother, but their role has extended far beyond this realm. To glamourize their roles as mothers is not only to ignore the actual conditions of childbirth, but to undermine the importance of other struggles and dilemmas many of these mothers had in reality – and to deny the action they took alongside men. More research is needed to understand the breadwinning roles undertaken by married women as well as the contribution single Jewish women made to the household economy. Greater attention also needs to be paid to the political action taken by married and single women both on an informal level through activities such as rent strikes, as well as the more formal structures of trade union organization. Further work is also required on the experience Jewish women had as clients of the communal agencies such as the Jewish Board of Guardians. Pregnancy, childbirth, and motherhood differentiated women's experience from men, making them seek different solutions to their problems and construct alternative types of support networks than those offered through institutions set up by men. For these women, migration and settlement raised different problems than those encountered by men. This was especially apparent in the case of the deserted wife, the unmarried mother or the prostitute whose situation challenged the traditional ideas concerning women's place and role within the Jewish family and community. Their plight raises questions about the specific vulnerabilities women faced when confronting a new society and strange cultural attitudes.

None the less, while women's experience was different from men, their history is intricately united with that of men. Their story cannot be treated as something separate from other areas in the Jewish community. Jewish women were present whether it was in the field of political mobilization, organization of the workplace, education, health, leisure, sexuality or family life. The history of Jewish women is one which questions the identities men themselves have taken in the past, and highlights the need for a more complete understanding of gender and its interrelationships with class and ethnicity. To study Jewish women in isolation or to ignore them would be to deny the very heritage of the Jewish community. As one man writing to the *Jewish Chronicle* in 1906 put it:

Is progress to be denied to our women in their inferiority! The Jew is brought up from earliest childhood to regard the Jewess as a very poor individual. He is taught to express his gratitude by a matutinal laudation of his God for not having made him a woman, whilst his less fortunate sisters are provided with a formula which expresses, if not complete satisfaction with their lot, at any rate, submissive reconciliation to it. With such a training, it is not surprising that a fixed apprehension regarding the relative importance of Jew and Jewess has become established in the minds of both sexes. With a meekness, highly desirable, no doubt, in so subordinate a creature, the Jewess is prepared to accept anything that may be thrust upon her; any attempt to raise herself out of the narrow sphere allotted to her is regarded as non-conventional, perhaps one would be more

correct in saying non-traditional, and the Talmudic equivalent
... is hurled at her, till, to secure peace, she is compelled to bury
her ambitions and return home to fry fish.[69]

NOTES

1. Mr J. Prag, member of the St Pancras Health and Insanitary Areas Committee, evidence to *Royal Commission on Alien Immigration*, PP 1903 IX II (henceforth PP 1903 IX), Minutes of Evidence, Q17877.
2. Rachel Biale, *Women and Jewish Law* (New York, 1984), pp.21–4.
3. Paula Hyman, 'The Other Half: Women in the Jewish Tradition', and Saul Berman, 'The Status of Women in Halakhic Judaism', in Elizabeth Koltun, *The Jewish Woman: New Perspectives* (New York, 1976); Linda Gordon Kuzmack, *Woman's Cause: The Jewish Woman's Movement in England and the United States, 1881–1933* (Columbus, OH, 1990), pp.4–5.
4. See, for instance, Richard Yellin, 'A Philosophy of Jewish Masculinity: One Interpretation,' *Conservative Judaism.*, Vol. 32, No. 2 (Winter 1979), p.93 and Moshe Meiselman, *Jewish Woman in Jewish Law* (New York, 1978), p.16; cited in Susannah Heschel, (ed.), *On Being a Jewish Feminist* (New York, 1985), p.xviii.
5. David Feldman, 'Immigrants and Workers, Englishmen and Jews: The Immigrant to the East End of London 1880–1906', Ph.D., Cambridge University, 1985, table 1.8, p.37.
6. Works which have examined the economic, social and political background of the Jewish community include Lloyd P. Gartner, *The Jewish Immigrant in England, 1870–1914* (London, 1960); Bill Williams, *The Making of Manchester Jewry 1740–1875* (Manchester, 1976; 1985); Jerry White, *The Rothschild Buildings: Life in An East End Tenement Block, 1887–1920* (London, 1980); Feldman, 'Immigrants and Workers'; David Cesarani (ed.), *The Making of Modern Anglo-Jewry* (Oxford, 1990), and V.D. Lipman, *A History of the Jews in Britain since 1858* (Leicester, 1990). The last two books have good bibliographic references and an overview of the literature on Jewish immigrants, but that of Lipman makes no reference to gender.
7. For more information on the ways in which this has affected scholarship on the Jews in Britain see David Cesarani's introduction to his edited book, *The Making of Modern Anglo-Jewry*, pp.1–3.
8. See, for instance, the hospital records of the New York Lying-In Hospital or Chicago Lying-In Hospital (New York Archives, New York City and North-Western Memorial Hospital Archives, Chicago).
9. Jewish women's experiences of migration to America have been examined in C. Baum, P. Hyman and S. Michel (eds.), *The Jewish Woman in America* (New York, 1975); Sydney Stahl Weinberg, *The World of Our Mothers: The Lives of Jewish Immigrant Women* (North Carolina, 1988); Susan Glenn, *Daughters of the Shtetl: Life and Labour in the Immigrant Generation* (Cornell, 1990). A comparative study of English and American Jewish women appears in Gordon Kuzmack, *Woman's Cause*. Comparative studies of different immigrant groups in America have also tackled gender in their work. See, for instance, Elizabeth Ewen, *Immigrant Women in the Land of Dollars: Life and Culture on the Lower East Side, 1890–1925* (New York, 1985); Doris Weatherford, *Foreign and Female, Immigrant Women in America 1840–1930* (New York, 1986); Louise Lamphere, *From Working*

Daughters to Working Mothers: Immigrant Women in a New England Industrial Community (Cornell, NY, 1987).

10. For critiques of the way in which social and economic historians have neglected the issue of gender and women's experience see, for instance, Sheila Rowbotham, *Hidden from History: 300 Years of Women's Oppression and the Fight Against It* (London, 1973); and Sally Alexander, Anna Davin and Eve Hosteteler, 'Labouring Women: A Reply to Eric Hobsbawm', *History Workshop Journal* (Autumn 1979, pp.174–82.

11. For a useful discussion on the importance of gender in historical research, see Joan W. Scott, *Gender and the Politics of History* (New York, 1988).

12. See, for instance, Jane Lewis, *Women in England 1870–1950* (Brighton, 1984); a collection of essays in Jane Lewis (ed.), *Labour and Love* (1986); Elizabeth Roberts, *A Woman's Place: An Oral History of Working-Class Women 1890–1940* (Oxford, [1984] 1986) and in Gail Malmgreen (ed.), *Religion in the Lives of English Women 1760–1930* (London, 1986).

13. A recent essay on the lack of historical attention to the history of black women in Britain is Ziggi Alexander's 'Let it Lie Upon The Table: The Status of Black Women's Biography in the UK', *Gender and History*, Vol.2, No.1 (Spring 1990), pp.22–34.

14. This research focused on the efforts of two well-established Jewish women, Lady Louisa Goldsmid and Fanny Hertz, to advance women's education. See Stella Willis, 'The Anglo-Jewish Contribution to the Education Movement for Women in the Nineteenth Century,' *Transactions of the Jewish Historical Society*, Vol.xvii, (1951–52) pp.269–81.

15. Miriam Steiner, 'Philanthropic Activity in the Manchester Jewish Community 1867–1914', M.A, Manchester University, 1974.

16. Rickie Burman, 'The Jewish Woman as the Breadwinner', *Oral History Journal*, Vol.10, No.2 (Autumn 1982) pp.27–39; 'Growing up in Manchester Jewry – The Story of Clara Weingard', *Oral History Journal*, Vol.12, No.1 (1984), pp.56–63; ' "She Looketh Well to the Ways of Her Household": The Changing Role of Jewish Women in Religious Life, c.1800–1930', in Gail Malmgreen (ed.), *Religion in the Lives of English Women 1760–1930* (London, 1986); and 'Jewish Women and the Household Economy in Manchester, c.1890–1920', in Cesarani, *The Making of Modern Anglo-Jewry*.

17. Lara Marks, 'The Experience of Jewish Prostitutes and Jewish Women in the East End of London at the Turn of the Century', *The Jewish Quarterly*, Vol.34, No.2 (126) (1987), pp.6–10; idem, ' "Dear Old Mother Levy's": The Jewish Maternity Home and Sick Room Helps Society, 1895–1939', *Social History of Medicine*, Vol. 3, No.1 (April 1990), pp.61–88; idem, 'Ethnicity, Religion and Healthcare', *Social History of Medicine*, Vol.4, (April 1991), pp.124–8; idem, 'Irish and Jewish Women's Experience of Childbirth and Infant Care in East London 1870–1939: The Responses of Host Society and Immigrant Communities to Medical Welfare Needs', Ph.D., Oxford University, 1990; 'Working Wives and Working Mothers: A Comparative Study of Irish and East European Jewish Married Women's Work and Motherhood in East London 1870–1914', in The Polytechnic of North London Irish Studies Centre, *Occasional Papers Series*, No.2 (London, 1990). Susan Tananbaum, 'The Anglicization of Russian Jewish Immigrant Women in London, 1880–1939', Ph.D, Brandeis University, 1990; Jerry White, *Rothschild Buildings: Life in an East End Tenement Block* (London, 1980). Iris Dove is also currently writing a Ph.D. at Thames Polytechnic on Jewish girls' clubs in East London.

18. Gordon Kuzmack, *Woman's Cause*; Eugene Black, *The Social Politics of Anglo-Jewry* (Oxford, 1988), Ch.8; Rachelly Cutting, 'The Jewish Contribution to the Suffrage Movement', unpublished B.A. thesis, Anglia Polytechnic, 1988 (copy held

at the London Museum of Jewish Life).

19. Tony Kushner, 'An Alien Occupation – Jewish Refugees and Domestic Service in Britain, 1933–1948', in Werner E. Mosse *et al.* (eds.), *Second Chance: Two Centuries of German-speaking Jews in the United Kingdom* (1991), pp.555–78.

20. The catalogue to the Anglo-Jewish exhibition primarily lists Jewish religious objects related to male religious practices. While some mention is made of the importance of religion within the domestic sphere, little reference is made of women's preparations for religious rituals within the home. See *Catalogue of the Anglo-Jewish Historical Exhibition* (London, 1888).

21. This can be seen in the evidence given to the *House of Lords Select Committee on Sweating System*, PP 1888 XX; PP 1889, XII, XIV; PP 1890, XVI; *House of Commons Select Committee on Alien Immigration*, PP 1888, XI; PP 1889, X; and PP 1903. An interesting analysis of the way in which perceptions of alien immigration impinged on more general discussions concerning social and political questions of physical deterioration, unemployment, high rents and poverty in Britain appears in David Feldman, 'The Importance of Being English: Jewish Immigration and the Decay of Liberal England', in David Feldman and Gareth Stedman Jones, *Metropolis London* (London, 1989).

22. For more detail on the connections between the fears of racial degeneration and the South African War and how these affected issues of infant mortality and maternal and infant welfare see Anna Davin, 'Imperialism and Motherhood', *History Workshop Journal*, Issue 5 (Spring 1978), pp.9–66; Carol Dyhouse, 'Working-Class Mothers and Infant Mortality in England, 1895–1914', *Journal of Social History*, 12 (1979), pp.248–67, and Jane Lewis, *The Politics of Motherhood: Child and Maternal Care in England 1900–39* (London, 1980).

23. PP 1903 IX, Dr Shirley Murphy, Q3960, p.203; see also Qs.17877, 17899, 18311; S. Rosenbaum, 'A Contribution to the Study of the Vital and Other Statistics of the Jews in the UK', *Journal of the Royal Statistical Society*, Vol. 68 (1905), Table XVII, p.528. *Royal Commission on Physical Deterioration*, PP 1904 XXXII Minutes of Evidence, Q1608. Infant mortality was surprisingly low in the Jewish community not only in East London but in other areas of Britain and Eastern Europe. For a fuller discussion of the low Jewish infant mortality see Marks, 'Irish and Jewish Women's Experience of Childbirth and Infant Care in East London', pp.47–56; and idem., 'Ethnicity, Religion and Healthcare', pp.125–6.

24. Colin Holmes, *Anti-Semitism in British Society* (London, 1979), p.40; *Jewish Chronicle (JC)* 8 Oct. 1897, p.18; 6 Oct. 1901, p.18.

25. For more information on the experience of unmarried Jewish mothers see L. Marks, 'Irish, and Jewish Women's Experience of Childbirth and Infant Care,' Ch.5 and idem, '"The Luckless Waifs and Strays of Humanity": Irish and Jewish Immigrant Unwed Mothers in London 1870–1939', *Twentieth Century British History* (forthcoming).

26. For a fuller explanation of the fears concerning prostitution see Judith Walkowitz, *Prostitution and Victorian Society* (Cambridge, 1980).

27. Cited in E.J. Bristow, *Vice and Vigilance* (London, 1977), p.180.

28. Approximately one thousand Jews were employed in the trade. The percentage of Jews arrested for prostitution was higher than for any other group. Data collected from before the First World War in the East End Borough of Stepney show that 20 per cent of the convictions for brothel-keeping were against Jews. (E.J Bristow, *Prostitution and Prejudice: The Jewish Fight against White Slavery 1870–1939* [Oxford, 1982] p.237.) Admittedly, such figures might reflect a bias against Jews, rather than an accurate gauge of the numbers of Jews involved in the trade.

29. Originally named the Jewish Ladies Society for Preventive and Rescue Work, the JAPGW was founded by Lady Rothschild and Constance Rothschild (later Lady

Battersea), Claude G. Montefiore and Arthur Moro. For more details on the Jewish involvement with the white slave trade and their campaign against it, see Lloyd Gartner, 'Anglo-Jewry and the Jewish International Traffic in Prostitution 1885–1914', *American Jewish Studies Review*, Vol.7–8, (1982–83), pp.129–78. Bristow, *Prostitution and Prejudice* (Oxford, 1983); L.V Marks, 'The Experience of Jewish Prostitutes and Jewish Women'; and idem, 'Race, Class and Gender: The Experience of Jewish Prostitutes and other Jewish Women in the East End of London at the Turn of the Century', in J. Grant (ed.), *Silent Voices* (forthcoming); Black, *The Social Politics of Anglo-Jewry*, pp.232–6.

30. *East London Observer*, 21 May 1910, p.2.
31. Barbara Drake, *Women in Trade Unions* (1920), p.44, cited in Jane Lewis, *Women in England 1870–1950* (Sussex, 1984), p.167.
32. White, *Rothschild Buildings*, p.210.
33. *East London Observer*, 17 Feb 1906, p.3; 21 May 1910, p.2.
34. See, for instance, Feldman, 'Immigrants and Workers'; Joseph Buckman, *Immigrants and the Class Struggle: The Jewish Immigrant in Leeds, 1880–1914* (Manchester 1983).
35. Burman, 'Jewish Women and the Household Economy'; idem, 'The Jewish Woman as Breadwinner', pp.56–63.
36. See Glenn, *Daughters of the Shtetl*.
37. Anzia Yezierska's autobiography gives a very clear description of how her family revolved closely around the father's religious scholarship. Her mother's spiritual status depended on maintaining her father and the rest of the family. See *Bread Givers* (New York, 1925).
38. S.M. Dubnow, *History of the Jews in Russia and Poland*, cited in Baum, Hyman and Michel, *The Jewish Woman in America*, p.55; Burman, 'Jewish Women and the Household Economy'.
39. Lodging constituted the provision of shelter as well as the contraction of services such as laundry, mending, tea and breakfast.
40. A comparison of the work roles undertaken by Jewish married women and others appears in Marks, 'Working Wives and Working Mothers'.
41. James Schmiechen, *Sweated Industries and Sweated Labour: The London Clothing Trades, 1860–1914* (Urbana and Chicago, IL, 1984), pp.67–9; Patricia Branca, *Women in Europe since 1750* (London 1978), pp.32–3; Peter Stearns, 'Working-Class Women in Britain, 1890–1914', in M. Vicinus, *Suffer and Be Still* (London, 1973), pp.113–14; Laura Oren, 'The Welfare of Women in Labouring Families: England 1860–1950', in M. Hartman and L.W. Banner (eds.) *Clio's Consciousness Raised* (New York 1974), p.227, cited in Gordon Kuzmack, *Woman's Cause*, notes 10 and 11, p.109.
42. Burman, 'Jewish Women and the Household Economy', pp.70–72.
43. This is discussed in greater detail in Burman, 'Jewish Women and the Household Economy'.
44. One exception to this is where she has appeared as the prostitute.
45. On average Jewish daughters gave 89 per cent of their earnings to the family income while sons gave 70 per cent. U.S. Congress, Senate, *Report on the Condition of Woman and Child Wage-Earners*, Vol.2, Senate Doc. 645, 61st Cong., 2d. sess. (Washington, DC, 1911), Table 13, pp.652–53; cited in Glenn, *Daughters of the Shtetl*, p.84.
46. Glenn, *Daughters of the Shtetl*, pp.81–2.
47. Ibid., Ch.5.
48. Ibid. See also Gordon Kuzmack, *Woman's Cause*, p.131.
49. Several explanations have been given for the more traditional outlook of Jewish unionists. Fishman has argued that unlike America where immigrant groups

constituted a large majority, in England the Jewish immigrants were much more of a minority and as such were more of a target for discrimination from both trade unions and the gentry (Bill Fishman, *Jewish Radicals, 1875–1914* [New York, 1974], p.xii). This restricted any radical tendencies and was reinforced by the attitude of the Anglo-Jewish establishment and its institutions which aimed to modify and anglicize the immigrants. One exception to this was the German anarchist Rudolf Rocker's Brenner Street Club which was open to men and women and was the centre for radical political and union activities in the Jewish communities in the years between 1898 and 1914 (Gordon Kuzmack, *Woman's Cause*, pp.107–14).

50. Gordon Kuzmack, *Woman's Cause*, p.115.
51. Ellen Ross, '"Fierce Questions and Taunts", Married Life in Working-Class London, 1870–1914', in David Feldman and Gareth Stedman Jones (eds.), *Metropolis London: Histories and Representations since 1800* (London, 1989).
52. For more information on Louisa Goldsmid see note 14. Emily Routledge was the half-sister of the publisher Edward Routledge. For more information on the trade union activities of Abraham and Routledge see Gordon Kuzmack, *Woman's Cause*, pp.107–8, 113–14.
53. Gordon Kuzmack, *Woman's Cause*.
54. For the role Jewish women played in improving healthcare for women see Marks, '"Dear Old Mother Levy's" '; Idem, 'Irish and Jewish Woman's Experience of Childbirth and Infant Care'.
55. For a fuller discussion of the ways in women's spiritual and communal synagogue roles were changing in England see Burman, 'She Looketh Well to the Ways of Her Household'. An overview of the development of women's philanthropy and its connection with religious changes and the rise of middle-class women participation in social reform in the nineteenth century appears in Anne Summers, 'A Home from Home – Women's Philanthropic Work in Nineteenth Century', in Sandra Burman (ed.), *Fit Work for Women* (London, 1979).
56. Bill Williams, *Manchester Jewry*, p.280.
57. For Jewish women's visitation to hospitals and Poor Law institutions see Marks, 'Irish and Jewish Women's Experience of Childbirth and Infant Care', pp.228, 249–51.
58. For a history of Jewish women's work as lady visitors and for more information on Jewish philanthropy in general see Steiner, 'Philanthropic Activity and Organisation in the Manchester Jewish Community'.
59. For Jewish communal work undertaken with unmarried mothers see Marks, 'Irish and Jewish Women's Experience of Childbirth and Infant Care', Ch.5; idem, '"The Luckless Waifs and Strays of Humanity"'.
60. JAPGW, Gentleman's Committee minutes, 14 May 1919.
61. J. Walkowitz, 'The Politics of Prostitution', *History Workshop* 13 (Spring 1982), pp.79–93; M. Kaplan, *The Jewish Feminist Movement in Germany 1904–1938* (1979), p.137
62. Sources for this organization are kept at the Anglo-Jewish Archives, Southampton University.
63. For more information on the help the UJW provided for midwives and nurses and the difficulties or recruiting Jewish women to the profession see Marks, 'Irish and Jewish Women's Experience of Childbirth and Infant Care', Ch.3.
64. At the turn of the century Jewish immigrants in East London were shown to have higher birth rates than the rest of the population. For more information on this and the fertility patterns of the Jewish community see Marks, 'Irish and Jewish Women's Experience of Childbirth and Infant Care', pp.63–6.
65. In the years 1855–1934 the maternal death rate in England and Wales averaged around 4.6 per 1,000 live births, totalling some 3,000 to 4,000 maternal deaths a

year. For more information on maternal mortality see Irvine Loudon, 'Maternal Mortality: 1880–1950. Some Regional and International Comparisons', *Social History of Medicine*, Vol.1, No.2 (Aug. 1988), pp.183–228; idem, 'Deaths in Childbed from the 18th Century to 1935', *Medical History*, Vol.30, No.1 (1986), pp.1–41.
66. Some exceptions to this are Marks, 'Irish and Jewish Women's Experience of Childbirth and Infant Care'; and Gerry Black, 'Health and Medical Care of the Jewish Poor in the East End of London 1880–1939', Ph.D., Leicester University, 1987. Some exploration of childbirth and women's health has been carried out in the American context. See Stahl Weinberg, *The World of Our Mothers*, pp.37–8; Neil M. Cowan and Ruth Schwartz Cowan, *Our Parents' Lives: The Americanization of East European Jews* (New York, 1989), Ch.6. For comparative experiences of Jewish immigrants with others during childbirth see Ewen, *Immigrant Women in the Land of Dollars* (New York, 1985), Ch. 8; Weatherford, *Foreign and Female*, especially Ch.1. For a study of the health of Jewish immigrants see Deborah Dwork, 'Health Conditions of Immigrant Jews on the Lower East Side of New York: 1880–1914', *Medical History*, Vol. 25, No.1 (1981), pp.1–40.
67. More information on this topic appears in Marks, 'Irish and Jewish Women's Experience of Childbirth'; idem, ' "Dear Old Mother Levy's" '. The difficulties encountered by one Jewish woman as a result of anti-Semitism during childbirth are explored in Judith Emmanuel, 'The Politics of Maternity in Manchester, 1919–1939: A Study from Within a Continuing Campaign', M.Sc, Manchester University, 1982, Ch. 3.
68. American scholars who have explored this area include Stahl Weinberg, *The World of Our Mothers*; Cowans, *Our Parents' Lives*; Ewen, *Immigrant Women*; and Weatherford, *Foreign and Female*.
69. ' "New Jewish Woman" letter by "New Jewish Man" ', *Jewish Chronicle*, 14 Sept. 1906, p.34.

Heritage and Community: The Rescue of Manchester's Jewish Past

BILL WILLIAMS

This article charts an attempt to salvage the physical and documentary heritage of Manchester Jewry between 1969 and the early 1990s. A serious obstacle was the general indifference of the local community. Communal leaders were preoccupied with meeting the urgent needs of the Jewish present. A second generation had turned its back on a past it had long outgrown and now preferred to forget. In this unpromising context a small pressure group worked to raise the community's historical consciousness and to set up mechanisms which would rescue, preserve and display the evidence of Manchester's Jewish past.

In 1969 Leonard Cohen, a Manchester businessman then living in retirement in Cyprus, conceived the idea of a commemorative history of Manchester Jewry. His own family had played their part in that history and so had he, most notably as an influential worker for the relief and rescue of European Jewry after the Second World War.[1] Almost simultaneously, Walter Wolfson, a prominent Manchester solicitor, wrote to the local *Jewish Telegraph* calling for support in exploring the local Jewish past. Wolfson's own roots lay in local Zionism, of which his father had been an early proponent, and in the many-sided activities of the Jewish Literary Society movement. His call was answered by the local playwright and impressario Hymie Gouldman, whose most notable work, *From Cheetham Hill to Cheadle*, written only a year or two earlier, had lovingly charted the successes and ambiguities which had accompanied the embourgeoisement and suburbanization of the working-class Jewish immigrant population. As all three came together in the early summer of 1969, Cohen provided the funds, Wolfson the co-ordination and Gouldman the powerful nostalgia which activated and then sustained a Committee for the Publication of a History of Manchester Jewry.

What they shared was a desire to see a history of Manchester Jewry written. Otherwise they had little in common. There was no agreement on how the history should be written, by whom, from what perspective or at what length. At first what they probably had in mind was a brochure rather than a book. They were not professional historians. Apart from his plays, Gouldman had written brief commemorative pamphlets on Manchester's Great Synagogue and the Manchester Jewish Board of Guardians.[2] Although both were scholarly men, neither Wolfson nor Cohen had more than a passing acquaintance with the reputed highlights of Manchester's Jewish history. What held them together was a largely sentimental but hugely stubborn refusal to allow Manchester's former Jewish Quarter and the institutional landmarks of an older Jewish community to disappear without trace. They were moved by much the same impulse which lay behind a burgeoning renaissance of local studies in the wider society: a determination to preserve at least the memory of a familiar world which was fast slipping away in the wake of 'urban renewal'.

They had little to guide them. Two short articles in which Neville Laski had sought to sketch the development of Manchester Jewry were riddled with error and characterized by a haughty disdain for the sources upon which a more accurate study might have been based.[3] Israel Slotki's studies of the Manchester Talmud Torah and the Shechita Board, however useful as sources, were celebratory chronicles (and semi-autobiographies, for Slotki had played an important part in the affairs of both) rather than critical histories.[4] References to Manchester's Jewish history in general works on Anglo-Jewry were as fleeting and faulty as one might expect from historians who saw developments in the provinces as little more than pale and rather insignificant reflections of changes in the metropolis.[5] Historians of Manchester had given the Jewish community short shrift. They were interested in Manchester Jews, and then only rarely, not as participants in a distinct communal life but as the occasional contributors to developments in the wider society. No professional historian had as yet taken on the study of Manchester Jewry or, for that matter, of any Jewish community in the English provinces.[6] The committee which Walter Wolfson now chaired and held together between 1969 and 1976 broke altogether new ground: it was the first body to take seriously the rich and vulnerable heritage of provincial Anglo-Jewry.

Little survived of the material and documentary evidence of that heritage. In Manchester, the upward social mobility of an immigrant Jewish population, the Blitz, slum clearance and radical economic changes in the immediate post-war years had effectively depopulated the former Jewish Quarter of north Manchester. Red Bank, the target of Eastern European settlers from the 1840s to the 1890s, was erased by the City Engineers during 1938. The other 'immigrant districts' on Cheetham Hill – Strangeways, Lower Broughton and Hightown – all of which had suffered severe bomb damage, were cleared by civic bulldozers during the 1960s. By that time, the bulk of their Jewish residents, rising out of the dire poverty of their immigrant forebears, had already moved northwards towards Prestwich, Whitefield and Bury or crossed the city to what were (quite incorrectly) seen as the more sophisticated suburbs of the south. The older residential property of Cheetham was almost totally destroyed: only one working-class home remained, in Park Street, where a single intransigent family had fought a successful rearguard action against compulsory purchase. Its former synagogues, which were increasingly out of walking distance, and other communal institutions had either been pulled down to make space for superstore speculators or converted to commercial use as hand-bag factories, textile warehouses and down-market cash-and-carries. Frankenburg House, formerly the offices of the Jewish Board of Guardians, now sold kitchen sinks. Maccabean Hall, once the headquarters of the Zionist Friendly Society, the Ancient Order of Maccabeans, now specialized in the wholesaling of cheap jewellery. Many buildings had passed into the hands of a new generation of enterprising immigrants, from India, Pakistan and Bangladesh: one late synagogue now served as a mosque.

Such a scenario was not unique to Manchester. During much the same period, similar forces swept away the Leylands district of Leeds, Glasgow's Gorbals and Liverpool's Brownlow Hill. In all three towns, the bulk of the surviving Jewish populations had migrated from inner-city slums to comfortable outer-city suburbs. And since no one had exercised any kind of restraining hand or evinced any interest in what was being endangered or lost, such upheavals were accompanied by the wholesale destruction of Jewish buildings, artefacts and archives. The devastation was probably greatest in Leeds. In Liverpool and Glasgow the 'cathedral synagogues', Princes Road and Garnet Hill, survived, although as islands in an urban wasteland. Liverpool alone appointed a 'communal archivist' (part-time, unpaid, but exceptionally dedicated) to monitor the fate of communal records: the losses were none the less considerable.

In Manchester, communal indifference opened the way for a chain of tragedies: whole segments of local Jewish history were rendered irretrievable by the stroke of a spade. The solid and stylish Higher Broughton Synagogue, built in 1907 to accommodate a new immigrant elite,[7] was demolished in the mid-1960s to make way for a block of flats. The written records of the congregation's activities, including its important literary society and Zionist branch, were buried in the debris. All that has survived of the interior furnishings is a pair of embroidered Ark curtains which found their way, by some circuitous and probably illicit route, on to a stall at Pendlebury Fleamarket, better known for its second-rate bric-a-brac and second-hand shoes. The loss, as in every such case, was more than material. With the records went evidence of the role in Jewish religious life of (amongst many other figures of importance in Anglo-Jewry) Michael Marks, founder of Marks and Spencer, Ephraim Sieff and his more famous son, Israel, Samuel Finburgh (Salford's first Jewish MP), Harold and Leslie Lever and Abraham Moss. No synagogue in Manchester boasted more magistrates, city councillors, mayors, MPs and aristocrats amongst its members: what they did *in* the synagogue will now never be known. The building itself had symbolized the newly-acquired status of the many entrepreneurs who, from the first decade of the century, had been rising from the Eastern European immigrant milieu to assume positions of leadership in commerce, the community and the city.

This notion of buildings as symbols was lost on the community of the late 1960s. As a result, their demolition was in no case preceded by the systematic creation of a photographic record. A handful of photographs survive by accident. The impressive facade of the North Manchester Synagogue in Strangeways – the creation of Galician immigrants in the 1890s – is represented in a brochure distributed by the commercial firm (manufacturers of dental accessories) which took over the premises. Other incidental snaps (including one of the entrance, no more, of the Higher Broughton Synagogue) were used occasionally to decorate the covers of commemorative histories. Interior shots are extremely rare. In the case of the Higher Broughton, four survive: snaps of a wedding ceremony of the 1950s taken surreptitiously by one of the guests. Most of Manchester's lost synagogues – well over 40 – have not left even a photographic imprint.

The evacuation of the Jewish Quarter was accompanied by the loss of documents on an equally dramatic scale. The records of voluntary

organizations, at risk at the best of times, became particularly vulnerable as Jewish institutions wound up their affairs, amalgamated,
moved to premises in newer areas of settlement or took the opportunity to 'rationalize' their operations. Ultra-efficient secretaries,
seeking economies or simply making space, put paid to the earliest
records of the Jewish Working Men's Club and the Manchester
Battalion of the Jewish Lads Brigade. The archives of the Manchester
Zionist Association were destroyed in the 1950s by a caretaker anxious
to create more room in new offices after the Association had vacated
the building at 67 Cheetham Hill Road which it had occupied at the
turn of the century. With them went the documented activities of the
literally hundreds of Zionist bodies which had flourished in Manchester since the late 1880s. The extent of this particular loss is best
evaluated by setting it against the central role played by Manchester
men and women in the evolution of Zionism, nationally and inter-
nationally. Weizmann and his 'Manchester School' were largely instrumental in negotiating the Balfour Declaration, Rebecca Sieff,
Miriam Sacher and Helena Weisberg in the creation of WIZO. What
ended up on a municipal rubbish tip was part of the prehistory of the
Jewish State.

Other gaps created by apathy and negligence are only a little less
significant. In their different ways, Jewish trade unions, literary
societies and friendly societies were the expression of radical social
change within the Manchester Jewish community of the 1890s. All
three flourished until the outbreak of the Second World War: some, if
in a rather attenuated form, into the 1950s. In the 1930s there were in
Manchester some 15 trade union branches, 30 literary societies and
over a hundred friendly society lodges. Of the records of all these
bodies, only those of one small friendly society (founded in 1919)
survive. The only written relic of Manchester's many Jewish Socialist
formations is a single membership book of the Jewish Workers Circle,
which happily (although, no doubt, improperly) fell into the hands of a
former comrade who appreciated its importance. Religious institutions fared little better. What remained of the records of the United
Synagogue, founded in 1904[8] and favoured by the ebullient workshop
masters of the Cheetham area, were discovered by members of
Wolfson's committee in 1970, strewn across the floor and yard of the
derelict building, soon to begin a new life as the Panorama Cash-and-
Carry.

Some losses were calculated: most happened by default. Synagogues were under no legal obligation to deposit their records in public archives. In the case of communal records more generally, no one on the Manchester Jewish Representative Council or the Manchester Council of Synagogues had thought to create a link with the city archive department. It may be that the idea of Jewish records passing into the public domain was viewed by some local Jewish leaders with some concern, particularly after Nazi Germany and its satellites had exploited just such documents to speed the process of genocide. No one had sought to allay their fears. Neither the Jewish Board of Deputies nor the Chief Rabbi's office had given any sort of national lead (or set any kind of good example). For their part, hard-pressed and traditionally-minded archivists had as yet shown little independent interest in Jewish records or, for that matter, in the records of any ethnic minority. No official system existed to acquaint them with the value, or even alert them to the existence, of Jewish communal documents. In the absence of recognized local mechanisms and a co-ordinated national plan, records simply 'disappeared', decayed or, like Ark curtains, slipped into the cavernous depths of Manchester's market for memorabilia. A volume of memoirs from a Refugee Hostel of the late 1930s surfaced at a church jumble sale. A tin trunk containing the personal papers and correspondence of another refugee from Nazi Europe fell into the hands of a dealer who rapidly converted the separated fragments into cash.

This kind of loss suggests the general fate of personal and business records. Few families moving 'up the hill' between the 1940s and the 1960s considered their family albums or the papers of their immigrant forebears of sufficient importance to warrant steps being taken to ensure their preservation. No one sought to persuade them otherwise. As the traditional Jewish tailoring, cap-making, rainwear and furniture trades collapsed in the wake of changing fashions, foreign competition and post-war slump, no steps were taken to make a photographic record, to draw in their archives or to preserve examples of their (mostly primitive) technology. A few factory buildings survive in new guises: their interiors have been gutted, their machinery scrapped, their order books junked.

In seeking to check these processes of archival loss, Wolfson's committee achieved some initial success. A broad strategy of retrieval was hammered out. The idea of a 'communal archive' was rapidly abandoned in favour of the channelling of Jewish records into public depositories. It seemed highly unlikely that funds could be found to

replicate within the community the specialized facilities and staffing
available in a public record office for the storage, conservation and
indexing of documents or for making them available to the public
under suitably safe conditions. Nor did such duplication seem in-
herently desirable. In a public record office, Jewish records would
coexist with the general archives of the city, perhaps encouraging the
historians of local Jewry to set communal history in a wider context and
historians of the city to accord the Jewish experience its proper place in
local history. Archivists unfamiliar with Jewish records might also
come to appreciate their special character, their volume and their
importance as a source of local as well as Jewish history. This is
precisely what happened. Within months, the committee and the city
archivist were working together to negotiate the deposit of Jewish
records. Before the end of 1970 these had included the substantial
collections of three major communal institutions: the Great Synagogue, the Jewish Board of Guardians (now Jewish Social Services)
and the Jewish Benevolent Society.

Negotiations did not always reach a successful conclusion. The
records of one Jewish charity, the Linas Hazedek and Bikur Cholim
Society,[9] founded in about 1910, were destroyed by their owners (the
society itself had become defunct) *after* the committee had signalled its
interest. In general, however, the system worked remarkably well, the
flow of archives broadening as it gathered pace. The first business
records to emerge, early in 1971, were the ledgers of an immigrant fent
merchant (and leading Clarion Socialist), Leon Locker: the first significant personal documents the detailed household accounts of a
German hat-band manufacturer who settled in Manchester's plush
Victoria Park in 1870. Publicity in the local Jewish press was deployed
to encourage further deposits: among them were the personal papers
of Jacob Nathan, the reputed founder of Manchester Jewry in 1780,
preserved by descendants who had long since abandoned Judaism.

The problem of saving buildings and artefacts proved more intrac-
table. There was no museum of social history in Manchester which
might have seen objects relating to the Jewish experience as lying
within its purview. The only Jewish Museum in the country, in
London's Woburn House,[10] was, to say the very least, unsympathetic
towards the kind of late-nineteenth century domestic objects and
economic artefacts which the committee was beginning to locate. A
narrow collecting policy at Woburn House appeared to exclude anything which was produced after 1880, any item which could not be

described as, in some sense, 'Jewish' and objects which lay outside the boundaries of Jewish ritual and elite culture. Plastic figurines of black slaves, made for a Jewish plantation owner in the West Indies, clothed in Manchester textiles (the plantation had strong links with the warehouses of Jewish cotton merchants in Manchester) and owned in 1971 by the Manchester Jewish philanthropist, Margaret Langdon, were refused entry for not being 'Jewish'. Thereafter the committee did not risk sending a schmearer's roller, the irons and oven of a Jewish presser or the workbench of a Jewish shoemaker. The Whitworth Art Gallery accepted the figurines: there was no home in Manchester for things more proletarian. All the committee could do was note what was on offer and encourage their safe-keeping.

In the case of buildings, the committee could do little to halt an escalating process of destruction and decay. In 1969, when Wolfson's committee began its work, only two of the older synagogues of Cheetham Hill continued to function as places of worship: the Great, opened in 1858 to serve an anglicized elite (it was still known to some as the 'Englischer Shool'), and the Spanish and Portuguese, built to the design of a local Jewish architect in 1874 to serve the north Manchester Sephardim. Neither flourished. Only notionally within walking distance of their orthodox congregations, sentiment alone dictated their precarious survival.

Early in 1974 the executive of the Great Synagogue finally decided to follow their members northwards into Crumpsall and to sell their older building on Cheetham Hill. Although perhaps not beautiful (one critic has described the style as 'Manchester Baroque'), the facade of the Great, set up in the 1850s in what was then a fashionable suburb, marked an important turning point in the early history of Manchester Jewry: the emergence of a substantial, economically successful and socially confident Jewish middle class. The ornate interior, with its Spanish mahogany pulpit, *bimah*[11] and seating, was equally impressive and symbolic. Wolfson's committee made a written plea to the executive to preserve, rather than sell, the building, possibly for future use as a museum (this was the point at which the idea of a Manchester Jewish Museum first emerged). It was ignored. The committee asked that steps be taken at least to protect the building and its furnishings from vandalization. They were not. Within ten days of its closure, the building had been wrecked by vandals of every variety. Scrap-metal vandals had salvaged the synagogue's two copper domes. Antique vandals removed everything that could be detached (and much that properly could not). Teenage vandals destroyed what was left. Stain-glass windows were shattered, the pulpit was split in half, the *bimah* reduced to splinters. A week later wooden candelabra which had stood before the Ark were on offer in one of Manchester's seedier antique arcades.

How were such monumental losses allowed to happen? How are we to account for the conspicuous inaction of the Manchester Jewish Representative Council (the community's 'parliament'), for the apathy of the Jewish press and the indifference of the Jewish public in the face of the very evident destruction of the community's heritage? Why is it that Wolfson's Committee was allowed to operate in a cultural vacuum? Wolfson and Gouldman apart, its members (never more than eight in total) were not men of consequence in the community. Why did the acknowledged leaders of Manchester Jewry remain aloof?

As the non-Jewish historian invited on to Wolfson's committee in 1969, I found such communal attitudes particularly difficult to explain. My none-too-informed perception of the Jews was as an 'historical people' par excellence, a people with an especially strong sense of their historical mission and whose festivals, religious customs and daily routines were firmly rooted in a cherished past. And yet what faced me in Manchester were the quite unmistakable symptoms of gross neglect. Even a beautiful synagogue in the old Jewish Quarter which was still functioning as a place of worship after 1974 – the Spanish and Por-tuguese – had long ceased to be watertight (buckets were ranged along the floor of the Ladies Gallery) and was gradually losing its battle against severe structural infirmity and galloping dry rot. A younger Jewish population driving into town from Prestwich and Whitefield were witnesses daily to the crumbling ruins of their parents' world. Sometimes they were moved to sadness, never to action.

The disjunction between the honour bestowed on distant traditions and the desecration of the local heritage was explained to me in a variety of ways. The community's commitments to the present, I was told, were far too onerous to allow time or energy to be devoted to preserving the past. There were at least 20 charities and over thirty synagogues to maintain, hundreds of ancillary organizations to keep afloat, in a complex voluntary *kehillah* of over 30,000 people.[12] Since the Second World War the Manchester community had been part of what has been described as an Anglo-Jewish 'renaissance' following the dislocations of the war and the devastation of the Holocaust. The

Jewish Day School movement was gathering pace. Both religious wings of the community were expanding. New synagogues and societies were emerging in the suburban districts in which the Jewish community was now centred. The Jewish State was undergoing a difficult infancy and required continual support, both human and financial. The refuseniks in Soviet Russia were in desperate need of assistance. Seeking experience from the local past in order to build a Jewish future was a luxury the community did not believe it could afford. In a divided community, with only a limited pool of active volunteers and a limited amount of disposable wealth, encouraging an active interest in the past could hardly be seen as a communal priority. On first hearing of the idea of a Manchester Jewish museum, one leading communal figure (who had been the prime agent for the raising of millions of pounds for Israel and for local charities) gave it as his firm opinion that the community's 'givers' would never be persuaded to back such a cause.

There was some truth in this prediction. At the same time, the strength of his reaction (he was not to be persuaded) suggested that apathy to the local past had as much to do with the *nature* of communal leadership as with the priorities of particular leaders in a busy present. Communal leadership in the English provinces is all about brokerage: between the local community and the national institutions of Anglo-Jewry, between the money available in the community and the institutions which depended upon it, between Israel and the Zionists of the local diaspora, between warring factions within the community, but, most of all, between the Jewish community and the gentile society with which it sought to live in harmony. During the struggle for political emancipation in the mid-nineteenth century, the leaders of Anglo-Jewry came to believe (or perhaps they were persuaded by liberal England to believe) that the full acceptance of Jews by English society depended upon their good (and very English) behaviour.[13] Their aim as leaders, as they came to see it, was to render Jewry acceptable by enhancing 'the character of our nation in the estimation of others'.[14] The leaders of Manchester Jewry took on this mission. Their community had to be seen to be anglicized, integrated, respectable, civic-minded and patriotic. They sought to promote these virtues through a myriad institutions. They became the agents of social conformity and Englishness.

Sometimes the past figured in their propaganda, but rhetorically and in a very partial and highly mythologized form. It was a past heavily sanitized to promote appropriate images. Unseemly blemishes were minimized, nonconformity largely hidden from view. In this idyllic history the Jewish immigrants from Eastern Europe were essentially devout, peace-loving, sober and hard-working. They were rarely seen before the city magistrates. They never abandoned their families or beat their wives. They were not dependent on the rates. Their enterprise boosted the local economy. They rapidly transformed themselves 'from Polish into English Jews'. If they sometimes found the route to integration hard-going, they turned to the tutelage and example of their communal betters. They aspired to bourgeois values. If at first sight they sometimes looked like slum-dwellers with insanitary habits, sweated workers who undercut their native colleagues, militant socialists or inveterate gamblers, in reality they were a respectable middle-class citizenry of the future.

In terms of the Jewish heritage, there were serious problems in this kind of deeply Whiggish and deferential view of local Jewish history. In the first place, the past did not exist in its own right. It was the ugly duckling which, under proper guidance, would emerge in due course as the swan of the present. It was a time of foreign and inferior ways: habits which the community had given up and of which it did not wish to be reminded. This was not a view of history out of which a determination to preserve the immigrant Jewish heritage was likely to evolve. It was also a false history, unlikely to survive a confrontation with the awkward realities which disinterested rescue work might unearth. Wolfson's committee was itself not free of these prejudices. When I presented the first draft of *The Making of Manchester Jewry*, I was taken to task for the space I had devoted to Jewish criminality. At all events, local Jewish leaders saw little to gain, and much to lose, from the enterprise of preservation.

One tragic aspect of the situation was that this ethos was shared during the 1970s by the leading historians of Anglo-Jewry. They were not really very interested in the activities of the Jewish working class in the era of mass immigration, except in so far as these could be used to throw into relief the philanthropic efforts of the anglicized elite. The first serious study of Eastern European immigration to England was left to one American scholar, the first tentative exploration of behavioural nonconformity in Anglo-Jewry to another. The former, by Gartner, appeared in 1960, the latter by Endelman in 1990. In the interval of 30 years nothing of genuine significance appeared on the Jewish immigrant experience.[15] Moreover, Anglo-Jewish history as it

was practised by Cecil Roth and his school was both a product and a
vehicle of the influences which had shaped communal leadership. It
perpetuated the same images. It was informed by the same apologetic
pleading. It celebrated the same notions of progress. Communal
leaders and Anglo-Jewish historians were locked in a close symbiotic
embrace. Communal leaders sought, in part by the manipulation of
images, to close the gap between communal realities and gentile
expectations: Anglo-Jewish history praised them for their success. The
victim was the complex and ambiguous reality of the Anglo-Jewry
past.

There were important consequences for the English Jewish heritage. The reactionary stance of the London Jewish Museum was one.
Another was the apathy of the Jewish Historical Society of England
which, since the 1890s, had served as the custodian and publicist of
traditional Anglo-Jewish historiography. Throughout the 1960s and
1970s the society failed to mobilize its many provincial members (or its
London members, for that matter) for the protection of the fast-
eroding Anglo-Jewish heritage. Anglo-Jewish Archives, set up by the
Society in University College London in the early 1960s, was both
inadequately staffed and resourced and typically preoccupied with the
metropolitan experience. A branch of the Society was formed in
Manchester in the mid-1970s under the chairmanship of Walter Wolfson. Perhaps it played a peripheral role in raising the historical
consciousness of Manchester Jewry. Its chief effect was to divert the
energies of Wolfson's committeemen away from the increasingly
urgent task of rescuing documents, artefacts and buildings. In the face
of this pressing need, the local branch, taking its cue from London,
inclined decisively towards celebratory lectures and collective historical narcissism. Communal leaders could argue that, as far as the local
Jewish heritage was concerned, they were under absolutely no
pressure from the historical establishment of Anglo-Jewry.

Nor were they under pressure from the ordinary members of the
community or from the local Jewish press. It would be far too facile to
attribute indifference to the local Jewish heritage to leaders with other
priorities or to Jewish historians with other interests. Also lacking was
a popular constituency to which leaders might have felt it necessary to
defer. The people were also indifferent. From the beginning Wolfson's
committee had faced critics who had given its objectives short shrift.
Who, it was asked, wanted to honour the rather dismal past out of
which the community had long since evolved? The immigrants from

Eastern Europe, or, at any rate, their children, had made good, become English, risen out of the slums, overcome anti-Semitic sentiment and established themselves as respectable and comfortable citizens in the bourgeois districts of Prestwich, Whitefield, Didsbury, Cheadle, Gatley and Sale. Who wanted to be reminded of their now distant origins? A journalist on the local *Jewish Gazette* put the point particularly cogently. Manchester Jewry needed a museum, she wrote (it was 1978 and the idea of a museum had re-emerged), like it needed a ham sandwich.

In this kind of attitude it was possible to detect the influence of communal leaders. But it was also an independent reflection of a wide gulf between the Jewish generations. Those who felt this way were essentially members of a second generation which had effectively turned its back on the immigrant past as a means of bolstering its own confident resting place in the social heartlands of English society. They lived in 'Jewish areas' certainly, but they shared the privileges, status and ambitions of their gentile peers. In the suburbs they had developed a sense of belonging. Instinctively they shied away from the legacy of those whose acceptance had been more problematic, whose social status had been more questionable, whose material resources had been more slender and who had clung rather tenaciously to the cultural baggage of Eastern Europe. A certain residual lack of confidence added edge to their desire for historical amnesia. And it was to this generation that most of Manchester's post-war Jewish leaders belonged. Neither leaders nor led felt inclined to reveal the skeletons of poverty and marginality in their family cupboards.

There was a sense, too, in which an older generation had come to dismiss its own history as 'unimportant'. This was in part a reflection of the low estimate put upon their experiences by communal leaders and by their own children. But it was also a function of the way in which English society in general had defined history. Like all working people, they had been led to believe that real history was about influential people and significant events. This did not include them. The daily texture of their lives lay below the level at which history begins. There was no one to tell them otherwise. The programme of lectures of the Jewish Historical Society of England, like Anglo-Jewish history in general, focused upon the real or imagined achievements of a communal elite. The earliest study to centre upon the everyday experience of Jewish working-class people in England – Jerry White's *Rothschild Buildings*[16] – was the work of a non-Jewish historian touched by the History Workshop Movement, by which Anglo-Jewish history had been left effectively unscathed. Since communal leaders offered no different perspective, Jewish people of working-class origin in effect condoned their own exclusion from the historical record. From the point of view of the local Jewish heritage, there was no popular pressure to offset the indifference of the communal elite.

The upshot of all these strands of opinion was that Wolfson's committee sounded a lone warning. Its legacy is all the more impressive. It set in motion a chain of events which culminated in the opening of the Manchester Jewish Museum.

The first was the creation of a Jewish History Unit at Manchester Polytechnic in 1974.[17] With the aid of the Leonard Cohen Trust, the work of Wolfson's committee was now provided with an institutional base. This opened the way to new initiatives. Oral history, then only in its beginnings in England, was now added to the work of archive retrieval. A programme of 'life-story' interviewing embraced Jewish immigrants to Manchester, their children and non-Jewish people who had spent their early lives in or near the areas of Jewish residence. It served several purposes. One was to provide a perspective substantially lacking in the documentary records. Institutions like the Manchester Jews' School, the Jewish Lads' Brigade, the Jewish Board of Guardians and the Jewish Working Men's Club, illuminated in the archival sources chiefly by the glowing pride of their founders and managers, could now be viewed again through the eyes of their constituents. One effect was to bring home the destructive component of 'anglicization'. In the Jews School, the speaking of Yiddish was prohibited to the children of immigrants whose first (and sometimes only) language was Yiddish. Children who joined the school with 'foreign-sounding' first names had them changed by authoritarian decree (so Tauba became Tilly). Yiddish and politics were also taboo at the Jewish Working Men's Club (founded for, not by, working men), where adult immigrants were wooed from anarchist politics and introduced to the more refined pastimes of English society. An oral history focusing on the routines and culture of the home, the neighbourhood and the workplace was also a means through which Jewish people of working-class origin were invited to place a higher value on their experiences than that accorded to it within the community. It was seen as one way of raising the community's historical consciousness and of suggesting an 'alternative' version of the communal heritage. By 1984 the Unit had put together a collection of over 400 taped interviews.

The systematic retrieval of personal documents and family photographs was another way in which the Unit complemented and extended the work of Wolfson's committee.[18] By 1984 the 10,000 prints in
the Unit's collection illustrated most facets of Jewish life in Manchester in the late nineteeth and twentieth centuries. Given the diverse
origins of Manchester's Jewish population, a substantial number related to the Jewish experience in Germany, Eastern Europe and the
Mediterranean world prior to emigration and to other English Jewish
communities. Apart from formal portraits, the collection included
(*inter alia*) shots of garment workshops, street scenes, neighbourhood
gangs, domestic interiors and leisure pursuits: particularly evocative
(and rare) were snaps of a strike by Jewish waterproof garment-
makers in the late 1930s taken, on a Kodak Brownie, by one of the
strikers. Photographs also provided a means of reconstituting, in part
at least, the lost physical, residential and institutional context of the
old Jewish Quarter: the Unit's photographer went out to capture
whatever remained (more or less) intact. The exploitation of census
data by the Unit's researchers provided a statistical dimension.

Using these resources, Rosalyn Livshin explored the education and
assimilation of the children of Jewish immigrants from Eastern
Europe[19] and Rickie Burman began her pioneering attempt to uncover
the 'hidden history' of Jewish women.[20] Rickie's choice of subject was
not accidental. The restoration of Jewish women to the historical
record was part of the way in which the Unit was seeking to redefine
the local Jewish heritage. The (male) elitism, romanticism and apologetics of an older Anglo-Jewish history were decisively rejected.

Meantime, in 1978 the Mahammad of the Sephardi congregation in
north Manchester finally decided to abandon the old Spanish and
Portuguese Synagogue in Cheetham Hill and to move northwards to a
new locale. Wolfson's committee had been disbanded two years
earlier, following the publication of the book it had nursed into
existence[21] (Walter Wolfson himself was already seriously ill: unhap-
pily he died in May 1979). With the fate of the Great Synagogue very
much in mind (what was left of it was pulled down by the city as a safety
hazard in 1985), four people met at the Prestwich home of Werner
Mayer, a prominent member and office-holder of the Spanish and
Portuguese congregation. There a Jewish Heritage Committee was set
up. A provocative article – 'Death of a Synagogue' – written for the
Jewish Chronicle in September 1978, drew attention to the likely
future of the building (the article was accompanied by photographs of

the Great in a state of advanced decay) and signalled the opening of a campaign to purchase the synagogue, effect its repair, restore it to its original condition and transform it into the Manchester Jewish Museum.

The Jewish Heritage Committee (soon to be translated into the Jewish Museum Trust) inherited the problems as well as the strengths of Wolfson's committee. It was yet another pressure group, working against the communal grain. Such communal leaders as were consulted gave it as their considered opinion that money for such a project could never be raised. They meant, of course, that it was not worth their trouble trying to raise it. Others asserted that the kinds of things a museum ought to display (they meant ritual silver and *objets d'art*) would not be forthcoming. Others cast doubt on the existence of a potential clientele (this was the time of the 'ham sandwich' jibe). The Jewish Historical Society of England and the London Jewish Museum could find no way of reacting to (let alone supporting) as subversive a notion as a museum with a provincial, modern and working-class focus.

This is not the place to describe in any detail just how the tables were turned. In one sense, the communal leaders were correct. The bulk of the initial funding came not from local Jewish donors, but from governmental, semi-governmental and local government sources and from national trusts, some of them Jewish. It remains true that neither the community's elite nor its official delegates (locally or nationally) have given the museum their solid support. An adequate package of funds was none the less put together. The building had been purchased by the beginning of 1981, repaired and substantially restored by the spring of 1984 and converted into a fully-equipped museum by the March of 1985.

It effectively brought together the general aims of Wolfson's committee, the expertise, resources and distinctive historical outlook which had evolved within the Jewish History Unit (which closed in 1984) and the punctilious attention to architectural and structural detail which was the hallmark of the museum trustees. It was the first time in Anglo-Jewry that a building of historic interest threatened with demolition had been saved and earmarked for permanent preservation. It marked a victory not simply for the Manchester Jewish heritage, but for a very particular view of the local Jewish past. It was not about an elite (still less, a male elite). It was about the everyday experiences of ordinary Jewish men and women. It implied no particular definition of 'Jewishness'. It did not celebrate (still less, propagate) any particular kind of communal 'conformity'. About things Jewish, it was assertive rather than deferential. The emphasis was on the Jewish experience in its own right rather than on the real or supposed 'Jewish contributions' to the history of the city. Nothing else about it lent any credence to the notion that the place of Jews in English society depended upon behaviour or images acceptable to English gentiles. It was not defensive or didactic in the face of anti-Semitism. The assumption was rather that the realities of local communal history offered their own rebuttal of hostile stereotypes and anti-Semitic clichés to all but the most inveterate and irrational of racists (whose prejudices lay well beyond the reach of truth).

Trickier for the trustees than agreeing a philosophy was providing it with a physical format. Built to accommodate well-to-do Sephardi Jewish merchants who had come from the Mediterranean coastlands to open textile warehouses in Manchester, the stylish design and lavish decoration of the synagogue (both 'Saracenic', according to the architect) were calculated to impress. The size was more modest: sufficient only for some 100 merchants and their families. The question facing the trustees was how to create a museum in such limited space without undermining the structure and atmosphere of the original synagogue. The solution, worked out with the help of the North-West Museum Service, was to retain the ground floor of the synagogue intact and to locate the exhibitions in a Ladies Gallery (this was an orthodox congregation) stripped of its tiered seating and in a *succah* which adjoined the rear of the Ark[22]. The look and 'feel' of the original building were thus preserved. In the gallery, a series of eight alcoves were installed to house the history of Manchester Jewry. The *succah* was reserved for a programme of changing displays, more wide-ranging in their content but each related, in some sense, to the local Jewish experience. The trustees were fortunate to inherit a Spanish and Portugese Synagogue. The distinctive Sephardi lay-out, unlike the typical ground-plans of Ashkenazi synagogues, provides a sizeable space between the Reading Desk and the Ark:[23] a natural 'theatre in the round' for plays, concerts, recall sessions and other events. The overall visual result is a warm, colourful and compact synagogue on to which a compressed (but three-dimensional) representation of the Manchester Jewish heritage has been unobtrusively grafted.

The exhibitions, permanent and temporary, arise out of the museum's unique collections and express its distinctive *raison d'être*.

Photographs, artefacts, reconstructions and extracts from recorded interviews are deployed to create a history readily recognizable to those who shared it rather than one dictated by the community's image-makers or shaped according to the narrow predilictions of traditional Anglo-Jewish history. Perhaps a third generation, too, will see it as their own. If so, it may be that they will come to believe (some as the communal leaders of the future) that still more of it is worth seeking out and protecting.

NOTES

1. Norman Bentwich, *They Found Refuge* (London, 1956), pp.131, 134, 138 and 163. Leonard Cohen died in 1971. The link between his family and trust fund and Wolfson's committee were maintained by his son, Dr Daniel Cohen.
2. H.R. Gouldman, *Manchester Great Synagogue: The Story of a Hundred Years* (Manchester, 1958) and *The Manchester Jewish Board of Guardians: The Story of One Hundred Years* (Manchester, 1967).
3. Neville J. Laski, 'The History of Manchester Jewry', *Manchester Review*, Vol.7 (1956), pp.366–78, and 'The Manchester and Salford Jewish Community, 1912–1962' *Manchester Review*, Vol.10 (1965), pp.97–108.
4. Rev. I.W. Slotki, *The History of the Manchester Shechita Board, 1892–1952* (Manchester, 1954) and *Seventy Years of Hebrew Education, 1880–1950* (Manchester, 1950).
5. For example, V.D. Lipman, *Social History of the Jews in England 1850–1950* (London, 1954), pp.25–6.
6. For passing references to Jews in histories of Manchester see, for example, N.J. Frangopulo (e.b), *Rich Inheritance* (Manchester, 1962), pp.114–16. Ernest Krausz, *Leeds Jewry* (Cambridge, 1964) is a work of sociology in which history is no more than an introductory background.
7. No author, *Higher Broughton Hebrew Congregation: The First Fifty Years, 1907–1957* (Manchester, 1957).
8. No author, *Manchester United Synagogues and Beth Hamidrash Hagodol, 1904–1954: Golden Jubilee Souvenir Brochure* (Manchester, 1954).
9. Literally, 'The Lodge of Righteousness and Society for Visiting the Sick'. 'The Lodge of Righteousness' was perhaps a hostel which offered overnight accommodation to the itinerant poor.
10. The Jewish Museum in Woburn House is not to be confused with the London Museum of Jewish Life set up more recently in Finchley on a pattern very similar to that of the Manchester Jewish Museum.
11. The *bimah* is the platform upon which stands the Reading Desk in most orthodox synagogues.
12. *Kehillah* was the name given to the autonomous Jewish communities of Eastern Europe: it is used loosely here to denote the political and administrative structure of an English Jewish community. 30,000 is an estimate, probably on the low side: there has never been a local Jewish census.
13. See Bill Williams, 'The Anti-Semitism of Toleration', in A.J. Kidd and K.W.

Roberts (eds.), *City, Class and Culture: Studies of Social Policy and Cultural Production in Victorian Manchester* (Manchester, 1985), pp.74–102.

14. Bill Williams, *The Making of Manchester Jewry, 1740–1875* (Manchester, 1976), p.94.
15. Lloyd P. Gartner, *The Jewish Immigrant in England, 1870–1914* (London, 1960) and Todd M. Endelman, *Radical Assimilation in English Jewish History, 1656–1945* (Bloomington, IN, 1990).
16. Jerry White, *Rothschild Buildings: Life in an East End Tenement Block, 1887–1920* (London, 1980).
17. The Jewish History Unit (which became part of a wider-ranging Manchester Studies Unit) was sustained by funds from the Leonard Cohen Trust donated by Dr Daniel Cohen.
18. Most photographs were loaned to the Unit for copying. On the technique involved for preserving and indexing the resulting contact prints and negatives, see Caroline Warhurst and Audrey Linkman, *Family Albums* (Manchester Studies Unit publication, 1982).
19. Rosalyn Livshin, 'The Acculturation of the Children of Immigrant Jews in Manchester', in David Cesarani (ed.), *The Making of Modern Anglo-Jewry* (Oxford, 1990), pp.79–96.
20. Rickie Burman, 'The Jewish Woman as Breadwinner: The Changing Value of Women's Work in a Manchester Immigrant Community', *Oral History* Vol.10, No.2 (Autumn 1982), pp. 27–39, and 'Jewish Women and the Household Economy in Manchester, 1890–1920', in David Cesarani, op. cit., pp. 55–75.
21. Bill Williams, *The Making of Manchester Jewry*, op. cit.
22. The *succah* was a building at the rear of the synagogue which served as a 'tabernacle' during the Festival of Tabernacles (*Succoth*). To accord with Jewish custom, the *succah* needed to be 'open to the heavens' during the period of the festival. The *succah* of the Spanish and Portuguese Synagogue had a roof which could be slid away on rollers to make way for a wooden lattice-work cover. The trustees were unable to preserve the roller system.
23. In a Sephardi Synagogue, the *bimah* is most often situated at the rear of the building, opposite the Ark. In most Ashkenazi synagogues, the *bimah* occupies a more central position.

Squandered Heritage: Jewish Buildings in Britain

SHARMAN KADISH

In the winter of 1987–88 the United Synagogue sold the magnificent East London synagogue in Stepney Green (1877) to property developers, without consultation nor apparent concern for its fate. This sale drew attention to an issue long neglected by the leaders of Anglo-Jewry: the conservation of the Jewish architectural heritage in the British Isles. Immediate steps must be taken to arrest the disappearance of historic Jewish landmarks: synagogues, cemeteries and secular buildings. This article recommends co-operation between the Jewish community and the general conservation agencies (especially English Heritage) in the systematic documentation of Jewish sites, in order to establish priorities for preservation and to draw up guidelines for the listing of Jewish buildings. It calls for Anglo-Jewry to put conservation on the communal agenda and for the education of the Jewish public to appreciate the importance of our architectural heritage.

... Let us at least record anything of value before we pull it down. Georgian synagogues have been lost without trace; the Vic-

This article is dedicated to the memory of LILY GREENBERG (*z.l.*) (1913–1990), mother-in-law of Sharman Kadish, who was a lifelong member of the East London synagogue.

Sharman Kadish became involved with the fate of the East London synagogue in November 1987. Her husband's family had been members of the *shul* for many years and he was its last marriage secretary. They were hoping to celebrate their own marriage there, but the events related above intervened.

Sharman Kadish gave a shortened version of this article as a paper at 'The Future of Jewish Monuments' conference organized by the Jewish Heritage Council of the World Monuments Fund, held in New York in November 1990. This version is to be published in the conference proceedings. She is grateful to the Department of History, at Royal Holloway and Bedford New College, University of London and to the Jewish Heritage Council for their generous assistance in enabling her to attend this international gathering.

148 THE JEWISH HERITAGE IN BRITISH HISTORY

torians are still with us. Systematic records should be made and kept. Jews don't care about synagogues once the congregation drops and non-Jews don't know about them and so they are little valued. Few are mentioned in Pevsner's *Buildings of England* and fewer still are listed buildings.

So wrote architect Edward Jamilly 20 years ago in an article published in a volume to mark the centenary of the United Synagogue.[1]

The Case of the East London Synagogue

Until 1988 the East London synagogue in Stepney Green was the oldest surviving building of the United Synagogue in London.[2] It was a magnificent edifice, designed by Davis and Emanuel in 1877, only seven years after the Act of Parliament which created the United Synagogue itself (the largest synagogal organization in Britain). £2,000 was raised by the Anglo-Jewish community at large to pay for the freehold and construction of the grand 'cathedral' synagogue in Rectory Square to serve the spiritual needs of the poor, but 'respectable' Russo-Jewish immigrants in the East End. In 1927, the synagogue celebrated its Golden Jubilee and the 40 years ministry of its most famous preacher, the Revd Joseph F. Stern, who was dubbed the 'Bishop of Stepney' for his social work in East London.[3] The East London synagogue was a fine, and increasingly rare, example of high Victorian Jewish architectural style. Its cavernous interior, with seating for 600, had a strongly oriental feel. It featured intricate wood-carving, brasswork, floor mosaics and leaded stained glass, all set off against a background of rich red brick. Above the imposing *aron kodesh* was a delightful rose window. There was even an eight foot tall solid mahogany pulpit. Yet, the plain, unadorned exterior on Rectory Square hardly merited a second glance, belying the riches within.

In November 1987 the East London synagogue was sold by the United Synagogue to a firm by the name of Ridleys apparently of Enfield, for £260,000. The first the Jewish public knew about the transaction was a report in the *Jewish Chronicle* London Extra (6 November 1987). A private approach by Peter Shore MP for Tower Hamlets to the Chief Executive of the United Synagogue elicited some predictably unimaginative apologetics for his organization's policy: since the dwindling number of Jews left in the East End no longer justified the upkeep of such a large synagogue, he argued, the building

had to be sold and 'the proceeds ... partly used to refurbish and re-
equip the community centre adjacent ... so that it [could] continue to
be used both as a social centre and a small synagogue for those
members who are still living in the area' (15 December 1987).[4]

Clearly, the United Synagogue defines its functions in strictly
limited terms, as a social service serving the needs of the present-day
Jewish community. Specifically in connection with the East London,
several points may be raised in response to the United Synagogue's
posture:

(a) The East London started life as a 'deficit synagogue'[5] as an act of
    charity on the part of 'West End' Jews for the benefit of their less
    fortunate East End brethren. Lionel Louis Cohen's United Syna-
    gogue Executive of 1877 obviously was governed by wider con-
    siderations than simply balancing the books.
(b) The enormous overheads entailed in the maintenance of the
    building were, it would seem, the product of years of United
    Synagogue neglect.
(c) If the United Synagogue was genuinely concerned about the
    'spiritual viability'[6] of its East End constituents, as its claims (there
    are still about 500 paying members), then why did it not see fit to
    consult them before going ahead with the sale?

The story does not end there, however. The land upon which the
synagogue is situated is potentially worth greatly in excess of what
Ridleys paid for it. On 3 March 1988, which also happened to be
Purim, the East London synagogue was up for auction by Hillyers for
an asking price of £400,000. This was barely seven weeks after the
initial exchange of contracts (15 January 1988). There were no takers.
Attempts to start the bidding below the reserve price of £350,000 failed
to stimulate any interest in the packed auction room, with the result
that the lot had to be withdrawn.[7]

Unable to dispose of their asset on the one hand, the developers had
great difficulty in obtaining planning permission on the other. East
London synagogue is located in a designated conservation area and, at
the time of the initial sale, was a Grade 3 locally listed building. On 11
March 1988, after news of the sale became public and after the abortive
auction, it belatedly received a more comprehensive Grade 2 Department of the Environment listing. By the time English Heritage had
been alerted it was already too late to save the East London.

During the subsequent three years several different development schemes were floated for the site. Originally Ridleys claimed that they were interested in providing sheltered housing for elderly Jews – an eminently socially-acceptable solution (even if the fact that this housing would in all probability be a private development and not council subsidized was overlooked at the time).[8] Accordingly, they drew up plans for the conversion of the synagogue into 28 one-bedroom warden-controlled flats, and even held unsuccessful negotiations with housing associations in the neighbourhood. Yet, at no point did they submit a formal application to Tower Hamlets Council for the sheltered-housing scheme. This, despite the fact that at a stormy public meeting called by the Stepney Neighbourhood Committee on 20 July 1988, the vast majority of local residents indicated their preference for this solution.[9]

The Stepney Neighbourhood Committee was keen to see the building retained as 'a place of worship' and was happy to acquiesce in negotiations between Ridleys and the Bangladeshi community in East London with a view to converting the synagogue into a mosque. However, this idea ran into opposition from non-Muslim local residents who got up a petition which collected 280 signatures.[10] At the turn of the year (1989) negotiations were held with the Settlement Synagogue, the Reform and Liberal congregation based at Beaumont Grove (Stepney), to lease out the basement of the former United Synagogue for their services. However, the Progressives eventually withdrew on the grounds that the premises offered were too small to meet their needs.[11] Yet another idea, mooted behind the scenes, was to use the old *shul* as a badly needed repository for documents from the Anglo-Jewish Archives. But discussions with the Greater London Record Office did not lead anywhere.

One month prior to the above mentioned public meeting of July 1988, Ridleys submitted their first formal planning application to the Tower Hamlets Development Control Group: to convert the synagogue into eight three-bedroom luxury town houses and four one-bedroom flats. Although this scheme was thrown out by the public meeting and the developers were advised to go away and reconsider the sheltered housing project, Ridleys came back that September with a modified proposal for 24 one-bedroom flats – above an open-plan office built in the 'nave' of the synagogue.[12] This would, it was asserted, overcome the objections voiced by English Heritage to any attempt to divide up the body of the synagogue into separate units.

Tucked away in the Property News section of the *Jewish Chronicle* of 10 March 1989 was the following report:

> EAST LONDON SYNAGOGUE SCHEME RECEIVES PLANNING CONSENT: Bradley's & Eckhardt are pleased to confirm that a scheme involving the East London Synagogue has now received Planning Consent to provide approximately 10,000 sq ft of B1 office use together with ten, one bedroom residential units with their clients, Ridleys Limited, providing approximately 1,000 sq.ft. for community use. Both agents and developers are delighted that the scheme will preserve and enhance this historic building.

Delighted, maybe: the cost of the project was estimated at £1 million.[13] The subsequent withdrawal of the Reform synagogue for whose 'community use' space was put aside, meant that the developers were forced yet again to revise their plans. At the end of April 1990 the Council approved the open-plan office scheme, modified to allow for three stories of flats at the top of the building, plus the space designated earlier for 'community use' to be utilized by the authorities for some as-yet-undecided purpose under the terms of a 25-year lease. At the end of June permission was granted for the use of the 'lower ground floor' as a day centre for the elderly with accommodation set aside for a small synagogue for the remaining congregation. However, by the end of October 1990 intelligence reached the author (through the grapevine, of course) that Ridleys had gone 'bust' and were now in the hands of the receivers.[14] In September 1991 it emerged that the site had finally been sold for a knockdown price of £150,000.

Meanwhile, the East London synagogue is falling into decay: it stands forlorn and derelict, an easy prey to the elements and to vandalism. Back in the winter of 1987–88 the *shul* was systematically stripped of its beautiful fittings: most of the stained-glass windows, brass donor plates and the like. Indeed, one of the original conditions of sale was the prior removal of religious items from the premises by the United Synagogue. The pulpit was specifically mentioned in this connection. In the event, the pulpit was left behind – apparently because it was too difficult to move. It was curious then to read in the *Jewish Chronicle* of 22 April 1988 that 'thieves' – with 'heavy lifting equipment[(?)]' – had easily entered the building and simply spirited it away! The veteran president of the *shul*, and some of his members were obliged to rescue books, including *seforim*, which were strewn on the floor of the *shul*, and paintings and plaques donated in memory of departed loved ones.[15] Meanwhile the archivist from the Chief Rabbi's office had to supervise the recovery of the East London's marriage registers which had been left, contrary to statutory law, to moulder in a damp strong room. The ravages of damp have rendered some of the registers beyond repair. It has been estimated that over 20,000 marriages were solemnized at the East London synagogue in the 110 years it enjoyed the services of a marriage secretary. These records represent an invaluable source of information on East End Jewry.[16]

Ironically, the United Synagogue *was* assiduous in the removal of almost all the stained glass windows. Yet, it is a moot point whether they actually *had* the authority to remove them.[17] Doubts were raised at the outset as to whether these exceptionally beautiful and delicate windows were covered by the local authority listing, which pertained to the exterior of the building only. They were certainly removed before the DoE listing came into force in March 1988. Moreover, the United Synagogue had declared that it intended to keep the windows and other religious objects such as *sifrei Torah* in store ready for future use in a new synagogue in outer London.[18] In the meantime, the question may be asked: where are these items? Enquiries to the Jewish Museum at Woburn House reveal that they are not there. Surely such important artefacts should be made available for viewing by the Jewish public.

More shocking still, the abandoned shell of the synagogue has been the victim of at least two arson attempts. On 2 July 1988 the wooden pews inside the *shul* were set on fire by juvenile vandals and the fire brigade had to be called. On another occasion taps were deliberately turned on flooding the courtyard. Clearly, lax security means that hooligans can get in and treat the building, in the words of an indignant local resident, as an 'adventure playground'.[19] Not much discernible effort has been made to protect the synagogue. If the structure becomes irredeemably dilapidated, the validity of the listing order may well be called into question, and the way be opened for the demolition and 'development' of the highly valuable site, with the great financial dividends this would entail. This possibility can hardly have escaped the minds of the developers. I predict that such will be the final debâcle.

So the derelict East London synagogue stands as a monument to Anglo-Jewry's collective indifference to its rich cultural heritage. The United Synagogue is particularly culpable, it seems, for disposing of a building of major importance without consultation nor apparent concern for its fate. The whole affair may serve as a cautionary tale and to prove the truth of Edward Jamilly's lament of 20 years ago with which this article began. What lessons for the future may be drawn from the failure to save the East London synagogue?

The Need to Put Jewish Heritage Conservation on the Jewish Communal Agenda

The United Synagogue is the largest synagogal body in the country – with an estimated 39,000 members and (despite its present financial difficulties) undisclosed assets totalling many millions of pounds.[20] The United Synagogue, as already observed in passing, evidently sees its role in terms of providing a social service for the benefit of London's Jewish community. No one doubts that social services – education, welfare, care of the elderly – are essential functions. But, given the shift of the Jewish community from depressed inner-city neighbourhoods to suburban greener pastures, new congregations are seeking funds at the expense of the old. Pressed to satisfy social needs, the United Synagogue remains alarmingly unmoved by cultural considerations and its responsibility towards Jewish history – much of which, in the form of property, is in its own hands. Yet, in the 1960s, the United Synagogue demonstrated its willingness to spend vast sums of its taxpayers' money on building a succession of over-large and expensive synagogues in the West End and North-West London. Sadly lacking, however, was the willingness to experiment. The United Synagogue has failed to patronize innovative modern architects or avant-garde artists and craftsmen in the design of its houses of worship. The only exceptions are the Art Deco Dollis Hill and the imaginative Kingsbury synagogues. Jamilly describes this failure as 'one of the lost opportunities of Anglo-Jewish architecture'.[21] It is, one suspects, a similar lack of cultural awareness that explains the United Synagogue's failure to set any store by its architectural heritage. The East London 'affair' was one long saga of United Synagogue negligence, secretive property deals and shameless disrespect for the remnants of East End Jewry. It graphically illustrates that, as Tony Kushner has written, preserving the Jewish heritage has been a non-existent priority on the Jewish communal agenda up until now.[22]

The need for education is obvious. Those who 'run' British Jewry, not only in the United Synagogue, the Chief Rabbinate and other synagogal bodies, but also in the Board of Deputies, must be made aware of conservation as an issue of importance to the community. But changing attitudes within Anglo-Jewry is a long process. The East London experience is a warning of the urgency of the situation. Immediate rescue, not long-term reform, is the job at hand. This is where assistance from outside the Jewish community has been, and will continue to be, vital.

The Role of English Heritage[23]

To this end, it is essential that the Jewish community co-operates with the general conservation agencies, government and private, local, national and international.

Principal among these is English Heritage, which is associated with the Department of the Environment and which has the authority to advance grant aid for restoration work, to recommend sites for listing and to enforce listed building control. Listing is not entirely watertight in the legal sense; designated 'places of worship', as long as they remain places of worship, enjoy partial exemption from control – with considerable implications for synagogues as well as churches. Certainly, listing provides no insurance against fire, flood or vandalism. However, the existence of statutory controls can clearly be of great value in deterring synagogue organizations from seeking to relinquish their assets and in deterring greedy City developers from seeking to acquire them. The case of the East London synagogue is sufficient proof of this point.

Thus English Heritage can play an important role in the preservation of synagogues in Britain. As Tony Kushner has shown: there is an issue of principle at stake here. If Britain is really the multi-cultural country it is claimed to be, then national conservation organizations like English Heritage, the Royal Commission on Historical Monuments and local record offices must take some responsibility, and some initiative, in preserving the heritage of ethnic minorities as well as of the host culture.[24] Within these organizations much good-will exists; it is largely a matter of education. Other voluntary conservation bodies with experience in the field, such as the Georgian Group, the Victorian Society and the Church of England's Council for the Care of Churches are also willing to offer advice.

In 1987, no more than three synagogues in London, and an as yet undetermined number in the rest of the country, had been officially designated by the Department of the Environment as listed buildings, compared with literally hundreds of churches. One of these synagogues is Bevis Marks (1701) in the City which was modelled on the Spanish and Portuguese synagogue in Amsterdam. Bevis Marks is the only synagogue in Britain to be designated a Grade 1 monument of outstanding national importance. It is thus sobering to recall that the building was saved from almost certain destruction only through the far-sighted efforts of a group of Victorian Jewish gentlemen. In 1885 Lucien Wolf and others set up the quaintly-named Anti-Demolition League to stop the synagogue's board of management from selling its building in order to effect economies.[25] In 1928 the Royal Commission on Ancient Historical Monuments in England hailed Bevis Marks as 'a building of outstanding value ... most worthy of preservation'. Ironically, that Bevis Marks is still with us no doubt also owes not a little to the fact that it is completely surrounded and dwarfed by the huge office blocks which have transformed the Houndsditch area over the last 30 years. The average mindless vandal would need more than average initiative even to find it.

The other two synagogues on English Heritage's books back in 1987, and both listed as Grade 2 are the New West End in St Petersburgh Place, Bayswater (1878) and Dollis Hill (1938). Both are constituents of the United Synagogue and are still in use. The New West End, designed by the United Synagogue's architect Nathan S. Joseph with the assistance of W. & G. Audsley (architects of Princes Road, Liverpool, 1874), was the up-market contemporary of the East London. Built to a similar ground plan, marble and gold-leaf replace the simple brickwork used at Stepney Green, reflecting the wealth and social pretensions of its West End clientele. Dollis Hill, designed by Owen Williams, remains the only 'modern' synagogue building in Britain to be listed to date. Its innovative 'pleated' concrete walls made it worthy of inclusion in Krinsky's British selection in her *Synagogues of Europe* (1985).[26]

Thus the debacle at East London drew attention to a huge gap in English Heritage policy in relation to synagogues. Listing surveys are carried out across the country by district and not by building type. The London Division of English Heritage, for instance, deals with all types of buildings in London, and only incidentally with synagogues. Listing is carried out on an *ad hoc* basis as and when a worthy example is brought to the organization's attention. English Heritage lacks the resources to go out and look for suitable buildings to list. The other regional divisions of English Heritage operate in the same way.

Consequently no one at English Heritage can actually tell just how many synagogues throughout Britain enjoy listed status. Only in the wake of the East London affair were they even made aware of this deficiency. Andrew Saint, a colleague of Susie Barson's at the London Division, has recently conducted a brief survey of synagogues in the capital.[27] As a result, a further three synagogues have been awarded Grade 2s. Two of these are the work of Davis and Emanuel, the architects of East London; namely the Spanish and Portuguese synagogue at Lauderdale Road, Maida Vale (1896) and the socially significant as well as architecturally important West London Reform, Upper Berkeley Street (1869–70). Two other Victorian synagogues built for the United, have also received equivalent listings. The Hampstead synagogue, Dennington Park Road (1892) designed by Delissa, the son of Nathan Joseph, shares some 'progressive' features with the West London, the incorporation of the *bima* with the *aron kodesh* and the introduction of a pulpit. The New London synagogue, Abbey Road (1882) is the only survivor of H.H. Collins' eight commissions for the United Synagogue. All of Collins' buildings were closed by United Synagogue head office between 1955 and 1970 and the synagogue in St John's Wood was intended for demolition, on the removal of its congregation to larger premises in Grove End Road – which cost a hefty £400,000 to erect in 1956. The old *shul* was rescued by the New London Masorti congregation under errant Rabbi Louis Jacobs and was lovingly restored by Misha Black in 1965.

Thus some progress has been made since the end of 1987. However, it must be said that the synagogues listed so far are almost entirely Victorian 'cathedrals' designed by the clique of established architects working for the United Synagogue in the latter part of the last century. In the light of the East London, the need to protect the dwindling number of Victorian synagogues in Britain is unquestionable. Yet the choice so far reflects not only the inevitable lack of knowledge of the whole subject of Jewish buildings on the part of English Heritage, but also the unwritten rule that an important building must be *big*. To be fair, to date, two other significant Jewish buildings which do not fall into the above category, and both to be found in the humbler environs of the East End, have qualified for preservation. The first of these is the 'Dutch' synagogue Sandy's Row in Artillery Lane, Bishopsgate. In 1867, the Jewish congregation of that name moved into the building which had started life as a French chapel, a hundred years earlier (1766). In the interim, the building 'was used by a whole series of religious groups, including the French Church, the Universalist Baptists, becoming Unitarian Baptists in 1801, the Scottish Baptists and the "Salem Chapel" '.[28] The Sandy's Row synagogue is thus an interesting, and not unique, example of a religious building being recycled by different denominations or different faiths. Its chequered career does not detract from its worth as sacred monument, architecture or piece of social history. Sandy's Row's survival no doubt owes much to its proximity to the busy thoroughfares of Petticoat Lane Market and Liverpool Street Station. The *shul* is thus conveniently situated for a lunchtime *minyan* of city gents. With an architect on its Board of Management, this independent congregation is the only synagogue I am aware of which has successfully applied to English Heritage for grant aid. Unfortunately, its battle against the rising costs of repairs is by no means over.[29]

The Jewish Soup Kitchen in Brune Street, Whitechapel, was listed by the DoE in September 1989. It was designed by Lewis Solomon, who worked for both the United Synagogue and the Federation of Synagogues, in 1902. The listing of the Soup Kitchen represents the first and very welcome attempt to define Jewish monuments in Britain not simply in terms of synagogues. Even less is known about surviving Jewish schools, almshouses, *mikvos* and public baths and no criteria exist whatsoever as to whether such buildings are worthy of preservation for architectural or historical reasons. Cemeteries fall into yet another category. The shocking spate of racist attacks on Jewish burial grounds in Britain, in the wake of the outrage at Carpentras in France (May 1990) achieved national headlines. But the neglect and decay of many of our cemeteries, especially and inevitably the most historic, which have fallen into disuse in run down inner-city areas, have continued unabated for many years. The need to honour the dead and to preserve the communal memory for the living is obvious.

Such has been the commendable effects of English Heritage to date. But a great deal more still needs to be done.

What must be Done?: The Need for Research and a Proper Survey

Susie Barson writes elsewhere in this volume that 'The study of Jewish buildings is still outside mainstream architectural history'.[30] In contrast to the situation in the United States and in Central Europe, especially since the War, the subject of synagogue art and architecture has received scant attention in the academic literature in Britain.

Certainly, communal histories of individual congregations abound, but this is not true of scholarly analysis of the fabric which houses them or of the social forces which shaped their style. A search of the secondary sources yields the sum total of four serious articles written by two British architectural historians over the past forty years. (American studies, most notably Wischnitzer (1964) and Krinsky (1985) have paid some attention to synagogues in the UK.) The above quoted Edward Jamilly, a Jewish associate of the Royal Institute of British Architects, read his seminal paper on 'Anglo-Jewish Architects and Architecture in the Eighteenth and Nineteenth Centuries' before the Jewish Historical Society of England back in 1954. In 1970 his devastating attack on the philistinism of the United Synagogue went largely unnoticed.[31] Jamilly's researches have concentrated on the great cathedral synagogues built by the established post-Resettlement Jewish community before the great wave of East European immigration at the end of the nineteenth century. These include the world famous Bevis Marks; the fine provincial synagogues of the Georgian period; the parent synagogues of the Ashkenazi Union of 1870, the Great, the Hambro and the New (1838) (the latter of which is the only survivor, being essentially still with us having been rebuilt in replica in Egerton Road, Stamford Hill in 1915[32]); such curios as Sir Moses Montefiore's private house of worship at Ramsgate (1833) and the not always happy products of the United Synagogue building boom in the last 20 years of the century. Jamilly described the group of architects, mostly Jewish, Ashkenazi and in some cases related, who dominated the scene during this period: Davis and Emanuel, H.H. Collins, Edward Salomons, Nathan and his son Delissa Joseph, Lewis Solomon.[33]

After 1881 pogroms and economic distress in Eastern Europe brought a flood of refugees to Britain's shores, especially to the East End of London but also to the growing cities of the industrial North: Manchester, Leeds and Glasgow. Jamilly writes:

> The immigrants in general did not feel at home in the *Englische Shools* of the Establishment. There they found men called 'Ministers', the very name an abomination imported from the church, with shaven chins and wearing canonicals and silken scarves ... synagogues furthermore, with top-hatted officers, well-heeled congregants listening rather than praying, leaving the vocal work to cantor and choir. There can be no doubt that in

its Victorian phase, the United Synagogue succeeded in establishing itself as the church of the Anglican Jew.[34]

But the social clash between immigrant and native, East End and
West End Jewry, as reflected in synagogue architecture, is left to Judy
Glasman's work of the late 1980s. Glasman has published innovative
articles in the *Jewish Quarterly*, the *London Journal* and also in this
volume, based on material gathered for a University of London
dissertation entitled 'London Synagogues and the Jewish community
c.1870–1900' (1982). Here, the synagogal organization of East End
Jewry is explored for the first time. The immigrants brought with them
the religious practices and habits of mind of the Old Country. They
worshipped in *chevras* (societies) using *shtiebls*, converted houses or
workshops (or even rooms undergoing a temporary change of use by
the introduction of an *aron kodesh*) as their 'synagogues', in the
densely populated streets of the Jewish quarter. To the established
community, the *chevras* represented a barrier to the acculturation of
the newcomers. They perpetuated religious 'superstition', the Yiddish
language, Old Country ties of kinship and craft – not to mention
insanitary conditions. Glasman argues that the United Synagogue and,
to a lesser extent the Federation of Minor Synagogues (established in
1887), were engaged in a form of 'architectural colonization' *vis-à-vis*
the East End. The East London synagogue was the foremost example
of a self-conscious attempt by established Jewry to educate the 'better
class' of immigrant in the ways of Englishness. The spread of the
United Synagogue and Federation into the East End was no less a
means of establishing social control over the new arrivals.[35]

Jamilly's and Glasman's valuable work demonstrates just how much
more needs to be done. It also graphically highlights the enormous
physical destruction of the Jewish architectural heritage in Britain.
The majority of synagogues they describe are no longer with us. Some
were the casualties of aerial bombardment during the Second World
War. Far more have become the victims of Jewish demographic shift
and the demands of urban renewal programmes. This, incidentally, is
not a phenomenon confined to the late-twentieth-century East End of
London, Cheetham Hill (Manchester), the Leylands (Leeds) or the
Gorbals (Glasgow). A number of Georgian and early Victorian synagogues, in both London and the provinces, built on leased land, had to
give way to new roads and railways in the heyday of the industrial
revolution. Today, only two synagogues dating from the Georgian

period remain, at Exeter (recently restored) and at Plymouth. Of many early synagogues, no pictorial record survives in the form of architects' plans or contemporary illustrations; in a number of cases, even the name of the architect has been lost. There has never been any concerted effort to document the existence of Jewish congregations in a methodical way. This in itself would be a worthwhile task for the social historian. The opening of a synagogue is the most reliable guide to the pattern of growth and shift of the Jewish population.

Primary sources, especially for the last hundred years, abound. Since 1896 the *Jewish Year Book* has provided an increasingly comprehensive list of Jewish places of worship in the British Isles. The *Jewish Chronicle* often reported the opening or closure of a synagogue – sometimes with pictures. The *Illustrated London News* and other Victorian illustrated magazines[36] produced some fine engravings of the more lavish edifices, whilst the Yiddish press may provide information on their more humble counterparts. The archives of the major religious groupings within Anglo-Jewry: the United Synagogue, the Federation, the Union of Orthodox Hebrew Congregations, the Reform and Liberal synagogues, as well as specialist collections such as Anglo-Jewish Archives (now being catalogued at Southampton University), could all yield material. The Federation archives contain a valuable photograph collection of East End synagogues, many of which are now extinct. Recently, the London Museum of Jewish Life, the Manchester Jewish Museum and the Scottish Jewish Archives Centre have begun to amass photographic collections. English Heritage is enjoined to do likewise and has the resources and expertise to ensure that threatened buildings are at least recorded on film before they disappear.

The definitive history of synagogue art and architecture in Britain has yet to be written. In the meantime, however, a more modest holding operation is urgently required. Systematic documentation of extant sites and artefacts must be encouraged – a task never before undertaken in Anglo-Jewry.[37] A detailed survey of the stock of synagogue buildings must be carried out before it is too late.

Such a survey should be nationwide and not just confined to the capital. Despite the valiant efforts of Bill Williams and others who managed to rescue the Spanish and Portuguese synagogue in Manchester by turning it into the city's Jewish Museum, the North is gradually being denuded of its historic Jewish buildings.[38] The Great Synagogue in Manchester was lost in 1986, Liverpool's Princes Road

(1874) in Toxteth – scene of inner city riots – has recently been in danger of being sold to developers and Leeds is at best a disaster area. The legal status of other surviving congregations, for instance, Singer's Hill in Birmingham, (1856), Garnethill in Glasgow (1879) and the historic Bradford Reform synagogue (1880) is unknown at the time of writing. Provincial congregations, independent of the big London organizations, may get into financial difficulties and be tempted not to renew the lease, or to sell the freehold of synagogue buildings which are too large for their needs or are situated in places no longer populated by Jews. Such has been the fate of most of the remote congregations in Wales: Bangor, Tredegar, Llanelli, Merthyr, Aberdare have all gone, and the Cathedral Road synagogue in Cardiff is on the verge of obliteration.[39]

Ideally, the survey must be broad enough in scope to cover the 'moderns' as well as the Georgians and Victorians. As noted above, only one twentieth-century synagogue has been found worthy for listing so far: Dollis Hill. Other Edwardian and 1920s' and 1930s' buildings have been put at risk or have already fallen foul of the notorious instability of London Jewry. The Art Nouveau Liberal Synagogue in St John's Wood (1925) has recently been rebuilt behind the original portico to include a new community centre on the site. Lewis Solomon's 'eclectic' 1903 Stoke Newington synagogue in Shacklewell Lane has essentially been saved by its conversion into a mosque.[40] Indeed, such cases in which a building has undergone a change of function, should not be excluded from the survey. Like Sandy's Row, the strictly Orthodox Machzike Hadas in Fournier Street, E1 (1892) was originally an eighteenth-century Huguenot chapel (1743) and is now a Bangladeshi mosque. Princelet Street synagogue has, since 1983, become the Heritage Centre of Spitalfields. Acquired by a Trust Fund, the museum hosts exhibitions reflecting the immigrant history of the East End of London; the Huguenots, Irish, Jews and Indians. This is appropriate, as the synagogue (1870) was a Victorian addition to a Georgian house originally occupied by Huguenot silk weavers in 1719.[41] The curious little Egyptian folly of a *shul* at Canterbury (1848) has been bought by the local grammar school for use as a music room and concert hall. In all these cases, ingenuity has been the key to physical survival.

In conclusion, let us return to the 'moderns'. The Golders Green United synagogue (Dunstan Road 1922) by Messrs Joseph was recently rejected as a candidate for listed status by English Heritage. I would agree with this verdict as its style is not to my taste. Architectural experts such as Wischnitzer and Krinsky have found merit in such creations as Belfast, Hove, Woodside Park, Pinner, Kingsbury, Carmel College and even the 'Rolls Royce' grille at Finchley (Kinloss Gardens) – all products of the 1950s and 1960s suburban building boom. Such valuations are subjective. The question of whether or not to protect new buildings does, however, throw up the whole issue of criteria. A full-scale survey of Jewish buildings throughout the country is an essential precondition before a rational conservation policy can be arrived at. The lamentable gaps in the historical record mean that there are few criteria against which to measure the relative value of extant buildings for listing purposes. This is particularly true in the case of small-scale buildings which present definitional and methodological problems of their own. The difficulties are immense. But in the light of data gathered nationwide, it should be possible to establish priorities for preservation and to draw up guidelines for the listing of Jewish sites. Alternative uses for redundant buildings might also be considered.

Until three years ago, the premier conservation organization in the land, English Heritage, had given no systematic thought whatsoever to the question of synagogue conservation. They can hardly be blamed for the omission, given that the Jewish community has taken, until now, precious little interest in the subject. Anglo-Jewry and English Heritage, together with cognate bodies, both public and private, must share responsibility for the preservation of the Jewish architectural heritage in the British Isles.[42]

Glossary

Aron Kodesh (Heb.) 'Holy Ark', focal point of synagogue in which Scrolls of the Law are housed

Bima (Heb.) Raised platform, traditionally centrally placed, from which the Scrolls of the Law and Portions from the Prophets are read

Mikva, mikvos, mikvaot (Heb.) Ritual bath

Minyan Quorum of ten males, over the age of 13, required for collective worship

Purim Jewish festival commemorating the Book of Esther, during which children put on fancy dress and get up to all sorts of pranks

Sefer, seforim (Heb.) Holy books

Sefer Torah Sifrei Torah (Heb.) Scrolls of the Law, containing the Pentateuch

Shabbat (Heb.) The Jewish Sabbath, from sunset on Friday to nightfall on Saturday

Shool/shul (Yiddish) synagogue

NOTES

1. Edward Jamilly, 'Synagogue Art and Architecture', in Salmond S. Levin (ed.), *A Century of Anglo-Jewish Life, 1870–1970* (London, United Synagogue, 1970), pp.75–91, quote p.91.
2. Excluding the New Synagogue which is no longer *in situ* in its original location (see below p.158 and note 32).
3. There is no history of the East London synagogue. But see Aubrey Newman, *The United Synagogue* (London 1976), pp.23–4, 48, 202 and Israel Finestein, 'Joseph Frederick Stern 1865–1934: Aspects of a Gifted Anomaly', in Aubrey Newman (ed.), *The Jewish East End 1840–1939* (London, Jewish Historical Society of England cited hereafter as JHSE, 1981) and Stephen Sharot, 'Religious Change in Native Orthodoxy in London 1870–1914: The Synagogue Service', *Jewish Journal of Sociology*, Vol.15 (1973), pp.57–78.
4. A copy of this letter was passed on to Dr Kadish by Mr Shore.
5. See Newman, op. cit. p.123.
6. See note 4.
7. Hillyers catalogue, Lot 49. Dr Kadish and her husband were present at the auction. See also *Jewish Chronicle* 'London Extra' (hereafter cited as *JC*), 26 Feb., 18 March 1988. There was apparently a subsequent attempt to sell the synagogue at auction.
8. *JC*, 6 Nov. 1987.
9. *JC*, 29 July 1988. Dr Kadish and her husband were present at this meeting.
10. Ibid. and 17 June, 8 July 1988; *East London Advertiser* (*ELA*) 15, 29 July, 4 Aug. 1988. At the public meeting local residents voiced strong objections to the mosque scheme, on the grounds that it would lead to noise, parking problems, decline in the value of adjacent property and disturbance by a possible prayer call. There were no representatives of the Bangladeshi community present at the meeting.
11. *JC*, 30 Dec. 1988, 13 Jan., 3 March, 3 Nov. 1989.
12. Ibid., 18 Nov. 1988.
13. Ibid., 3 March 1989.
14. Information provided in telephone conversations between Dr Kadish and the Planning Department of Tower Hamlets Borough Council, 8 May, 5 Nov. 1990. A reliable source unwittingly provided the intelligence on the property company's current financial problems. It has been extremely difficult to get at the truth throughout the whole affair, given that little is made public until after the fact (if at all). The synagogue hall has been used as an alternative place of worship since the old building was sold and friendship club meetings are held for the benefit of elderly Jews in the neighbourhood on a regular basis. See the description in Stephen Brook, *The Club* (London, 1989), pp.259–62.
15. *JC*, 13 Jan. 1989. Fortunately the East London synagogue's Roll of Honour of First World War dead was rescued by the retired chairman of the United Synagogue Burial Society, Alf Dunitz, and was rededicated at Waltham Abbey Cemetery. See *JC*, 29 June 1990 and *Ajex Journal*, Vol.16, No.7, Parade 1990, p.7 where it is

wrongly stated that the synagogue has been demolished. Acknowledgements to Charles Tucker for the latter reference.

16. See *Inventory of the Archives of the East London Synagogue* dated Nov. 1969 in Anglo-Jewish Archives (AJ/80) where the poor state of the marriage registers is referred to. This list also alludes to other material which cannot now be traced including two important pictures which may or may not still be on the premises:

   (i) Portrait of Revd Solomon Herschel. Engraving of painting by F.D. Barlin dated 1808, and dedicated to Benjamin and Abraham Goldsmid.
   (ii) Drawing of the East London Synagogue from *The Architect*, 8 April 1876.

   See also *Jewish Tribune*, 23 July 1982, p.1 for the theft of the synagogue's Victorian Silver.

17. Except the rose window above the Ark and several windows in the children's synagogue which were subsequently smashed by vandals.

18. *JC*, 6 Nov. 1987; *ELA*, 18 Dec. 1987.

19. Ibid., 16 Sept., 30 Dec. 1988; *ELA*, 4 Aug. 1988; taps *JC*, 3 Nov. 1989.

20. See the brochure *The United Synagogue: Serving London Jewry* published to mark the 120th anniversary of the organization (Sept. 1990). Judy Glasman states: 'By 1970 [the United Synagogue] had been a major force in the building of approximately eighty-three London synagogues.' See her 'Architecture and Anglicization: London Synagogue Building 1870–1900,' *Jewish Quarterly*, Vol.34, No.2 (126) (1987), pp.16–21, quote p.16.

21. Jamilly (1970), op. cit., p.86.

22. Tony Kushner, 'Auto-Destruction: The Loss of the Jewish Heritage in the United Kingdom', *Hamaor*, Vol.25, No.2, Rosh Hashanah 5751/1990, pp.11–14.

23. See the contribution by Susie Barson, pp.166–70 below.

24. Kushner, op. cit., p.14.

25. Lucien Wolf, Origin of the JHSE (Presidential Address 15 Jan. 1912), *Transactions JHSE*, 1911–14 (London, 1915), pp.206–21; p.214 on the Anti-Demolition League; Rachel Wischnitzer, *The Architecture of the European Synagogue*, (Philadelphia, PA, 1964), p.104. Edward Jamilly informs me that the late Dr Vivian Lipman, Anglo-Jewish historian and one time Director of the Ancient Monuments and Historic Buildings Department of the DoE, tried to interest the United Synagogue in the establishment of an Advisory Committee on Jewish buildings, many years ago, but without success.

26. Carol Herselle Krinsky, *Synagogues of Europe* (London and Cambridge, MA, second revised edition, 1985), pp.419–21.

27. *Hampstead & Highgate Express*, 15 July 1988, p.21.

28. Glasman (1988) see note 35 below, p.146 citing *Survey of London*, Vol.XXVII, pp.36–7.

29. *JC*, London Extra, 6 Oct. 1989, p.1 reported that Sandy's Row received £15,696 in grant aid from English Heritage and Tower Hamlets Borough Council in 1988. See also *The Times*, 3 Nov 1990. The Historic Buildings Commission (DoE) together with the now defunct Greater Manchester Council contributed towards the repair and restoration of the city's Spanish and Portuguese synagogue which became the Jewish Museum. English Heritage, the successor of the HBC, now assists the Museum. Acknowledgements to Bill Williams.

30. See her contribution in this volume.

31. *Transactions JHSE* XVIII (1953–55), pp.127–41. Helen Rosenau's *A Short History of Jewish Art* appeared in 1948. Her more recent *Vision of the Temple* (London, 1979), deals with Britain only in passing.

32. See Jamilly (1970), op. cit., p.78 and Wischnitzer op. cit., pp.186–8 where the famous engraving by H. Melville from T.H. Shepherd, *London Interiors* (1841) is

reproduced. See also *Illustrated Times*, 8 Dec. 1855 for a later version. The future of the New Synagogue on its present site in Stamford Hill is uncertain and its omission from the ranks of synagogues listed by the DoE so far needs to be rectified urgently (Listed Grade, 3 Sept. 1991).

33. Jamilly is highly critical of what he terms the oriental 'mish-mash' of late Victorian revivalism. See his article, 'The Architecture of the Contemporary Synagogue,' in Cecil Roth (ed.), *Jewish Art* (London revised edition, 1971), pp.273–85.

34. Jamilly (1970) p.83.

35. Glasman (1987), op. cit.; 'London Synagogues in the late nineteenth century: Design in Context', *London Journal*, Vol.13, No.2 (1988), pp.143–55.

36. Some of which are reproduced in the delightful *Victorian Jews through British Eyes* edited by Anne and Roger Cowen (Oxford, 1986); see also Gina Glasman, *East End Synagogues*, a Museum of the Jewish East End (now the London Museum of Jewish Life) pamphlet (London, 1987).

37. Calls for such a survey throughout Europe were made at the end of the Second World War – but in the case of Britain were never taken up. See George K. Loukomski, *Jewish Art in European Synagogues from the Middle Ages to the Eighteenth Century* (London, 1947), p.54 and Rosenau (1948), op. cit., p.5.

38. See Tony Kushner, 'Looking Back with Nostalgia? The Jewish Museums of England', *Immigrants and Minorities*, Vol.6, No.2 (July 1987), pp.200–11. The Scottish Jewish Archives Centre, set up in 1985, is housed in the Garnethill synagogue, Glasgow which is still in use. Acknowledgements to Harvey Kaplan.

39. A fruitful source of information on the synagogues of Wales is *CAJEX*, magazine of the Association of Jewish Ex-Service Men and Women (Cardiff) founded 1950. See especially 'The Synagogues of Wales', as drawn by Olwen Hughes in *CAJEX*, Vol.XXXVIII, No.1 (March 1988), pp.36–42. Acknowledgements to Anne Yardley. The interior of the tiny Bangor synagogue was rescued and formed the centrepiece for an exhibition mounted by the Manchester Jewish Museum in 1985. It is being donated to the Welsh Folk Museum. See Kushner (1987), op. cit., p.203 and note 25.

40. Wischnitzer, op. cit., pp.220–21 on Stoke Newington. On the Liberal Jewish Synagogue, see *Stone Industries*, Vol.26, No.4 (May 1991), cover and p.33. A similar case to that of St John's Wood, although of later date, is that of Ernst Freud's London Jewish Hospital synagogue (1958). Wischnitzer's praise for this tiny bijou *shul* did not prevent its demolition in the early 1980s when the hospital site was acquired for development as a private clinic. This took place in the teeth of local Jewish opposition. A petition was mounted against the closure of a public facility which had been opened after the First World War as a result of voluntary donations by the Jewish poor. See G.D. Black, 'Health and Medical Care of the Jewish Poor in the East End of London 1880–1939', unpublished Ph.D., University of Leicester, 1987.

41. On Canterbury see *Church Building* (Whitsun, 1985), p.75 On Princelet Street, see *The History of 17–19 Princelet Street* available from the Heritage Centre, Spitalfields, London E1 6QH, and Samuel Melnick, 'Living Heritage: The Princelet Street Project', *Hamaor*, Vol.26, No.2 (Rosh Hashanah, 1991), pp.16–17.

42. See Sharman Kadish, 'Anglo Jewish Heritage is Under Threat' (Rosh Hashanah 5752/1991), 15 Feb. 1991, p.21; 'Disused Synagogue a Monumental Disaster', ibid., 11 Oct. 1991, p.15.

English Heritage, Statutory Control and Jewish Buildings

SUSIE BARSON

English Heritage was created in 1984 to take over historic buildings and monuments responsibilities of the Department of the Environment. It has direct responsibility for almost 400 historic sites and monuments in England, including Stonehenge and Hadrian's Wall. English Heritage advises the government on all conservation issues, and exercises special statutory powers in London. The annual grant budget is around £30 million. This article explains the role of English Heritage in the conservation of Jewish buildings, particularly synagogues, through listing and grant aid.

English Heritage was set up by the Conservative government in 1984 as a 'QUANGO' directly responsible to the Secretary of State for the Environment. Taken out of the Department of the Environment (DoE), to which it is still indirectly linked, English Heritage was to be the main national body concerned with the care and protection of English historic buildings and ancient monuments.

There are effectively three ways in which English Heritage can take positive steps in carrying out its responsibility for protecting buildings of historic or architectural importance: through the listing procedure and listed building control, through giving advice (even when a building is not subject to listed building control), and finally by offering grant aid towards the cost of urgent structural repairs. I will expand on these measures in turn, and consider their particular relevance to synagogues, the most important specifically Jewish building type.

Listing: Statutory lists were begun by the Ministry of Works, predecessor of the DoE, just after the Second World War. Today English Heritage compiles the lists which are issued by the DoE in the name of the Secretary of State. The list contains buildings and structures of all periods and types, giving a brief description and grading them I, II* or II. The premise that the older the building, the rarer it is therefore the more valuable, guides the principles of selection in listing. Buildings that qualify are all those before 1700 which survive in anything like their original condition; most between 1700 and 1840, though selected; after 1840, the best examples only are considered. Buildings of exceptional interest (less than five per cent of the total) are listed grade I, those of particular importance given II*, but most buildings are grade II. In the official wording, these grade II buildings are 'of special interest, which warrant every effort being made to preserve them'.

Listing surveys are carried out across the country by district, not by building type. Consequently, in the absence of an overall study or survey on the nation's stock of synagogues or specifically Jewish buildings, listing is ad hoc and the total number listed is still unknown. In the London Division, my colleague Andrew Saint looked into the position on synagogues and found that only five were listed. A brief survey added another five purpose-built synagogues to the list, bringing the total to ten, mostly nineteenth century, all listed grade II. Specific policy guidelines on the listing of synagogues are currently being formulated for the benefit of those revising older lists. I understand that it is hoped to extend this exercise into a broader study of the historical development of synagogue buildings in England, but whether this will ever materialize I cannot honestly say: clearly it is something where the assistance of the Jewish community will be vital.

Once a building is listed (here I mean a secular building), alterations to the exterior or interior can only legally be carried out with listed building consent, granted by the local authority or District Council. In London, English Heritage has the veto power to direct the local authority to refuse listed building consent; in the rest of the country our role is only advisory. We are consulted as a matter of course about all proposals affecting grade I and II* buildings and about the proposed demolition of grade II buildings. Listed building consent is in theory only granted if the proposals do not adversely affect the character of the building.

Listed Building Control: A synagogue may be listed for its architectural or historic interest, but like Church of England churches, Roman Catholic churches, non-conformist chapels, Quaker meeting houses etc. it is classed as a 'place of worship' and therefore enjoys 'ecclesiastical exemption' from listed building control. This means in practice that consent is not required for interior alterations, or for partial demolition as long as part of the building continues to be used as a place of worship. Conditions for ecclesiastical exemption are set out most usefully in the government circular on conservation law, 8/87 paragraph 103–5.

Not surprisingly, there is considerable opposition to the exemption, most conspicuously from the national amenity societies, but also from English Heritage. Apparently some rethinking by the DoE is currently going on which may narrow the scope of the exemption, making it more difficult, for example, to remove external features such as towers, spires or domes. But the interior would remain vulnerable, which has worrying implications for buildings like synagogues or nonconformist chapels where the interior is often of more interest than the comparatively modest exterior.

There is a limited safeguard against unsuitable development which affects the site of a place or worship listed grade I or II*. Where development requires planning permission, extensions for example, the Local Authority must seek the advice of English Heritage. It is not, however, bound by law to take advice which may be given.

Grant Aid: There are two types of grants available from English Heritage: Section 3A grants are given towards the cost of urgent structural repairs on buildings deemed to be of outstanding architectural or historic importance. The grants are usually 40 per cent of the cost of the eligible works and can run into tens or even hundreds of thousands of pounds. The award of such grants is based on a rigorous assessment of the 'specialness' or 'outstandingness' of the building. Age, rarity, historical importance and architectural quality are all taken into account. English Heritage will also take into account the congregation's own resources before making an offer. 'Section 77' grants, usually much smaller sums, are given for external works on buildings of interest in some conservation areas. 'London grants' are also available to help restore a particular feature of interest such as railings or stained glass in buildings in the Greater London area.

Grant aid is usually given on conditions, of which perhaps the most significant is that 'no works of addition, alteration or redecoration' will be carried out subsequently without English Heritage approval. These conditions can deter congregations from applying because they do not wish to be beholden to English Heritage in the future. I think such fears are mostly groundless, and should not prevent an application for grant – the building may then suffer on two counts: no grant money, and no outside vigilance on alterations.

The Church of England already has a fairly rigorous system for keeping a check on works done to its buildings through what is known as the 'faculty' procedure. Indeed this is the original justification for the ecclesiastical exemption, and this system undoubtedly helps Anglican churches in their dealings with English Heritage (because many of the limitations are the same and the idea of outside control, though irksome, is not unfamiliar). Most of the 3A grants for places of worship are made to the Church of England, and this will always be the case because of the huge number of mediaeval and Victorian churches, but English Heritage is keen to redress the balance with other denominations as far as is possible with the money available. The difficulty is that we do not have the staff or the time to take the initiative and seek out deserving recipients for aid, and must for the most part deal only with those who apply.

What more can be done? Clearly there are shortcomings in the present system of caring for historic religious buildings of all denominations, in terms of both listing and grant-aid. Nevertheless there are some measures that can be taken to help preserve the buildings in the face of less-than-perfect legislation. Applying for grant aid is the most obvious. It would also be extremely helpful if a list was compiled of listed synagogues, and also those worth listing, and sent to our Chief Inspector's Branch at Fortress House (which scrutinises listing proposals), so that there could be a basis for informed decisions affecting historic synagogues.[1]

Local authorities are often less than vigilant when it comes to listed building control over places of worship, and need to be watched to see how they respond to applications – whether or not English Heritage advice is taken into account. By joining voices with amenity societies such as the Victorian Society, Georgian Group, and Thirties Society, or by protesting directly to Local Authorities or even to English Heritage, public opinion can alter the outcome of unpopular proposals, as Local Authorities have the power to withhold planning permission, and may be persuaded to do so. Another point to remember is that when a listed religious building ceases to be used regularly for worship, it is no longer enjoys ecclesiastical exemption, and like a secular building, is subject to listed building control. Finally, it is clearly helpful to know the intentions of the owners; the United

Synagogue itself could be approached directly on controversial proposals before they take action. Unfortunately it is impossible to stop
people destroying a building if they are determined (for whatever
reason) to do so, as was the case with the East London Synagogue.

I feel sure that the more that is known about Jewish buildings,
synagogues, meeting halls, soup kitchens, etc., the more they will be
valued. The study of Jewish buildings is still outside mainstream
architectural history. It is therefore with help from the Jewish community, as well as with constructive criticism, that bodies such as
English Heritage, and presumably equivalents in other countries, can
more effectively save the buildings. You are the experts and
specialists; we need your knowledge and commitment.[2]

NOTES

1. Such a list has now been complied (November 1991).
2. A Working Party on Jewish Monuments has now been set up by Dr Sharman Kadish;
   Susie Barson represents English Heritage at the meetings.

Assimilation by Design: London Synagogues in the Nineteenth Century

JUDY GLASMAN

Nineteenth-century synagogues are discussed in relation to Anglo-Jewish and immigrant Jewish socio-economic characteristics and the operations of specific organizations. A variety of buildings are examined, including the purpose-built 'West End' type, the converted chapel and the smaller, less easily researched, workshop-type room. Material and ideological forces are shown to be at work, with assimilation achieved through design and education within a politically threatening context.

Few synagogues have found their way into the standard texts of architectural history. Late-nineteenth-century synagogal buildings, accused of 'aesthetic failure',[1] have received only cursory attention.[2] Historical surveys have typically concentrated on summarizing the essential style and characteristic plan of any period broadly in relation to the degree of freedom/restriction within which Jewish communities operated. In addition there has been an assumption in existing literature of an increasingly emancipated Jewish social position, where collective progress marches forward to a goal of political, religious and civic equality. Between the 'ghetto' synagogue and the 'emancipated' synagogue lies the perceived indecision of the Victorian period.[3] More recently the 'modern' synagogue building is interpreted as making a 'genuinely' Jewish statement.

Histories of Anglo-Jewry, however, do not substantiate these views. V.D. Lipman's article 'Synagogal Organisation in Anglo-Jewry'[4] has shown that far from developing in social isolation, the change in synagogal constitutions, from oligarchy to democracy between 1845 and 1890, resembled contemporary English institutions such as municipal corporations or parish vestries. Furthermore, Lipman and others[5] discuss the essential diversity of the London Jewish population towards the end of the last century.

This essay attempts to close the gap between methodologies of architectural history and general history. It concentrates less on the aesthetics and more on contexts, including that of institutions at work. Such a focus brings into centre-stage smaller synagogues and the architecture of religious buildings which have often been bypassed as insignificant.

In 1850 there were about 18,000–20,000 Jews in London, out of roughly 35,000 in Britain as a whole.[6] 1881–82 and 1891–92 were peak periods of emigration from Russia and Poland due to political crisis and the deteriorating economic position in Eastern Europe. Estimates of immigrants arriving in London between 1881 and 1888 were calculated at between 20,000 and 30,000, and from 1890 and 1902, 50,000 and 60,000. These immigrants, clustered within a small area, were highly visible and differentiated at a time when longer established generations of Anglo-Jewry were reaching legal and political parity. In 1891 an Association for Preventing the Immigration of Destitute Aliens had been set up under the auspices of the Earl of Dunraven and Arnold White. The Conservative government was committed to an Aliens Bill as an election gambit. The Jewish worker was blamed for sweating, unemployment and a general lowering of wages. In response to this pressure Anglo-Jewry undertook a programme of anglicisation. Improvement took the form of a three pronged attack; model dwellings would replace slum housing; Hebrew classes would be substituted by schools and, lastly, small religious groups meeting in private dwellings would be superseded by large scale synagogues.

It must be stressed that synagogues[7] built between 1870 and 1900 were far from being isolated 'art products', resulting from an agreement between a single architect and the local congregation. Instead such buildings were generally only approved where there was an obvious overlap between local needs and the protection of metropolitan Jewish status. Throughout this period the United Synagogue, the union of large London congregations of Central and Eastern European origins, encouraged and ensured the building of synagogues in a certain form. Within this contractual relationship, the function of design was just as much a part of the local congregation's dependence on, and integration into, the Anglo-Jewish body as was, for example, the control of ritual.

In the East End, immigrant working-class and lower middle-class religious buildings did not come within the United Synagogue fostered tradition, which was one of large custom-built design. Instead, they used converted or extended buildings, occupied by small groups centred around country of origin, type of employment or religious faction. This form of religious worship was not just a temporary measure resulting from lack of money, where large scale worship in the United Synagogue type would have been preferred if available, but was in fact a necessary part of immigrant society. The *chevrot*[7a] came to be seen as a direct threat to the stability of the native Jewish population. Through the United Synagogue the latter allowed a number of compromises in building policy, which would promote the 'West End' church-like synagogue type, thereby suppressing *shtiebl*[7b] worship. It was hoped that by the building of these synagogues, the immigrant Jews (who were the subject of an increasingly anti-alien and anti-Semitic campaign) would be enticed out of the congested East End areas – particularly of Whitechapel and Spitalfields. The assumption was made that design could effect social, religious and behavioural change.

The large synagogue building itself was regarded as a tool of anglicization. With the abandonment of previously rigidly maintained regulations, the 'Colossal Synagogue' Scheme of 1890 represented a peak in the efforts by the Anglo-Jewish establishment to bring about the integration and 'uplift' of the alien Jew. The Federation of Synagogues, set up by Samuel Montagu in 1887 for immigrant Jews, continued to pursue these aims, although using slightly different means. The enforcement of sanitary regulations provided an excuse for widespread intervention and, by limiting the allocation of building funds to proposed 'model' buildings, synagogue provision and design were tightly controlled. The source and control of material means proved to be vital determinants of design.

II

The United Synagogue Act of Foundation of 1870 defined constituent status for local congregations. The building of synagogues by these congregations took place within a relationship which was characterized by sound commercialism and a detailed financial agreement. Shortly after the Foundation the qualifications of entry to constituent status had evolved into a standardized format, developed partly through experience and partly on lines of principle. It is within a defined spread of local and central control that the responsibility for building finance and the function of design were carried out. By 1970 it was estimated that this system had resulted in the building of some 83 synagogues.

A critique of the United Synagogue appears in Israel Zangwill's classic novel of immigrant life, *Children of the Ghetto*:

> I have always maintained (said Sidney Graham) that the United Synagogue could be run as a joint stock company for the sake of a dividend and that there wouldn't be an atom of difference in the discussion if the councillors were directors. I do believe the pillars of the community figure the Millenium as a time when every Jew shall have enough to eat, a place to worship in and a place to be buried in. Their state church is simply a financial system to which the doctrines of Judaism just happened to be tacked on.[8]

The United Synagogue building programme was a corporate enterprise and through an understanding of the workings of this institution, aspects such as building design, style and location can be explained. The United Synagogues Act and Deed of Foundation recognized five constituent synagogues as making up the Union. These were the Great Synagogue, the Portland Street Branch Synagogue (also known as Central Synagogue; see illustration 2), the Hambro Synagogue, The New Synagogue and the Bayswater Synagogue. By 1905, nine further synagogues had been built. These were St John's Wood, East London, New West End, Dalston, Hammersmith, Hampstead, Hackney, Stoke Newington and Brondesbury. They were funded under Clause 5 of the Act of Foundation which specified 'the maintaining, erecting and founding, and carrying on in London and its neighbourhood, places of worship for persons of the Jewish religion who conform to the Polish or German ritual'.[9]

Other provisions included places of burial, poor relief and maintaining a chief rabbi. The structure of local synagogue boards of management and central management arrangements were all laid down. Buildings, burial grounds and any other land were to be kept and used as the United Synagogue Council directed. Income from funds belonging to the Great, Hambro and New Synagogues was to be used for a building and repair fund.

The dates of foundation of suburban synagogues provide a realistic guide to Jewish demographic change. Synagogue provision followed the move into the suburbs, often accompanied by social mobility. This

Illustration 1: Interior of the Central Synagogue
Source: The Builder, 6 Nov. 1869.

was described by the Reverend J.A. Gouldstein discussing his congregation at the North London Synagogue:

> the people are practically all middle-class. They suffer from movement to Hampstead where fashion is now taking the Jews. In earlier years North London was more habitually the first place for Jews to move to from East London, some moving on North West or West afterwards, the North was called 'the filter, because of all the impurities left behind' ... At the present time they very often skip the North and go straight to Hampstead or wherever else they are bound for. It is all a question of fashion, and whereas Bayswater used to be the fashion, the Jews now go to Hampstead, Kilburn, Cricklewood etc. but they always go where gentile fashion leads.[10]

There were similarities between congregations applying for building loans. Most had some kind of temporary provision and were collecting money towards a permanent structure and were usually linked to the United Synagogue by membership of the Burial Society. However, the United Synagogue was only prepared to satisfy a well-organized demand. Criteria for membership was strict – immediate need and future increase had to be demonstrated. Financial security and commitment to long term building maintenance as well as prompt voluntary donation were necessary. The new congregation had to find a geographical location in harmony with the whole metropolitan spread of synagogues – without infringing the local 'trading rights' of any nearby synagogue. Even if an application fulfilled these rules, the congregation had to be of a certain size and was rejected even if a small efficiently run building was quite within their capabilities. The United Synagogue fostered the creation of large synagogues, small buildings were not thought to be economically viable. In addition these synagogues were to be established 'for the honour of the Jewish Community, [and] for the stability of the Jewish religion'.[11]

Often, once the parent body had agreed to loan money and allow the issue of debentures, the congregations were encouraged to erect a larger building than they needed at the time. Thus provision for building extension was an integral part of the design brief. The Council and Executive Committee showed an awareness that synagogue building encouraged suburban settlement, and the planning of synagogues was to some extent a deliberate operation of social and geographical engineering.

Current and potential congregants were carefully enumerated. For example in the case of Dalston, the United Synagogue Committee had

> every hope that the endeavours of the Gentlemen who are promoting the erection of a permanent synagogue at Dalston will be successful; their congregation appears to possess the elements of stability and of increase, while the regular attendance of the worshippers at Divine Service in the present temporary and inconvenient structure affords evidence of strong religious attachment to their synagogue.[12]

The congregation had to be seen to be able to maintain loan repayments and collect donations. The donation of money for building was a very public act. Lists of donations for buildings or charity were constantly published in the *Jewish Chronicle*. The principle of voluntary donation supplemented by central loan developed into the two-thirds rule; that is, when two-thirds of the necessary finance had been collected voluntarily, the United Synagogue would provide the last third of the cost. When the Dalston Committee proposed a larger fraction in 1876, they were told:

> In the case of other synagogues, the public subscriptions have usually amounted to two-thirds of the cost of site and building and the communal funds have not been trenched on to something like a third of the cost. These proportions, in the case of the projected synagogue, are reversed, and stand in marked contrast to what was done in the case of the Bayswater, Central and the East London Synagogues, and what is proposed to be done in the case of Nottinghill and St. John's Wood.[13]

It was the aim of the conditions laid down that the synagogue should open free from debt and thereafter be able to concentrate on paying interest on debentures, repayments on the Building Fund loan and collecting communal taxes. Part of the protection of synagogues' economies was achieved by careful geographical placement almost amounting to a definition of a synagogal parish, with synagogues approximately two miles apart. Brondesbury was concerned not to encroach on St John's Wood and Hampstead. Hampstead agreed not to poach the members of St John's Wood.

Although the conditions of association were stringent, they were

178   THE JEWISH HERITAGE IN BRITISH HISTORY

also sensible. If congregations had not become Constituents the possibilities of building their own synagogues would have been greatly lessened and, if possible at all, would have been a long and arduous affair. Advantages included security of existence, ideological unity and donations from community leaders. The United Synagogue, however, became sole legal owner of site and building, controlling budget, rates of pay, design and repair, personnel and ritual. Decorous worship was encouraged, which generally meant using the synagogue less as a meeting place and more as a place solely for religious worship. Such a model was presented as a contrast to East European practice. Discipline during religious service was considered a measure of anglicization, likened to church practices. Moreover, synagogue design was to endorse the perceived need for decorum.

The buildings of this period were all designed by a handful of Jewish architects who were, as a rule, active in communal affairs. N.S. Joseph (1832–1909) was Architect and Surveyor to the United Synagogue. He was deeply involved in almost every aspect of the institution, being Chairman of the Conjoint Committee of the Russo-Jewish Committee and the Board of Guardians and Chairman of the Sanitary Committee of the Board of Guardians. He designed the Central Synagogue (1870), and participated in the designs for Bayswater (1863), the New West End (1878) and Dalston (1885), and was architect to the Guinness Trust and to the Four Per Cent Industrial Dwellings Company. Delissa Joseph designed Hampstead (1892), Hammersmith (1890), Finsbury Park and South Hackney (1897). H.H. Collins (1833–1905) designed North London, Barnsbury (1868), the Borough New, Walworth (1867) and St John's Wood, Abbey Road (1888). Lewis Solomons (1848–1928), Honorary Architect to the Federation of Synagogues, eventually superceded N.S. Joseph in 1904 at the United Synagogue and designed the new Hambro in Whitechapel (1891) and Stoke Newington (1903). Other architects associated with synagogue buildings were Messrs Davis (1838–1915) and Emanuel (1841–1904) and E. Salomon. All these architects were Jews, most of them actual congregants, sometimes of the synagogues that were being built. Many of them were part of, or intimately connected with, the Anglo-Jewish establishment.[14]

At the United Synagogue the job of Architect-Surveyor was laid down.

He shall report to the Building Committee and advise generally on all works and repairs to be carried out ... With reference to new synagogues to be erected by other Architects, he shall report to the Building Committee as to accommodation, convenience of planning, and sufficiency of exits, also as to probable outlay both for construction and maintenance of the fabrics, and whether their erections is likely to involve litigation. He shall also peruse the specifications, chiefly in relation to the permanent nature of the materials employed, and make generally such suggestions, both on the plans and specifications, as may seem to him desirable in the interests of the United Synagogue as paramount owner.[15]

It seems reasonable to speculate that a series of formal and informal measures, including the employment of a handful of known and intimately connected architects, reinforced the adoption of a standardised plan type and accommodation provided in late nineteenth-century synagogue design.

Certain aspects of design were centrally enforced. The main concerns were provision of seating in the body and gallery of the synagogue, which affected synagogue income. Poorly arranged seats were notoriously difficult to let and much attention was paid to seeing and hearing religious proceedings. This was probably also due to the assimilation of design to church practice; previously, for example, the view from the women's section had been considered unimportant. A Committee Room was usually provided, and circulation and placement of staircases standardized. Towards the end of the century, classrooms in the synagogue appropriated the function of religious education from the unqualified foreign teachers, or provided teaching accommodation where none existed in suburban areas.

The usual design type adopted was a rectangular ground plan orientated as far as possible to the east with galleries for women on the north, west and south walls. The main entrance was usually at the west end with entry into a vestibule and staircases at the north-west and south-west corners. Considerations of overall effect were mainly discussed in connection with the largest and more expensive buildings. Gothic invention outshone previous modest Italianate designs when a group from Bayswater synagogue, seeking to house the overflow of people, financed the New West End as (see illustration 2) a copy of the Liverpool Synagogue built two years earlier in 1874 by Messrs. W. and G. Audsley. The same architects were employed and N.S. Joseph also brought in. Liverpool had been a deliberate departure from previous synagogue design, interestingly employed first by a provincial congregation. 'The Mooresque style which has almost universally been adopted for the modern synagogues, is in this building entirely absent, the architects believing that the Mooresque is both unsuggestive and inappropriate for a Jewish place of worship.'[16] The justification of interior and exterior design was that it had been selected 'with the sole view of producing a pleasing composition, with enough of the Eastern feeling to render it suggestive and enough of the Western severity to make it appropriate for a street building in an English town'.[17]

III

Anglo-Jewish 'West End' establishments and their practices contrast with arrangements in London's East End, occupied by the most recent immigrants. East End religious organizations can be roughly divided into two groups. First, the medium-sized congregations relatively well defined, worshipping most frequently in converted building previously used by other denominational groups, such as chapels or Mission Halls. Secondly, those practising on a small scale in *minyan*[18] rooms or *shtiebls* probably converted or extended houses or workshops, or a room undergoing a temporary change of function by the setting up of a piece of furniture to be used as an Ark. Some of the constitutents of the second group present a seemingly insoluble problem for historical and architectural analysis. The problem is the result of inaccessibility through lack of complete documentation, made worse by architectural history's focus on new, purpose-built and consciously-designed buildings. Yet the use of building conversion, housing immigrant religio-social organizations was a highly emotive subject for the Jewish community of the 1880s onwards. It is only by acknowledging the importance of the small converted negligibly-documented *shtiebls* of the East End, that the degree of vehement insistence on the West End United Synagogue building type and their tight design control over synagogue projects becomes understandable.

The Jewish Directory of 1874[19] includes the three City synagogues which were part of the 1870 Act of Union. These were the Great Synagogue (Aldgate); the Hambro (Fenchurch Street) and the New (Great St Helen's). These synagogues, and particularly the Great, were occasionally used by East End inhabitants. Of the other East

Illustration 2: Exterior of the New West End Synagogue
Source: The Builder, 27 July, 1878

London synagogues included in the Directory three were founded in the eighteenth century – Prescott Street (founded 1748 seating 100), Scarborough Street (founded 1792 seating 262) and the Polish synagogue, Carter Street (founded c.1790). Six congregations had been established in the mid-nineteenth century – the German Synagogue (1858), Sandy's Row (1851), Princes Street (1870 seating 270), Fashion Street (1858), White's Row (1860 seating 160) and the 'Lovers of Peace' Society, Tewksbury Buildings (1863). These existed before the larger immigrant influx of the last 20 years of the nineteenth century and were mainly made up of earlier Dutch and German immigrants of the later eighteenth century and first half of the nineteenth century. Nonconformist places of worship, previously supported by the lower middle and tradesmen classes were often taken over by these congregations. Chapel conversions were not only freely available in the East End, as their users had moved elsewhere, but also the character of the building was sympathetic to synagogue conversion. Charles Booth whilst commenting acidly in *Life and Labour of the People in London* on the undemonstrative appearance of Nonconformist places or worship also, indirectly, highlighted their suitability as potential synagogues

> There is about the doctrines and practices of the Baptists a sternness which no other religious body exhibits ... Their buildings are entirely without religious sentiment or architectural charm of any kind. It is enough if the hall is so shaped and the seats are so arranged that everyone can see and hear the preacher.[20]

The Sandy's Row Synagogue was one of the largest independent congregations in the East End. A *Jewish Chronicle* report of 20 May 1881 placed its membership at 420, income at £517 and expenditure at £464.[21] Started by a small group of Dutch working men, its objects were somewhat analagous to those of an ordinary Friendly society – benefits granted during periods of mourning and payment for the necessary prayers.[22] In 1867 they moved into a French chapel in Artillery St, Bishopsgate, purchasing a short lease and converting the building into a synagogue. In 1870 the congregation obtained a new lease for 21 years with the option to perpetually renew it on the condition that the building was thoroughly repaired. It was resolved at this stage to establish a regular synagogue. The building is of rectangular plan

48' x 36' with a gallery extending round the north, south and west sides reached by open staircases in the north-west and south-west angles. Between its opening in 1766, and occupation by Dutch Jews in 1867, it was used by a whole series of religious groups including the French Church, the universalist Baptists becoming Unitarian Baptists in 1801, the Scottish Baptists and the 'Salem Chapel'.[23] With the purchase of the new lease the original entrance from a narrow passageway, in Parliament Court, was closed and a new entrance opened in Sandy's Row. The plans were prepared by N.S. Joseph, the £1,100 cost was paid for partly by subscription and partly by a loan from the builders, annual repayments of £70 being paid.[24] The new entrance ensured an easterly orientation.

From the surviving evidence it is clear that while other denominations practised either in the small-scale dissenting mode or imitated the state church model, Jews practised in both ways. This was partly the result of staggered immigration over a period of two-and-a-half centuries which meant that recently-arrived immigrants adopted dissenting building habits. In contrast, those of longer residence, while initially worshipping in this way, had graduated or assimilated to a building use analagous to the more permanent state church model.

There is also an important connection between general East End building activity and methods of synagogue building. In East End streets, spaces left by loosely arranged housing built earlier in the century had all been filled in by small cottage properties. Open spaces consisted only of a few churchyards and old burial grounds. Such increases in density included the building of small houses back-to-back and building workshops at the back of housing and therefore mitigated the need for new independent approaches. The *chevra* at 35 Fieldgate Street was said to have been 'approach[ed] through a somewhat dingy passage, and is built in the same way as many workshops in the locality on what was originally an open space at the back of the house. There are between 80 and 90 seats for males and no provision for female.'[25]

A similar arrangement was made in Princes St, where a synagogue was built at the back of house number 19. In the East End strict division of function between the workplace and the dwelling place was not made. Unsurprisingly, both in terms of spaces for worship and spaces for work, the poorest people made do with a temporary conversion of an area with a different function; mainly rooms in houses. Less poor congregations and more substantial employers could afford to engage special premises for praying and working.

Descriptions of the interiors of spaces used for worship are rare. Beatrice Webb gave some indication of interior appearance and atmosphere:

> it is a curious and touching sight to enter one of the poorer and more wretched of these places (chevrot) on a sabbath morning. Probably the one you will choose will be situated in a small alley or narrow court, or it may be built out in a back yard. To reach the entrance you stumble over broken pavement and household debris; possibly you pick your way over the rickety bridge connecting it with the cottage property fronting the street. From the outside it appears a long wooden building surmounted by a skylight, very similar in construction to the ordinary sweater's workshop. You enter; the heat and odour convince you that the skylight is not used for ventilation. From behind the trellis of the 'ladies gallery' you see at the far end of the room the richly curtained Ark of the covenant, wherein are laid, attired in gorgeous vestments, the sacred scrolls of the law.[26]

The provision for women here was on the same level as the men. The 'gallery' in the synagogue visited by Zangwill's heroine is somewhat different.

> ... she crossed the threshold of a large chevra she had known in her girlhood, mounted the stairs and entered the female compartment without hostile challenge ... This room had no connection with the men's; it was simply the room above part of theirs and the declaration of the unknown cantor came but faintly through the flooring; though the clamour of the general masculine chorus kept the pious *au courant* with their husbands. When weather or the minds of the more important ladies permitted, the window at the end was opened; it gave upon a little balcony below which the men's chamber projected considerably, having been built out into the backyard. When this window was opened simultaneously with the skylight in the men's synagogue, the fervid roulades of the cantor were as audible to the women as to their masters.[27]

Other reports indicate how rooms in houses were used. Harry Blacker, in his East End autobiography reveals how a small congregation was not only made up of members of one family but also members of the same economic group.

> Any room large enough to hold ten men or more was established as a synagogue ... Uncle Charlie was my great uncle ... like my father he was a cabinet maker ... Because of his large family, Charlie rented a complete house. The front room, ground floor was used as a synagogue on the Sabbath. A portable beautifully made wardrobe served as an ark for the solitary scroll it housed. On a shelf beneath it, the prayer books and Pentateuchs were stored, so that the sin of carrying on the Sabbath could be avoided. Every Saturday without exception at least fourteen men would assemble for the service, Uncle Charlie providing five of them as well as leading the prayers ... The service itself was simple, Uncle Charlie stood on a high desk facing the ark, and in the traditional sing-song voice, led us through the intricacies of the Sabbath prayers ... Before the concluding prayers and following the reading of a weekly portion of the Torah, and impromptu sermon would be delivered by a visiting learned man. This was invariably in Yiddish, besprinkled with Hebrew quotations and English grace notes.[28]

The nature of the service in the *chevra* was different from that of the United Synagogue and it was incomprehensible to Anglo-Jewry. An essay written by a university graduate (an assimilated Jew, H.S. Lewis), for the Toynbee Trustees explained that 'East End synagogues are perhaps not calculated to impress favourably a casual visitor to whom the whole service is unintelligible. There is no decorum and during parts of the service there is much talking and noisy movement ... a devotion full of self-abandonment.'[29] The *chevrot* functioned within the socio-economic organization of the East End. A majority of East End Jews found employment in the tailoring, boot-making and cabinet-making trades. Generally this work was carried out in small workshops either attached to a house or in converted rooms. What was known as the 'Jewish method of production' involved a team of workers with highly specialized jobs and miniscule differences between wages. Small masters often earned less than their employees. Such small-scale production was easily set up and apparently just as easily liable to fail. Within these unstable conditions the *chevrot* provided some slight insurance and additional social support for the worker. Beatrice Webb described the *chevrot* as 'self-creating, self-supporting and self-governing communities'[30] and while the workshop was of course dependent on the larger economy, to some extent her adjectives are applicable in this context. Certainly the *chevrot* complemented the working of the economic unit.

The congregation of one synagogue might be made up of members of the same trade; for example, at 21 Cheshire Street, cabinet-makers had fitted out their own synagogue for the United Workmen's Congregation.[31] More often the *chevra* was made up of *'landsmann'*, people from the same town, area or country. Polish or Russian *chevrot* were generally named after the town or district from which they emigrated, such as the *'Kalisher'*, *'Crawcour'* or *'Plotskar'* societies. The master of the workshop was likely to give preference of employment to his *'landsmann'*.[32]

These *chevrot* looked away from the British Chief Rabbi, the so-called 'West End Goy', and back to eminent rabbinic figures in Eastern Europe for adjudications according to Jewish law. These figures concentrated on the traditional responsibilities of scholar, communal arbiter and advanced teacher. In fact from 1893 to 1912 East End orthodox Jews looked to the authority of the schismatic *Machzike Hadath* religious leader Rabbi Werner. The question then is posed as to how these small autonomous *chevrot* financed any building. The smaller ones obviously did not build; they extended existing buildings themselves. Those who were slightly more ambitious paid off loans from the builders over long periods and may have been donated money.

Perhaps one of the most interesting conversions was the Spitalfields Great Synagogue (see illustrations 3 and 4) which occupied the Neuve Eglise, Fournier Street originally constructed in the 1740s. In March 1897 the Executive Committee of the Talmud Torah classes agreed with the trustees of the French Church to take a lease of the chapel, which they did in 1898. The leasees were said to have put a new roof on it. This was to provide 12 additional classrooms above the synagogue which was subleased by the *Talmud Torah* to the *Machzike Hadath* Community (Defenders of the Faith). The chapel interior was reconstructed by Maple and Company at a cost of £4,500. The interior was a rectangular plan measuring 80 feet from east to west and 54 feet from north to south, with a gallery on the south, east and west sides reached by open staircases inside the south-east and south-west angles. The Neuve Eglise used a reredos placed against the north wall, in front of which was the pulpit, raised above the communion table enclosure.

Illustration 3: Exterior of Spitalfields Great Synagogue, Fournier Street (probably photographed c. 1957)
Source: Survey of London, Vol. XXVII: Spitalfields and Mile End New Town 1957.

The adaptation of the building into a synagogue involved removing the middle section of the east side gallery to make a space for the ark, and regrouping the pews around the centrally placed reading platform.[33]

Gartner explains the nature of the Spitalfields Great Synagogue and its organization:

> [It was] the most categorical challenge from immigrants to established English Judaism ... Their outlook may tersely be summarised as a rejection of the official Judaism of England as a heterodoxy to be combatted, and with which truly pious Jews ought not to be associated. They were convinced that Judaism as practised by native Jews was not true Juddaism, and that its pretence to orthodoxy was false.[34]

In 1891 they established an independent *Shechita*[35] system breaking the United Synagogue monopoly. When the Chief Rabbi refused to endorse the *Kashrut*[36] regulations, an independent *Kehilla*[37] was set up. This *Kehilla* carried out marriages and divorces in conjunction with the District Registrars but without reference to the Chief Rabbi. Rabbi Werner had become the unofficial head of orthodox immigrant Jews in Britain.

What is of relevance here is that the heavy cost of transforming the chapel into a synagogue imposed an intolerable burden on the members of the congregation. £1,400 was already owing to Messrs Maple and Company for reconstruction work in the *Talmud Torah* next door, the additional £4,500 and other financial obligations connected with the independent *Shechita* organization meant an overall debt of at least £6,000. The result of the building debt was the loss of autonomy, and dependence on the very establishment which they had been set up to oppose. By 1905, the *Machzike Hadath Shechita* organization was forced to amalgamate with the official Chief Rabbi's Board. The congregation joined the Federation and its Burial Society, and asked to borrow a thousand pounds. Rothschild and Montagu, members of the Jewish aristocracy, each lent £500 through the Federation but in exchange a number of concessions had to be made. Members of the Spitalfields Great Synagogue and its minister 'shall recognise in all religious matters the jurisdiction and authority of ... the Chief Rabbi of British Jews.[38]. The lessons of the *Machzike Hadath* seem clear. The cost of independent building was the loss of religious autonomy.

It was hoped that these efforts to control immigrant synagogues would disprove anti-alien criticism – like that made in 1892 and

Illustration 4: Interior of Spitalfields Great Synagogue
Source: Survey of London, Vol. XXVII: Spitalfields and Mile End New Town 1957.

included in Arnold White's *The Destitute Alien in Great Britain*: 'As
they come, so they remain – aliens, children of another race, amongst
us, yet not of us. And the East End produces no type of man or woman
so unfit, so un-English and morally and personally so alien, as the
pauper immigrant when he becomes a settler in the ... East End.'[39]

Criticism from within the Jewish Community itself had initially
concentrated on attacking the *Chevrot* for their isolationism and lack
of contribution to communal philanthropy. By 1883 the future of the
City synagogues and the safety of the United Synagogue were seen to
be endangered.

> There can be no question that these minor places of worship are
> formidable rivals of the larger city synagogues, and that as long
> as no attempt is made to diminish the severity of the competition
> it is hopeless to expect a revival of the fallen fortunes of the older
> fanes. Unless the Council of the United Synagogue is reconciled
> to the prospect of certain collapse of one or more of its con-
> stitutent synagogues, energetic steps must be taken to divert to
> its exchequer some of the contributions which at present help to
> swell the funds of the *Chevrot* ... The subject, however ... is not
> a financial one only. If the morale of the community is con-
> sidered, it is clear that the growing strength of the *Chevrot* is an
> undesirable feature ... .[40]

As far as the buildings were concerned their position was seen as
encouraging congestion, being unsuitable for women and also insanitary. The advantages of West End type worship seemed to be self-
evident to the *Jewish Chronicle*:

> surely it must be more agreeable, for instance, to sit in a
> handsome spacious well ventilated place of worship like that in
> Great St. Helen's and hear two good readers with a suitable choir
> ... and to have a chance of hearing a capital sermon in the
> English language by a competent preacher – than to sit on
> uncomfortable seats in a stuffy little room up a close court,
> suffocated from want of fresh air, disturbed by the discordant
> noises of closely packed worshippers inside the building and the
> more discordant noises of street boys outside it.[41]

Besides this, the format of the *chevra* service, and its feature the
sermon, or *darasha*[42] of the *maggid*[43] as practised in the *Chevrot* were
said to be a 'travesty of holy things':

The first and great lesson a Polak ... has to learn is to adapt himself to his new country ... and to cease to be a Polak. This he never will or can do if he form a little Poland in an English city. He should on the contrary, do all in his power to associate with Englishmen and to ally himself with English institutions ... I cannot help thinking and saying that what is termed '*Magiduth*'[44] in connection with existing *chevras*, is a monstrous mistake and the sooner it dies out the better. Apart from the fact that it perpetuates a language which indeed is no language at all, but a jargon which defies classification and shuts out progress, the *darasha* in itself if utterly worthless as a civilising medium.[45]

Most threatening of all, anti-alien criticism often failed to distinguish between the immigrant and the native Jew. As the organ of Anglo-Jewry wrote: 'Our fair fame is bound up with theirs; the outside world is not capable of making minute discrimination between Jew and Jew ...'.[46]

IV

The provision of synagogue accommodation for poorer congregations in east and to some extent north-east London can thus be seen as a response to the pauper alien problem. Synagogues and classrooms provided at some geographical remove from the East End were to relieve Jewish working class congestion and make the alien Jew less 'visible'. Within this category can be included the Constituent synagogues of East London, Stepney Green (1876) (see illustration 5), South Hackney (1879) and Stoke Newington (1904) (see illustrations 6–9) areas of second settlement at one move from Whitechapel and Spitalfields. It will be seen that these efforts were marked by an importation of the West End synagogue type into the 'foreign' territory of east London in the hope of accomplishing some sort of social change, a kind of architectural colonization.

The placement, design and staffing of these synagogues were calculated to act as aids to migration[47], effecting large, orderly congregations and bringing them into the Anglo-Jewish fold. Religious, racial and class unity were to be accomplished by educating immigrants in the ways of British citizenship. The use of the middle-class building type identified these synagogues with other synagogues of the United Synagogue.

The solution of the United Synagogue was to allow a series of

Illustration 5: East London Synagogue, interior
Source: The Architect, 8 April 1876.

The solution of the United Synagogue was to allow a series of compromises in its financial arrangements with poorer congregations. Such allowances were not of great importance in themselves, but were nevertheless significant because they transgressed the rigidly maintained rules of commercial hard-headedness which characterized synagogue building operations outside the East End. The norm of strong local initiative, with some United Synagogue support, was changed. The parent body became directly active in stimulating local interest – for example, the public meetings held in connection with the founding of the East London Synagogue.[48]

The five-twelfths loan promised to Stoke Newington was changed to voting half the amount needed as 'it would be fatal to delay building this Synagogue'[49] and when it was found that South Hackney could repay neither the interest or recoupment of the principle on money loaned, interest payments were waived for three years[50]. Religious accommodation previously used in these areas was classified as unsuitable. The United Synagogue building type presented a deliberate contrast to this unsatisfactory accommodation. The Hackney congregation had been meeting in a temporary iron structure where the lack of a women's gallery had been remarked upon. In Stepney, Jews were formed into small *Chevrot* using the local schoolroom for larger services held on the high holydays. There was provision for worship but obviously not the right sort: 'a place of worship should be erected so that the inhabitants of the district could worship their God in a proper manner'.[51]

In order to ensure the buildings had all the correct architectural features, design was strictly supervised from the centre, whereas the sites were normally selected by the congregation before application for Constituent status. The East London site was only approved after conference with the Council. A report on the site was made by the District Surveyor for the Eastern Division of the City of London and rough plans and estimates prepared by N.S. Joseph, then Honorary Architect to the United Synagogue and Messrs. Davis and Emanuel, the designers of Stepney Jewish Schools who had also participated in various working class housing and dwelling schemes. At Stoke Newington all plans, estimates or contracts connected with the erection of the building were to be submitted to the Building Committee for approval, no designs were to be considered before consultation with Council and the choice of architect was no longer the prerogative of the local congregation but was left to the joint discretion of the Building Committee and the Provisional Committee.

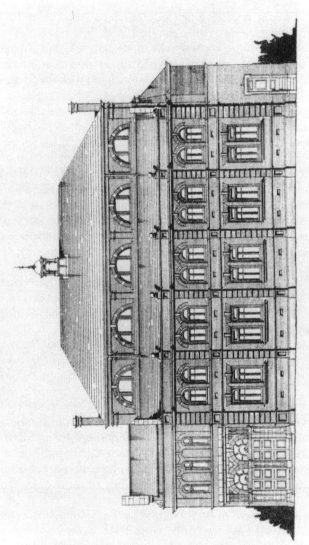

SOUTH ELEVATION (FRONT)

Illustration 6: Stoke Newington Synagogue, front elevation
Source: *The Architect and Contract Reports*, 22 Nov. 1903.

Illustration 7: Stoke Newington Synagogue, interior showing east end
Source: The Architect and Contract Reports, 22 Nov. 1903.

At South Hackney it was decided that the protection of the United Synagogue interests warranted a change of normal procedure:

> Hitherto it has been customary to add one of the Honorary Officers and the United Synagogue to the Building Committee of the incoming synagogue. This course has not worked well, as the United Synagogue which eventually has to assume all responsibility for the building has no control over its erection. It is therefore contemplated that the plans of the proposed building together with all the necessary estimates and contracts connected with its erection, shall be subject to the approval of the Building Committee of the United Synagogue.[52]

As was usual with the United Synagogue type, it was built on a larger scale than was immediately demanded. Before the East London Synagogue had become the philanthropic project of Anglo-Jewry, only 140 seats in total had been needed. By the time the building was finished it would house 604. It was this synagogue that was to be 'a pride to its promoters, an honour to the district and a glory to the community of Israel'.[53] The synagogue was to be 'of the plainest character consistent with propriety ... The plans have been prepared in the most economical way, without any architectural decoration. For example, it is contemplated to erect the synagogue of brick, inside and outside, so as to save the expense of plaster'.[54] With this sort of degree of intervention, the West End plan type was safely secured for east London. The three buildings were designed by different architects, but looked remarkably similar. The exterior of the buildings running alongside the street merged with the housing, no obvious imposing statement being made. The street facades depended mainly on the arrangement and grouping of doorways and windows. At East London the only articulation of the main front was the two houses attached to the synagogue hall at either end.

In the rectangular the three-sided gallery was standard. The reading desk was placed centrally in Stoke Newington and East London (although where seating capacity was at a premium, as at South Hackney, the reading desk was integrated with the Ark platform and latitudal seating filled the space). Significantly at Stoke Newington and South Hackney the pulpit occupied a central and commanding position. The pulpit, which had come to dominate the synagogue interior and superceded even the Ark as the main focal point, was considered a tool of anglicisation. This feature was to be used to induce

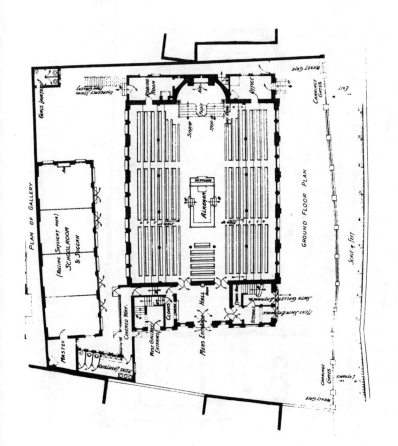

Illustration 8: Stoke Newington Synagogue, ground floor plan
Source: *The Architect and Contract Reports*, 22 Nov. 1903.

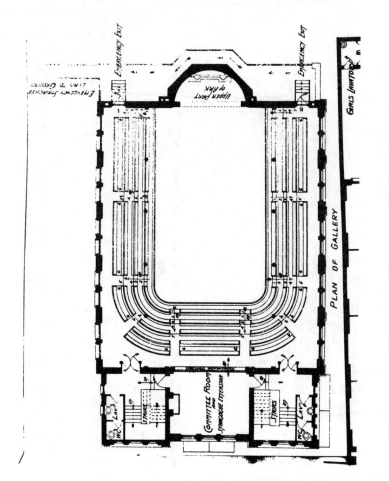

Illustration 9: Stoke Newington Synagogue, plan of gallery level
Source: The Architect and Contract Reports, 22 Nov. 1903.

a more thoughtful and critical attitude to religion on the part of the foreigners. The Chief Rabbi himself was constantly urging the values of British culture and the duties of citizenship. The qualifications for the ministry were sound grammatical and fluent English. Such a ministry, with these required skills would, from their especially prominent position, inculcate the 'British' way of life. In addition these efforts to provide suitable accommodation were enhanced by supplementary concessions such as allowing cheaper marriages and funerals in the East End. All cheap rate marriages took place initially at East London. The prices of seats were reduced and the money was to be collected weekly or monthly to make it easier for the poorer congregants to pay.

V

The founding of large synagogues outside the confines of Whitechapel and Spitalfields could only provide religious accommodation for a small fraction of immigrants. Between the years 1885 and 1898 a number of schemes were prepared by the United Synagogue administration which aimed to provide a solution to the problem of remaining immigrant Jewry. Earlier measures for ameliorating the condition of the Jewish poor, such as the reduction in the cost of marriage and funeral charges and the operations of the Four Per Cent Industrial Dwellings Company, of which Rothschild was president, were no longer considered adequate. According to the United Synagogue perception:

> in recent years the Jewish question in East London has become more and more acute ... It has been shown that the number of the Jewish population in East London has increased enormously, that its character has changed, as was natural from the arrival of so many foreign Jews, and that the characteristics of the latter differ very widely among themselves. It follows that different organisations, and more ample provision than that which might have sufficed under former circumstances, have now become necessary. Nor is it only in the conditions of the poor Jews themselves that changes have taken place. The migration of the wealthier classes of the community to all parts of London, distant from the centre occupied by the poor, has naturally tended to

widen the gulf which divides the richer from the poorer classes of
the community ... sympathy now takes the form of charitable
organisations, there is not and there cannot be, that close touch
between the two classes which is begotten of association of the
one with the other. Moreover, ... the residence and sphere of
action of many of the Jewish Clergy has necessarily been in some
degree removed from the poorer Jewish quarters ... .[55]

The wider implications and candid explanation of motives were given
by Noah Davis, a United Synagogue Committee Member, when he
warned that 'Our motives are not wholly philanthropic; our own
personal interests are involved, for we will have to take care of
ourselves in looking after them'.[56]

In February 1885 the East End Inquiry Commission presented its
report. It had been appointed by the United Synagogue Council to
report on the circumstances affecting the social condition of the poorer
classes of the East End Jews. East European Jews had been found to
be dirty, untrained and oppressed.

> Habituated by centuries of grinding oppression to look with
> suspicion on everyone outside his own immediate personal
> circle, the foreign Jew ... seeks and finds such aid as he requires
> mostly among compatriots of his own creed. He and they es-
> tablish for themselves a social ghetto which their exclusiveness
> locks from the outside, and within which he has but little
> opportunity to shake off the habits which have accompanied him
> from his home ... Unaccustomed ... at home to an unlimited
> water supply, the Jewish immigrant cannot be expected to be at
> once scrupulously clean in his habits.
>
> First steps must be taken to cause the foreign poor to imbibe
> notions proper to civilised life in this country; secondly, the
> physical conditions of the poor and their surroundings, must by
> improved.[57]

At this stage the Commission found that these Jews were tied to a
social and economic framework based in the East End and were less
susceptible to the strategy of dispersal used at Stepney and Hackney.
The first proposals for what became known as the 'Colossal Synagogue' were mooted in the 'Scheme for the Foundation of a Synagogue
and Provident Society' dated January 1890 and chaired by Rothschild.
This scheme provided the basis of discussion for the next five years,

being irrevocably abandoned in June 1898. The key part of the scheme was the association of large synagogue with a Provident Society, which amounted to a co-option of the *chevra* principle although on a much bigger scale. The 1890 Scheme had intended building a synagogue which would be the largest of all the Constituent synagogues and would rival the continental synagogues of Berlin and Paris.

The strict stand against congestion was relaxed and it was recognized that for reasons of employment (the example cited being the necessity for tailors to be near city warehouses), complete dispersion was not feasible. There were to be 1,000 seats in the body of the synagogue and 400 in the gallery. Two hundred men's seats were to be free, while 500 were to be let at prices ranging from 3d to 1s per week. Seventy men's seats were to be let at £5 5s annually to the wealthy and generous who, it was hoped, would leave the seats empty and thereby increase the number of free seats – a form of endowment. The cheapest seat charge was to include all the costs imposed by the statutory regulations of the United Synagogue, conferring at the same time all the rights and privileges of membership. Gallery accommodation would only initially be provided against one wall, justified as a measure of economy and by the knowledge that female attendance tended to be small. The synagogue complex would also include a large hall to be used as a Court for the Beth Din, providing extra space for worship meetings and general purposes.

The principle of the funds of a local congregation being supplemented by central resources was abandoned. East End Jewry was in no position to finance such an immense structure. However the most controversial measure (perhaps proof of the sensitivity to and fear at that time of pressure from anti-alien sentiment), was the renunciation of the balanced income and expenditure rule. The synagogue building itself was to be run with the expectation of a permanent deficit. The running of the synagogue was to be carefully controlled. The election of salaried officers normally in the hands of the congregation, was to be vested initially in the Council, and the Secretary was always to be chosen from candidates approved by the Honorary Officers of the United Synagogue.

VI

The East End Schemes run parallel with the efforts of Samuel Montagu and the Federation of Minor Synagogues to obtain direct representation for the smaller synagogues on the Boards of *Shechita*, Deputies and Guardians. It undertook to render available to the members the services of a minister certified as holding orthodox opinions by the Ecclesiastical authorities. Just as with the United Synagogue, a large part of its activity was concerned with the regulation of buildings as a lever of social change. The Secretary, J.E. Blank, claimed in 1898 that 'the Federation was formed in 1887 with the general object of improving the general position as regards methods of worship and places of the poorer congregations'.[58] Within the framework of the Federation's building policy, progress was made towards the same ends as the Anglo-Jewish body but using slightly more circumscribed means. In concluding, the Federation Annual Report of 1896 begged

> to remind members of the Federated synagogues that great as is the work which has yet been achieved, more remains to be done. When the Federation of Synagogues was called into existence, the model synagogue was then the exception but is now general. Until every Federation Synagogue is in every respect irreproachable, the members should not rest satisfied. To the smaller and weaker *chevras* the history of the Federation should serve as a lesson and an encouragement, prompting their members to put forward their utmost efforts to reconstruct their synagogues[59]

The purpose of this building policy was rarely explicitly stated. It may be argued that it was not unreasonable for buildings to be made more sanitary or generally improved; however it becomes clear that the type and state of the synagogue building and the size of congregation affecting whether converted rooms or a purpose-built synagogue were affordable, were the immediate criteria of acceptance for Federation membership. Visitation by the Building Committee to the premises and the Architects' Reports were the sole documents on which the Board based their decision. If the place of worship was considered nearly suitable, efforts were made to pressurise the congregation to conform with generally acknowledged architectural standards. The carrot offered – membership of the Burial Society, unobtainable without membership of the Federation – was very tempting, such facilities on consecrated land were difficult and expensive to provide. The stick of amalgamation with another congregation, architectural improvement or the building of a model synagogue was often accepted, probably with varying degrees of tolerance. There can be no doubt that the building policy of the Federation deliberately changed the nature of synagogue accommodation in the East End.

Small-scale *shtiebl* worship was clearly identified as an obstruction to anglicization.

> The policy of the Federation is to make every synagogue a considerable centre and none is federated that has not at least fifty members. They [the Federation] constantly urge the amalgamation of small bodies of worshippers ... such amalgamation has often brought about conditions leading to the building or equipment of a model synagogue ... The motive for the formation of the small detached 'room' synagogue springs from the tendency for foreigners from the same district or town to wish to worship together. [The objections to this are numerous, the most important being that they remain apart, exclusive, suspicious and thus take longer to come under the general influences of the Anglo-Jewish community and of the freer atmosphere of England.][60]

It was with this object in mind that all applications for membership were referred to an Advisory and Building Committee. When the Federation was first set up, Lewis Solomon, the architect, inspected and reported on the condition of 15 of the synagogues. Copies of this report together with a request that defects be remedied were sent to the congregations concerned. Membership was withheld from those congregations worshipping in inadequate premises.

> Applications from the *Kehol Chassidim* Synagogue 16 Union St, Whitechapel and *Chevra Tehillim*, 30 Heneage St, Whitechapel were rejected on reports from the Honorary Architect on the unsuitability of the buildings for places of worship ... Applications from the *Blukha* Synagogue, 66 Spelman St, Brick Lane and the 34 Lucas St Synagogue, Commercial Road, were deferred until such time as essential alterations suggested by the Honorary Architect had been made ... An application for admission into the Federation from the *Chevra Shaas*, 36 Old Montagu St, a newly constructed synagogue[61] [was accepted].

Congregations with potentially suitable places of worship were induced to improve the buildings as a condition of acceptance. Those with recently built synagogues gained admission more easily.

Federation facilities were withheld until the numerical requirement was fulfilled and sanitary and decorous premises acquired. A medium-sized congregation could not worship in a room and would be more likely to be able to contribute towards the building so as not to be 'pauperized' by a donation covering the total cost. Amalgamation with another group increased the numbers, improved their spending capacity, and made for a more cohesive community. By 1892 Prescot and New Castle Street had merged and *Beth David* and Crawcour Synagogue were proposing to move from their separate premises both in Fieldgate Street, in order to share a model synagogue to be erected in New Road. There is evidence that the Committee was torn between approving membership in the hope that faulty premises would be remedied at a further date and the congregation kept within the communal fold, or isolating that group perhaps hoping to force amalgamation. It is not known how many or how long these prayer groups practising in rooms or converted workshops were able to survive.

The Federation promoted the 'model' synagogue:

> The Federation of Synagogues may with pardonable pride point to the long list of suitable synagogues which have been erected or reconstructed either by direct assistance or as a result of the high standard which is now consistently set before its members for a house of worship. These include the New Road; Old Castle Street; *Shaas*, Old Montagu Street; Spital Square; Dunk Street; Princes Street; Lodz; Davis Mansions; Greenfield Street; Great Garden Street; Vine Court; Great Alie Street; a notable achievement in the comparatively brief period of nine years.[62]

The sponsorship of the 'model' synagogue was only made possible by the material means supplied by Samuel Montagu, the Federation having no funds of its own. Montagu, using the Federation as his agent, finalized arrangements with the congregations and seemed to have often presented the Board with a *fait accompli*. He donated money, but at the same time specified to a large degree its expenditure. In 1899 for example, he acquired a freehold for a synagogue in the Nottinghill destrict, advanced £500 for the Fieldgate Street Synagogue, and proposed lending money to the Cannon Street Road Synagogue, repayment due to the Federation. No evidence has been found of Samuel Montagu's direct influence on the designs of Lewis Solomon, however there seem to have been a number of fixed requirements for a 'model' synagogue building plus a number of more subjective qualities thought to be inherent in just such a design. What then constituted a 'model' synagogue? The buildings were to be of a moderate size, the last synagogues mentioned housed between 280 and 300 worshippers. One of the benefits of the larger congregation should be that it could open free from debt. The replacement of dingy rooms by a commodious building preferably purpose-built was a much discussed change. Converted rooms in houses were unacceptable. This type of indecorous worship was so abhorred that when the *Kalischer* Synagogue moved to its newly constructed model building, the congregation undertook 'to remove all the fittings from the old synagogue in order to prevent as far as possible its being again utilised for the same purpose'.[63]

Many of the minor repairs were concerned with ingress and egress. The danger from panic or fire were to be considered but more abstract notions had to be satisfied. In the Architect's report on the Kurland Synagogue, 133 Cannon Street Road, Lewis Solomon did not recommend 'this synagogue being admitted to the Federation on the grounds that there is no accommodation for women, that the synagogue is too small to be taken into account, that the building is not such as to command respect, and that it is unsafe from a fire point of view . . .'.[64]

The *chevra* at 35 Fieldgate Street embodied all that was considered unsuitable. It was small, without any street frontage and undifferentiated from the commercial buildings surrounding it. As we have seen, it was disliked due to its unsavoury approach, workshop style design and lack of provision for women.[65] In such a state admittance to the benefits of the Federation was not granted. The opening of such model synagogues, financed in this way, was reviewed by the *Jewish Chronicle* although they paid more attention to the social event than the building.

> It is an unpretending structure, the plainess of which was relieved by a judicious arrangement of banners lent by Messrs J. Defries and Co. and of palms and flowers specially sent by Samuel Montagu M.P. from his country house near Southampton. Altogether the synagogue presented a pretty appearance reflecting the greatest credit on the Honorary Secretary of the Building Committee, Mr J.E. Blank.[66]

Significantly the opening was made an occasion for apparent communal unity – Lord Rothschild and the Chief Rabbi being present, and

more importantly the whole ceremony emphasized the practice of
Jewish religion within an English environment.

> It was a happy thought to have fixed the consecration of the New
> Road Synagogue on the Queen's birthday; and a still happier
> thought to have made reference to that auspicious anniversary a
> dominant feature of the service and the attendant proceedings.
> The members of this *Chevra* are all foreigners, mostly Poles, and
> it was touching to hear 'God Save the Queen' heartily sung in
> Hebrew by the congregation. Fittingly, the Chief Rabbi made
> loyalty the subject of his impressive discourse on the occasion;
> and his fervent words had living force lent to them by the
> presence of the first Jew who had been made an English peer,
> and who attended the service as President of the United Syna-
> gogue [Lord Rothschild], and by the no less significant presence
> of the other occupant of the Warden's box, the Member of
> Parliament for the Constituency in which the humble Bethel is
> situated, Mr. Samuel Montagu:[67]

A synagogue reconsecrated a few months earlier was opened with
slightly less ceremony. The Old Castle Street Synagogue was also
designed by Lewis Solomon, Honorary Architect to the Federation
and was said to provide an architectural example to other *chevrot* in the
area. The synagogue, closed due to action taken by the Sanitary
Commission of the Jewish Board of Guardians, had been re-erected on
the same site.

> The transformation has been remarkable [enthused the *Jewish
> Chronicle*] in the place of the narrow and dingy building, there
> now stands a synagogue which might well serve as a model for
> any other *chevra* in the East End. The present building, which is
> approached through a neat and roomy vestibule, is forty feet in
> length and thirty feet wide. There are seats for 285 persons, 120
> being in the ladies gallery. The difficulty of providing good light
> and ventilation has been successfully surmounted by an open
> roof with lantern light ventillators. The Ark which is of fine
> proportions is surmounted by two glass tablets on which the Ten
> Commandments are written and these in their turn have on
> either side a handsome stained glass window having been all
> formerly in the St. John's Wood Synagogue and presented by the

congregation to the new building with the approval of the Council of the United Synagogue.[68]

In conclusion, both the United Synagogue and the Federation exerted pressure on immigrant Jews to assimilate, partly in response to perceived anti-semitic threats. This was actively pursued through building finance and design policies, which succeeded in establishing the 'West End' synagogue norm in the 'foreign' territory of the East End. In the process, small religious groups, independent from any British organisations and informal in religious practice, were brought into line under the guise of benign philanthropy and sanitary objectives. The Jewish population in London, rather than being a unified homogenous group alienated by and alienating the natives was, in fact, composed of various conflicting sub-groups. By 1914 anglicization had in the main been accomplished by design, both in the sense of the conscious adoption of objectives, and by specific building programmes and arrangements.

NOTES

1. B. de Breffny, *The Synagogue* (London, 1978), p.72.
2. Taking the last 30 years of the century, R. Wischnitzer in *The Architecture of the European Synagogue* (Philadelphia, PA, 1964) and de Breffny, *The Synagogue* only include Stoke Newington and the new Hambro. H. Rosenau in 'The Architectural Development of the Synagogue' (London University thesis, 1939) includes no examples.
3. de Breffny, chapter on 'The Search for a Style'.
4. *Jewish Journal of Sociology*, Vol.1, No. 1 (April 1959).
5. For instance, in the work of Lloyd Gartner.
6. V.D. Lipman, *The Social History of the Jews in England 1850–1950* (London, 1954), p.66.
7. The traditional functions of the synagogue have been threefold. It has served simultaneously or in different combinations as a place of prayer, study or meeting. In the period under discussion the interior arrangement was reasonably standardised relying on the elements of ark (container for scrolls), *bimah* (reading platform) and seating. The appurtenances in the smaller synagogues might well be furniture whereas in the larger purpose-built synagogues the ark and *bimah* reached architectural proportions and mostly became an integral part of the building itself. There are certain Halakhic (an accepted decision in rabbinic law) rules governing the construction, use, design and location of the synagogue and regulating ownership and disposal of the building. Accommodation for women was segregated, usually a gallery was provided or a section of the hall partitioned off. Most of the activities of the synagogue service took place between the ark and the bimah, the scrolls being opened up at the reading desk on the platform. The reading platform was generally placed centrally although there were various attempts to combine the

bimah and ark at the east end by the Reform movement or in an effort to provide additional seating accommodation. Preaching could either take place from the reading platform or from a pulpit usually on one side of the ark. The duties of synagogue administration were divided between religious and lay officiants.

7a. *Chevrot:* plural of *chevra* meaning literally 'society'.
7b. *Shtiebl:* literally 'small room', sometimes with religious function.
 8. Israel Zangwill, *Children of the Ghetto* (London, 1892), Vol.2, p.247.
 9. Polish German ritual practised by Ashkenazi Jews.
10. Booth notebook 27, Interview, 13 Dec. 1897 p.63 (unpublished); North London Synagogue opened 1868 and Hampstead in 1892.
11. *Jewish Chronicle*, 24 Jan. 1873, p.607, Walter Josephs quoted. The *Jewish Chronicle* will be referred to hereafter as *JC*.
12. Executive Committee of the United Synagogue in Council Minutes of the United Synagogue, Vol.1, Part II, pp.377–8; report, Nov. 1881, p.3. The Executive Committee of the United Synagogue will hereafter be referred to as EC and the Council Minutes of the United Synagogue will be referred to as CMUS.
13. EC report, CMUS, Vol.1, Part II, pp.377–8; CMUS, Vol.1, Part 1, pp.219–20, July 1876, p.9.
14. E. Jamilly, 'Anglo-Jewish Architects and Architecture in the 18th and 19th Centuries', *Transactions of the Jewish Historical Society*, Vol.XVIII, pp.127–43.
15. Regulations for the Appointment of an Architect and Surveyor to the United Synagogue, CMUS, Vol.3, 26 April 1904.
16. *Builder*, 12 Sept. 1874, p.773.
17. Ibid.
18. *Minyan:* quorum of ten adult males for divine service.
19. A.I. Myers, *The Jewish Directory for 1874* (London, 1873).
20. Charles Booth, *Life and Labour of the People in London*, 3rd series: Religious Influences (London, 1902–3), Vol.2, p.82.
21. L.P. Gartner, *The Jewish Immigrant in England 1870–1914* (London, 1960), p.200.
22. *JC*, 17 Nov. 1876, p.518.
23. *Survey of London: Spitalfields and Mile End New Town* (1957), Vol.XXVII, pp.36–7.
24. *JC*, 17 Nov. 1876, p.518.
25. Federation of Synagogues: Minute Book of the Council, Vol.1, Oct. 1887–March 1903, 19 Jan. 1897 (unpublished) (hereafter referred to as FM).
26. B. Webb, Ch.4, 'The Jewish Community', *Life and Labour of the People in London* (London, 1889), 1st series, Vol.1, p.170.
27. *Children of the Ghetto* (London, 1892), Vol.2, p.326; see also description of 'Sons of the Convenant', Vol.1, p.254.
28. Harry Blacker, *Just Like It Was: Memoirs of the Mittel East* (London, 1974), pp.71–2.
29. C. Russell and H. Lewis, *The Jew in London: Being Two Essays Prepared for the Toynbee Trustees*.
30. *Life and Labour of the People in London* (London, 1889), 1st series, Vol.1, p.172.
31. *JC*, 17 Nov. 1876, p.518.
32. Russell and Lewis, ibid., p.193. Although this view of romantic national harmony within the workshop contrasts with William Fishman's view of class conflict among East End Jews.
33. *Survey of London: Spitalfields and Mile End New Town* (1957), Vol.XXVII, p.223.
34. Gartner, ibid., p.209.
35. *Shechita:* slaughter of animals for food according to Jewish law.
36. *Kashrut:* Jewish food laws.
37. *Kehilla:* Jewish community.

38. B. Homa, *A Fortress in Anglo-Jewry; The Story of the Machzike Hadath* (London, 1953), p.67.
39. White, p.84.
40. *JC*, 15 June 1883, p.3.
41. *JC*, 10 Oct. 1873.
42. *Darasha*: sermon.
43. *Maggid*: preacher.
44. *Maggiduth*: teachings/preachings.
45. Letter to *JC* signed M.D., 28 July 1876, p.250.
46. *JC*, 12 Aug. 1881 cited by J. White *Rothschild Buildings: Life in An East End Tenement Block 1887–1920* (London, 1980), p.16.
47. Booth notebook 27, 3rd series, Vol.1, pp.9 and 11.
48. See three-page supplement in *JC*, 25 April 1873.
49. EC Report, p.5, CMUS, Vol.2, pp.4, 25–6.
50. CMUS, Vol.2, p.271, 11 April 1899.
51. Supplement to the *JC*, 25 April 1873, p.65.
52. EC Report, 23 Nov. 1894, Vol.2, pp.94–5.
53. *JC*, 25 April 1873, p.66.
54. CMUS Report, Vol.1, Part II, Dec. 1875 pp.180–81.
55. East End Scheme, 7 Jan. 1890, pp.1 and 2; CMUS, Vol.1, Part I, pp.565–6.
56. *JC*, 8 May 1891, p.8.
57. East End Inquiry Commission, 16 Feb. 1885, pp.1–2; CMUS, Vol.1, Part II, pp.451–2.
58. Interview with Booth and investigation team. Notebook B197, p.75, 28 Jan. 1898 (unpublished).
59. Annual Report FM considered at meeting, 22 Nov. 1896.
60. Interview with Booth's team, 28 Jan. 1898, Notebook B197 (unpublished).
61. FM, pp.334–5, 10 March 1903.
62. Montagu FM, 19 Jan. 1897, p.201.
63. Federation Report 1893/94.
64. FM, 13 May 1900, p.274.
65. 19 Jan. 1897, Building Committee Report.
66. *JC*, 27 May 1892, p.8.
67. Ibid., p.5.
68. *JC*, 17 April 1891, p.14.

210 THE JEWISH HERITAGE IN BRITISH HISTORY

ILLUSTRATIONS

1. Interior of the Central Synagogue

Closely linked to the United Synagogue foundation and administration, this synagogue typifies the 'West End' building type both in design and ornament, as well as in terms of management and the nature of services. The building was designed by N. S. Joseph, costing £24,000 and seating 860 people. The Synagogue's Building Committee specified that the bimah should be nearer the west doors than the east, with sermons delivered from a central reading desk. The original plans were prepared in both Moorish and Italianate styles, with a modified version of the Moorish designs being found to be acceptable. Interior ornament encodes references to the status of the building and its inhabitants (classical elements), non-secular function (gothic) and indications of ethnic origin (Moorish details). The view was taken that despite the noise of a major thoroughfare, the principal entrance would be in Portland Street as befitted a building of importance.

2. The New Synagogue (New West End)

Designed by Messrs Audsley, in collaboration with the United Synagogue Architect-Surveyor N. S. Joseph, as a copy of the Liverpool synagogue. The design, which mixed Moorish and gothic elements from various centuries, is nevertheless presented within a classically symmetrical framework. The building's appearance was said to rely on recent excavations of the Hebrew temple in Jerusalem. Contemporary comment suggested that although the site was enclosed, the frontage remained impressive.

3. and 4. Exterior and Interior of Spitalfields Great Synagogue

This synagogue is a key example of a non-aligned synagogue using a converted chapel building. It occupied the Neuve Eglise, designed by Thomas Stubbs in the 1740s. The building has been occupied by various religious groups, most recently the Moslems. Changes in occupants have reflected the history of waves of immigration into the East End.

The drawing (4) shows the original building before Maple and Co. re-grouped the seats around a centrally-placed reading platform, and put an ark against the east wall. The 'Machzike Hadath' community which converted the building, spearheaded the immigrant challenge to Anglo-Jewry. They received financial help between 1905 and 1910 in return for recognizing the Chief Rabbi's authority in all religious matters.

5. East London Synagogue: Interior, Plan and Perspective

As part of the 'pauper alien solution', three large synagogues were built at a deliberate distance from Whitechapel and Spitalfields. The synagogue at

Stepney Green marked the importing of the middle class synagogue type into East London, transgressing the formerly strict financial arrangements which were part of the admission into the United Synagogue. The building design, controlled from the centre, was seen as both civilising and anglicizing the religious practices and social behaviour of its mainly working class occupants. Messrs Davis and Emmanuel together with N.S. Joseph used the contained site with some ingenuity (see top plan and perspective), setting the length of the synagogue hall back from the street line. Ornament relied on different coloured bricks, a technique recently and ironically nicknamed 'streaky bacon'. The cast-iron nave arcade reduced the size of columns, allowing a clear view of proceedings.

6. to 9. Stoke Newington Synagogue: Front Elevation, Interior and Plans, designed by Lewis Solomon in 1903

The building was planned according to the standard United Synagogue type, although its overall demeanour was more modest in decoration, both inside and out. The elevation (6) employed a restrined classical vocabulary of paired windows between bays. Two sets of doors allowed separated entrances for the sexes, the ladies' entrance leading up to the south gallery (9). The plan (8) shows the use of the west end for circulation and east end position of office and robing room. Three particular features indicate an east London position and anglicizing role – firstly, the schoolroom, educational reform was seen as a necessary part of the programme of assimilation; secondly, the maximizing of seat numbers, raked for focus on the service; lastly, the key position of the pulpit (7) dominating the interior, even obscuring the ark. The values of British life were to be spread from the pulpit.

Directory of Jewish Historical and Heritage Resources in the United Kingdom

This directory is by no means comprehensive and should not be viewed as a definitive list. Indeed it is intended as a first step in the creation of a database of sources for those interested in Jewish history and heritage in the United Kingdom. An enormous amount of material exists in archives and libraries of a general nature and the vast majority of these holdings are not referred to in this directory – for example, there is much useful material on Leicester Jewry in the Leicestershire Record Office – see their guide *The Descent of Dissent* (London, 1989). There is also a great deal of material in private hands which is hard to locate and at great risk; many records, including those of whole local Jewish communities, have already been lost. Attempts have been made since 1988 to raise the money required to provide a detailed archive listing – a task that will involve several years' intensive work. Locating material (or indeed buildings and artefacts) is the initial stage required before preservation can take place. In the absence of proper funding, informal listing of archives is beginning to take place at Southampton University and, as Susie Barson and Sharman Kadish indicate in this volume, progress is taking place on the building front with English Heritage encouraging a survey of relevant monuments.

   The directory here partly reflects a bias towards those organisations and individuals who participated in the 'Preserving the Jewish Heritage' conference in Southampton, July 1990. It indicates the wealth of material that survives and is already available as well as the excellent institutions in the form of local and national projects in existence in the United Kingdom. Despite their achievements and appeal, one common theme emerging from the Southampton conference was the shortage of resources which hinders these organizations' progress. It is vital that Jewish (and non-Jewish) funding bodies give the support required for these varied and important initiatives. This directory, to repeat, gives only a hint of all the resources available in this country. The editor should be grateful to hear from any project or organization not mentioned for a future, more thorough survey. The directory is concerned only with material located in the United Kingdom although there is relevant documentation in other countries. See, for example, Stuart Cohen, 'Sources in Israel for the Study of Anglo-Jewish History – An Interim Report', *JHSE Transactions*, Vol. XXVII (1982), pp. 129–47; Marion Dacy, *Archive of Australian Judaica* (Sydney, 1987) and J. Casper and M. Dellenbach, *Guide to the Holdings of the American Jewish Archives* (Cincinatti, OH, 1979).

TONY KUSHNER

Organization

The directory is divided into various subheadings. Inevitably, there is some overlapping – for example, some museums and libraries contain archives and manuscripts and many have oral history collections. Moreover, the division between modern and non-modern libraries is sometimes arbitrary. Addresses, telephone numbers and opening times are correct at the time of writing (October 1991).

A. MUSEUMS

1. Irish Jewish Museum

3 & 4 Walworth Road (off Victoria Street), Portobello, Dublin 8

Open – May–September: Sunday, Tuesday and Thursday – 11.00 a.m.–3.30 p.m. October–April: Sunday only – 10.30a.m.–2.30 p.m.

Memorabilia of the Jewish community in Ireland covering the last 150 years, and restored synagogue on view.

2. The Jewish Museum

Woburn House, Tavistock Square, London, WC1H OEP
Telephone: 071–388 4525

Open Tuesday to Thursday (and Friday during the Summer) 10.00

a.m. to 4 p.m. Sunday (and Friday during the Winter) 10.00 a.m. to 12.45 p.m. Closed: Mondays, Saturdays and Jewish Holidays. (Sundays now open 10.00 a.m.–4.00 p.m.)

A collection of ceremonial art, portraits and antiques illustrating Jewish life, history and religion, particularly in Britain.

Among items of interest and fine craftsmanship are the elaborately carved synagogue Ark made in Italy in the sixteenth century, illuminated marriage contracts. Torah bells by the fine eighteenth-century London silversmith Abraham Lopes de Oliveira, and a small Byzantine gold votive plaque embossed with Jewish symbols.

Important among historical pieces are an eighteenth-century silver salver and two loving cups presented to the Lord Mayor of London by a City congregation.

The Museum offers two audio-visual programmes explaining Jewish festivals and ceremonies.

3. The London Museum of Jewish Life

The Sternberg Centre, 80 East End Road, London N3 2SY
Telephone: 081-346 2288; 081-349 1143

The London Museum of Jewish Life, founded as the Museum of the Jewish East End in 1983, is dedicated to the rescue and preservation of the social and cultural history of London's Jewish population from 1656 to the present day. While the East End remains an important focus in its work, the Museum is also concerned to reflect the diverse backgrounds and experiences of Jewish people in Britain, including both Ashkenazi and Sephardi Jews; those who came as refugees from Nazism, and more recent immigrants from India and the Middle East.

The Museum's collections include an Oral History Archive with some 250 tape-recorded interviews; a Photographic Archive with over 6,000 images and a wide range of documentary archives and social history artefacts. These are available for consultation by arrangement.

In addition the Museum offers the following resources:

A Permanent Exhibition tracing the history of Jewish London, with reconstructions of a tailoring workship, an immigrant home and an East London bakery;

Temporary Exhibitions and Travelling Displays on a wide range of themes; details of exhibitions available for loan are available on request;

Educational Programmes with activities, advice and resources for students and teachers;

A Research Programme, with lectures and research workshops, family history workshops, guided works and a research publication series.

4. The Manchester Jewish Museum

190 Cheetham Hill Road, Manchester M8 8LW
Telephone: 061-834-9879

Open: Monday – Thursday 10.30 a.m.–4.00 p.m.
      Sunday 10.30–5.00 p.m.

The Museum, housed in the beautifully restored Spanish and Portuguese Synagogue (1874) has a permanent display in the former Ladies' Gallery tracing the history of the Manchester Jewish community from the late eighteenth century to the present day. Temporary exhibitions in the former communal hall have included 'Jewish Weddings', 'Immigrant Trades and Skills', 'Before the Holocaust', 'Elevating Influences'. Walking tours and craft demonstrations regularly take place. School and other parties are most welcome but should be booked well in advance.

The Museum has played an instrumental role in locating and rescuing Jewish records which have been passed on to the local record offices. The Museum itself has over 1,000 individual photographic collections with over 10,000 photographs in total. In addition there are over 400 oral history recordings, all with summaries and some with transcripts. These cover the experience of Jews from Eastern Europe and their children as well as refugees from Nazism. There is a partial computer index to the collection compiled by Rickie Burman. The Museum has many artefacts not on display and also a fine textile collection.

B. MODERN LIBRARIES

5. The Brotherton Library

University of Leeds, Leeds LS2 9JT
Telephone:(0532) 431751
Librarian: R.P. Carr, ext. 5501 (or Direct Dial 335501)
Sub-Librarian for MSS and Special Collections : P.S. Morrish, ext. 5525 (or Direct Dial 335523)

Assistant Librarian (Semitic): M.C. Davis, ext.5526 (or Direct Dial 335526)

Opening hours for Special Collections, Mondays–Fridays, 9 a.m.–5 p.m. except Bank, Public or certain other official holidays

Holdings *c*. two million items, including major Judaica collections: Travers Herford Collection; Leeds Academic Assistance Committee papers; Roth Collection (*c*. 350 MSS, *c*. 800 pre 1850 printed books, *c*. 6,000 modern printed books plus pamphlets and offprints, letters, postcards and press cuttings).

All *bona fide* scholars welcome to consult the Library's collections; they should write in the first instance to the Librarian at The Brotherton Library, University of Leeds, Leeds LS2 9JT, enclosing an appropriate recommendation.

6. Institute of Contemporary History and Wiener Library Limited

4 Devonshire Street, London WIN 2BH
Telephone: 071-636 7247;   Fax: 071-436 6428
Director: Professor Walter Laqueur
Open: Monday to Friday 10 a.m.–5.30 p.m.

Holdings: 30,000 books
           2,500 runs of periodicals
           2,500 microfilms, e.g. complete NSDAP Hauptarchiv
           8 Press archives
           Photo Archives
           Documents and eye-witness accounts
           The Oscar Joseph Audio-Visual Archive
           The Eric Colebeck Stamp Collection on the Holocaust
           Posters, Ephemera, Artefacts.

The Library, a leading source for the study of totalitarianism, contains works on Nazism, fascism, anti-Semitism, the history of Germany since 1914, history of German nationalism, contemporary Jewish history, history of German Jewry – nineteenth and twentieth centuries (emphasis on Palestine, Israel, Zionism).

7. Institute of Jewish Affairs Library

11 Hertford Street, London W1Y 7DX
Telephone: 071-491-3517 Fax Number: 071-493-5838
Librarian: Cynthia Shiloh;   Assistant Librarian: Pat Schoten
Open: By appointment only on Tuesdays to Thursdays

Founded in 1941 in New York as the research arm of the World Jewish Congress, the Institute of Jewish Affairs came to London in 1966. As an international research body it is concerned with the contemporary social, political, legal and cultural issues affecting world Jewry.

The reference Library is both a research source for the Institute's own staff and an international information centre for scholars. Twenty thousand books in 14 languages, 300 periodicals received annually, and some archives dating back more than 30 years cover the fields of anti-Semitism, the Holocaust and racism; Zionism, Anti-Zionism and the Middle East conflict; terrorism; human rights; inter-faith relations; the USSR and Eastern Europe; and Jewish communities world-wide.

Publications of the Institute are the journals *Patterns of Prejudice*, *Christian Jewish Relations* and *Soviet Jewish Affairs* as well as regular *Research Reports*. Among books published are *The Jewish Communities of the World, Fourth edition* edited by Antony Lerman, an annual *Survey of Jewish Affairs* edited by William Frankel and *Anti-Zionism and Anti-Semitism in the Contemporary World* edited by Robert S. Wistrich.

8. Jewish Studies Library (formerly the Mocatta Library)

University College, Gower Street, London WC1E 6BT
Telephone: 071-387 7050 (ext.2598)
Librarian: F.J. Friend, B.A.

The Mocatta Library was founded upon the Library formed by Frederic David Mocatta and presented to University College by the Jewish Historical Society of England in 1905. This Library was largely destroyed in 1940, with the exception of the most important manuscripts, the Lucien Wolf collection and the collection of early editions of Josephus. The library had been reformed by the Jewish Historical Society by purchase, gift or deposit, and now includes the Hebraica and Judaica section of the Guildhall library, the Asher Myers and A.M. Hyamson collection of Anglo-Judaica, the de Sola and other collections from the Jewish Museum, and the major part of the Judith Lady Montefiore College Library and the Gaster Papers. The restored Mocatta Library and Museum and the Gustave Tuck Lecture Theatre were reopened in September 1954. In 1990 the Altmann and Mischon Collections were added and put together in the Arnold Mischon Reading Room.

9. Jews' College Library

Albert Road, London NW4 2SJ
Telephone: 081-203 6427
Open: (During term)Monday–Thursday 9 a.m.–6 p.m.
           Friday and eve of Jewish Festivals 9a.m.–1 p.m.
           Sunday 9.30 a.m.–12.30 p.m.
July and August: Monday–Thursday 9 a.m.–5 p.m.
           Friday 9–1 p.m.

The Library contains 70,000 volumes, 20,000 pamphlets and 700 manuscripts. The Departments include Biblical Studies, Rabbinics, Liturgy and Music, Theology, Philosophy, Philology, History, Anglo-Judaica, Zionism, and reference books and leading periodicals in English, Hebrew, French and German.

10. Kressel Collection

Oxford Centre for Postgraduate Hebrew Studies, Yarnton Manor, Yarnton, Oxford OX5 1PY
Telephone: Kidlington 6895
Librarian: Dr Noah Lucas

The Oxford Centre for Postgraduate Hebrew Studies houses the archive and Library built up by Mr G. Kressel that consists of 500 box files of Hebrew newspaper and periodical cuttings on 13,500 Jewish personalities and Institutions; and 35,000 volumes mainly in Hebrew, covering Jewish and Israeli topics.

11. Leo Baeck College Library

The Sternberg Centre for Judaism, 80 East End Road, London N3 2SY
Telephone: 081-349 4525

The Leo Baeck College Library contains currently 25,000 volumes, 1,500 pamphlets and a range of periodicals and reference books in English, Hebrew, German, French and Yiddish. It provides a basic library of Judaica for rabbinical students, and also materials for research on Jewish topics for advanced students, staff and visiting scholars. Special items are: graduation theses of past students of the College, a small collection of rare books and a growing tape library of recorded College lectures. Library loan facilities are available for obtaining books from other libraries in Great Britain and America. The College is a member of the Judaica Conservancy Foundation and is developing its own manuscript collection.

The subjects covered include Biblical studies, Rabbinics (including Responsa), Kabbalah, Hasidism, Theology, Philosophy, Folklore, Liturgy, Education, Language, Literature, Arts, History, Bibliography, Anglo-Judaica, Israel and Zionism.

The library is housed on the lower ground floor of the Manor House. Sufficient space has been allowed to enable it to expand to double its present size.

12. Parkes Library

Hartley Library, University of Southampton SO9 5NH
Telephone: 0703 593335
Open: 9 a.m. – 4.50 p.m. Mondays to Fridays

Everything that it can afford to buy about the relations of Jewish Communities with their neighbours, throughout the world and at all times. This includes the history of Jews in all countries, the history of Palestine, the foundation of the National Home, and the position of Israel in the Middle East. The collection was started by the late Rev. Dr J.W. Parkes in 1929, as part of his opposition to antisemitism, and has been continued by the University since 1964 when Dr Parkes gave his collection to the University.

The collection now (1991) consists of about 14,000 books and pamphlets, most of them available for loan with over 360 periodical titles.

Readership

Just as students and staff of the University can borrow most of the books, so members of the public who are interested in the subject represented in this collection may apply for an External Borrower's ticket should they need to carry out prolonged study at home.

Arrangement

The collection is arranged according to a local classification scheme based on the way Dr Parkes saw the subject. It begins with information about Jews and Judaism, then traces the history of Jewish communities in different countries, goes on to describe the Middle East, Palestine, Zionism and the history of Israel, and ends with Jewish/Christian relations, anti-Semitism and fascist movements. All the collection appears in the general catalogues of the University Library and there is a catalogue of the Parkes Library in the Special Collections reading room.

Location

The Parkes Library is in the Special Collections area on Level 4 of the Hartley Library. Readers should present proof of identity and sign the register in the Reception Office.

13. School of Oriental and African Studies

University of London, Malet Street, London WC1E 7HP
Telephone: 071-637 2388

Ancient Near East, Semitics and Judaica Division (Librarian: P.S. Salinger) contains over 10,000 Hebrew items covering modern Hebrew Language and literature as well as the Jewish history – especially Palestine/Israel and Biblical studies. The acquisition of the Stencl and Leftwich collections has created a Yiddish collection of some 3000 books. There are 200 Hebrew periodical titles.

C. EARLY AND MEDIEVAL LIBRARY COLLECTIONS

14. The British Library

Department of Oriental and India Office Collections
197 Blackfriars Road, London SE1 8NG
Telephone: 071-412 7000
Open: Monday–Friday 9.30 a.m.–4.45 p.m.
      Saturday 9.30 a.m.–12.45 p.m.

The Hebrew collection (including Samaritan and Jewish Aramaic) comprises more than 3,000 manuscript volumes and 10,000 fragments (including Haham Moses Gaster's collection and many fragments from the Cairo Genizah); Hebrew printed books, about 70,000 titles, including 100 incunabula, thousands of responsa, comprehensive coverage of talmudic and rabbinic publications of all periods, about 3,000 Yiddish and a large selection of Ladino and Judeo-Arabic books, Haskalah and early Zionist works, modern Hebrew literature, some

400 periodicals and newspapers from the earliest to circa 100 current titles; and microfilms.

15. Bodleian Library

Broad Street, Oxford OX1 3BG
Telephone: (0865) 277000
Open to holders of a reader's ticket: Monday–Friday 9a.m.–7 p.m.
Saturday 9 a.m.–1 p.m.
Hebrew Specialist Librarian – R.C. Judd, M.A., M.Phil.

The Hebrew and Yiddish collections comprise 3000 manuscript volumes and 60,000 printed books, including many incunabula, fragments from the Cairo Genizah and the Oppenheimer library, the finest collection of Hebrew books and manuscripts ever assembled. Intending readers should either bring an academic recommendation and adequate identification or contact the Admissions Office in advance.

16. The John Rylands Library

University of Manchester, Oxford Road, Manchester M13 9PP
Telephone: 061-273 333.

Collections of Hebraica and Judaica comprise over 10,500 fragments from the Cairo Genizah, manuscripts from the Crawford and Gaster collections, Samaritan manuscripts from the Gaster collection. In addition there are 6,600 printed items of Hebraica and Talmudic literature in the Marmorstein collection and 5,000 volumes in the Near Eastern collection on Hebrew language and literature.

17. Taylor-Schechter Genizah Collection

Taylor-Schechter Genizah Research Unit, Cambridge University Library, West Road, Cambridge CB3 9DR
Telephone: (0223) 333129 (direct); (0223) 333000 (messages) Fax: (0223) 333160

The Taylor-Schechter Genizah Collection is housed at Cambridge University Library and consists of about 140,000 fragments of Hebraica, Judaica and Semitica dating from the seventh to the nineteenth century in a variety of languages and dialects and relating to most areas of Jewish studies. A Research Unit is currently engaged on preparing descriptions of the items in various subject areas and the resulting catalogues are being published by Cambridge University Press for the Library's Genizah Series. Microfilms and photographs of items in the Collection are available from the Library's photography office and those wishing to consult the originals should present themselves to the library's admissions officer during normal weekday working hours, with an academic letter of reference. A complimentary newsletter is published twice a year and is available on application to the directory of the Unit.

D. NATIONAL ARCHIVAL BODIES

18. Greater London Record Office and History Library

40, Northampton Road, London EC1R OHB
Telephone: 071 633 7132 or 4431

Recently acquired the records of the United Synagogue and the Chief Rabbi's Office; the Federation of Synagogues and the Central British Fund as well as some of the records of the West London Synagogue (others located at Southampton University).

19. Public Record Office

Kew, Richmond Surrey TW9 4DU
Telephone: 081-876 3448

Chancery Lane, London WC2 1AH
Telephone: 071-405 0741
Open: Monday-Friday 9.30 a.m.–5.00 p.m.

No list of Jewish archives as such but an immense amount of material from both the medieval and modern periods on Jews in Britain and abroad.

20. Royal Commission on Historical Manuscripts

Quality House, Quality Court, Chancery Lane, London WC2A 1HP
Telephone: 071-242 1198; Fax: 071-831 3550

The Commission was appointed by Royal Warrant in 1869. A new warrant in 1959 enlarged its terms of reference as follows:

to make enquiry as to the existence and location of historical manuscripts, records or archives of all kinds of value for the study of history (other than the public records);

with the consent of their owners or custodians to inspect and report upon them;

to publish or assist the publication of such reports;

to record particulars of such manuscripts and records in a National Register;

to promote and assist their proper preservation and storage;

to assist those wishing to use them for study or research;

to advise upon general questions relating to their location, preservation and use to promote the co-ordinated action of all professional and other bodies concerned with their preservation and use;

to carry out the statutory duties of the Master of the Rolls in respect of manorial and tithe documents.

The Commission's unique accumulation of information and experience in more than a century of investigation enable it to provide expert, independent and disinterested advice on a wide range of problems concerning the care and use of historical records.

It advises owners on:
The care, storage and listing of their papers;
access by scholars for research or publication;
the choice of a record office or library in which to deposit their papers;
private treaty sales, tax concessions and grants.

custodians and their governing bodies on:

management and staffing of repositories;
design of new buildings;
acquisitions of historical records;
availability of grants.

government and government agencies on:

legislation affecting archives;
implementation of the Local Government (Records) Act 1962;
the appointment of repositories for manorial and tithe documents;
matters relating to the export of manuscripts;
the allocation of manuscripts accepted in lieu of tax and other heritage matters;
grants for the purchase and conservation of manuscripts research grants.

grant-awarding bodies on:

aid for the purchase, conservation and cataloguing of historical manuscripts.

professional associations on:

national policies and co-ordinated action concerning the preservation and use of historical records.

E. JEWISH ARCHIVES (NATIONAL, LOCAL AND PRIVATE)

21. Anglo-Jewish Archives

University of Southampton, The Hartley Library, Southampton SO9 5NH
Telephone: 0703 593335
Open: Monday–Friday 9 a.m.–5 p.m.

Collections relating to Anglo-Jewry and relations between the Jews and other people. The Division has more than 400 collections of manuscripts in this field, embracing many aspects of Anglo-Jewry, especially in the nineteenth and twentieth centuries. Holdings include the papers of Dr James Parkes, the archives of the Council of Christians and Jews, the Christian Council for Refugees, the papers of Revd W.W. Simpson and material connected with the consideration of the Jewish question at the congress of Aix-la-Chapelle. Recent accessions number the papers of the Anglo-Jewish Association; the papers of Rabbi Solomon Schonfeld, largely relating to the Jewish communities from Germany and Eastern Europe in the 1940s; the archives of the Union of Jewish Women; the papers of Chief Rabbi Hertz; early records of the Board of Shechita; Archives of the Federation of Jewish Relief Organisations; and the papers of the Jewish Board of Guardians and the Jewish Blind Society.

22. Ben Uri Art Gallery

21 Dean Street, London W1V 6NE
Telephone: 071-437 2852

Permanent collection of works by Jewish artists.

23. The Birmingham Jewish History Research Group

10 Lenwade Road, Oldbury, Warley, West Midlands B68 9JU

The Birmingham Jewish History Research Group has published three volumes dealing with the social history of Birmingham Jewry from the mid-eighteenth to the mid-twentieth century. It is now cataloguing the synagogue archives and is in process of compiling a 'pack' for the use

of schools and universities based on the experiences of refugees from
Nazi Germany between 1933 and 1945. Records and oral history
recordings deposited with local record office.

24. Board of Deputies of British Jews

Woburn House, Tavistock Square, London WC1H OEP
Telephone: 071-387 3952

Formed in 1760 the Board has extensive archives reflecting the history
of Anglo-Jewry and its relationships with Jewish communities abroad.
At present there are only limited facilities for researchers but permission may be granted to *bona fide* scholars.

25. Edmonton Jewish Research Group

Founded in 1978 to promote an understanding of how the local Jewish
community of North London developed and also to preserve records.
Has published three 'Heritage' volumes on the Jewish inhabitants of
North London. Enquiries to the Hon. Secretary, Mr J.C. Baum, 25
Harington Terrace, Edmonton, London, N18 1JX.

26. The Grimsby Jewish Community

24 Park Hill, London W5 2JN

Daphne and Leon Gerlis are interested in the history of the Jews of
Grimsby. Their work was published in 1986 as "The Story of the
Grimsby Jewish Community" by Humberside Leisure Services, Al-
bion Street, Hull, N. Humberside HU1 3TF (£4.00 + 50p postage)
1SBN O 904451 33x. This gives a brief account of local Jews listed in
mediaeval times followed by a detailed account of the rise and fall of
the present community from 1861 to 1982. The several appendices
include demographic analyses of births, deaths, marriages, domiciles,
trades and occupations and population changes.

Grimsby played an important role in modern Jewish history as a
major port of immigration and transmigration from the Baltic and
other European centres. Unfortunately there is a dearth of documentary records and the historical account must contain many gaps.
They would welcome any information about the subject, documentary
and anecdotal.

27. Jewish Music Festival

The London Jewish Music Centre, PO Box 2268, London. NW4 3UW
Telephone: 081 203 8046

Has catalogue of tapes, songbooks, etc. of Jewish interest.

28. Leeds District Archives

Chapeltown Road, Sheepscar, Leeds LS7 3AP (Archivist W. Connor)
Telephone: Leeds (0532) 628339

Jewish material includes minutes of the Order of Ancient Maccabeans
(1933–70); material relating to the Leeds Jewish Kosher Kitchen and
the Leeds Refugee Committee in the 1930s and 1940s.

29. Liverpool

The Merseyside Jewish Representative Council has a communal archivist; J. Wolfman, 29 Edale Road, Liverpool L1B 5HR. Substantial
material has been deposited with the Record Office, The Library,
William Brown Street, Liverpool.

30. Newcastle

Like Liverpool, its Representative Council set up a position of Communal archivist and all material (including the records of the Newcastle United Hebrew Congregation) are deposited with the Tyne and
Wear Archive Services. The present communal archivist is Walter
Sharman, 2 Carlton Close, Newcastle Upon Tyne.

31. Rothschilds Archive

New Court, St Swithin's Lane, London EC4P 4DU (archivist: Simone
Mace). Records from the Rothschilds family. References required for
admission.

32. Scottish Jewish Archives

Jewish Archives Centre, Garnethill Synagogue, Hill Street, Glasgow
G3
Director: Harvey L. Kaplan MA, 1/L 11 Millwood St. Glasgow G41
3JY
Telephone 041-649 4526
Archives Officer: Ben Braber Telephone 041-959 5708

The Scottish Jewish Archives Centre is located in Garnethill Synagogue, Hill St., Glosgow G3 – the oldest surviving Jewish building in

Scotland, which was opened in 1879. Its remit is to collect, preserve, and display material relating to the history of Jewish settlement in Scotland. This covers the existing communities of Glasgow, Edinburgh, Dundee and Aberdeen as well as the small communities which once existed in Ayr, Dunfermline, Falkirk, Greenock and Inverness.

Displays are being mounted on aspects of communal history and the centre is open to the public on one Sunday afternoon each month, as well as for public meetings. These are advertised in the local 'Jewish Echo'.

33. Spanish and Portuguese Congregation Archives

Lauderdale Rd, London W9 1JY
Telephone: 071- 286 2153

Archives of the Spanish and Portuguese congregation from the seventeeth century. Archives are not open to the public but admission may be given to *bona fide* researchers after requests are submitted in writing to the archivist.

34. Working Party on Jewish Archives in the United Kingdom

Convenor: Dr Tony Kushner, Department of History, The University, Southampton SO9 5NH

Formed in 1988 with representatives from national archival bodies, Jewish communal bodies and historians. Aims are to carry out a thorough survey of Jewish records in the UK and to develop a rational strategy for the depositing of archives. A booklet by Bill Williams, 'The Preservation of Jewish Records' has been produced by the Working Party and is available from the convenor.

F. ORAL HISTORY

(see also London Museum of Jewish Life, the Manchester Jewish Museum, the Birmingham Jewish History Group and Scottish Jewish Archives).

35. Imperial War Museum

Lambeth Road, London SE1 6HZ
Telephone: 071-416 5363; Fax: 071 416 5379
Open: Monday–Friday 10a.m.–4.30 p.m. by appointment

Sound archive established in 1972, 15,000 hours of recordings including sound effects and speeches but primarily an oral history collection with interviews following a biographical pattern and concentrating on conflict in the twentieth century both from military and civilian points of view. Most interviews recorded in English. All recordings catalogued and indexed. Copies of some recordings for sale. Interviews with Jewish participants in a wide range of events; topics which may be of particular interest include refugees from Nazi Europe, internment in Britain, British Union of Fascists, wartime civilian life in Britain, concentration camp survivors, Nuremberg Trials, Palestine Crisis and the foundation of Israel.

36. The National Life Story Collection

The British Library National Sound Archive
29 Exhibition Road, London SW7 2AS
Telephone: 071 823 7760 and 071 589 6603
Open: Monday to Friday 10.00 a.m.–5.00 p.m. with late opening until
9.00 p.m. on Thursdays

The National Sound Archive (NSA) opened in 1955 and became part of the British Library in 1983. It is one of the world's largest sound archives, with over a million items of recorded sound. These include wax cylinders, three quarters of a million discs, 50,000 hours of tape, audio and video cassettes, and compact discs. The very earliest recordings date from the 1890s and range from the voices of people like William Gladstone and Florence Nightingale to aboriginal chants from Australia.

Oral History is just one of the Archive's very wide range of subject areas, which include classical and international music, pop and jazz, drama and literature, wildlife and industro-mechanical sound, language and dialect. The NSA is now developing as a new national centre for oral history in Britain and Europe.

A major project has been undertaken, 'The Living Memory of the Jewish Community', involving an extensive collection of interviews of Jewish men and women. The initial focus has been on refugees and survivors from Nazi Europe.

G. BUILDING CONSERVATION

37. English Heritage

Chesham House, 30 Warwick Street, London W1R 5RD
Telephone 071- 973 3789 contact Susie Barson

Able to offer advise on listing Jewish buildings and monuments and grants available for repair and conservation.

38. The Future of Jewish Monuments in the United Kingdom

Conference organized by Dr Sharman Kadish, October 1991 to act as a focus for future action. Dr Kadish is based at Department of History, University of London, Royal Holloway and Bedford New College, Egham Hill, Egham, Surrey TW20 OEX.

39. The Heritage Centre, Spitalfields

19 Princelet Street, London E1 6QH
Telephone: 071-377 6901

Project to restore Georgian building and provide exhibition reflecting its role as a home for successive immigrant groups including Huguenots, Jews and Bengalis.

40. Jewish Heritage Council of the World Monuments Fund

174 East 80th Street, New York, New York 10021

Established in 1988 to create awareness of the significance and the preservation needs of Jewish monuments, provide technical and survey reports and sponsor restoration and preservation projects.

Index